Developing a
TOUGH-MINDED CLIMATE
... for Results

Contributors

E. M. ANSON
H. J. BATTEN
ROBERT L. CHASE
LEONARD C. HUDSON
NORMAN LOVETT
JOE E. McBRIDE
JAMES McMAHON
CHARLES H. RICHARDS
DALE H. STOUDER
JAMES L. SWAB
HARRY M. WILLITS

Developing a
Tough-Minded Climate
... for Results

By J. D. Batten

Resource *Publications*

An imprint of *Wipf and Stock Publishers*
199 West 8th Avenue • Eugene OR 97401

Resource Publications
 An imprint of Wipf and Stock Publishers
199 West 8th Avenue, Suite 3
Eugene, Oregon 97401

Developing a Tough-Minded Climate for Results
By Batten, Joe D.
Copyright©1965 by Batten, Joe D.
ISBN: 1-59244-405-9
Publication date 10/22/2003
Previously published by American Management Association, 1965

Contents

Foreword		9
I.	THE WINNING EDGE: SELF-DISCIPLINE	13

A Profile of Self · Attitudes Are the Key · The Profit Priority · The Practical Man · Theory—for What? · Prescription for Productivity

II.	THE ULTIMATE TEST IS PROFIT	25

What Profit Really Is · Tooling for Profit · Cost Planning Versus Profit Planning · Innovation: Charting for Profit

III.	ORGANIZATION AND THE TAUT SHIP	37

Formal Versus Informal Organization · Change and Its Uses · Why Organize? · How the Principle Works · A Climate for Results · The Organization Chart—Results or Esthetics? · Creativity and the Organization · Results-Oriented Job Descriptions

IV.	TOUGH-MINDED MARKETING MANAGEMENT	49

Preparing Oneself for the Future · Creating a Marketing Orientation · Developing a Marketing Plan · Organizing the Marketing Job

V.	THE PRODUCTION EXECUTIVE TODAY AND TOMORROW	63

Management Know-how and the Production Man · Steps Toward the Productivity Climate · Acting like a Top Executive · Conscientiousness Properly Applied · Attitudes—Performance—Balance—Stability

VI.	MAKING SYSTEMATION WORK	75

Work Standards/Standard Work? · Information Systems—for What? · EDP Must Sell Itself · Computers That Pay Their Way · Measuring the Contribution

CONTENTS

VII. DECISION MAKING IN THE SPACE AGE 89
It's Our Play · The Decision Making Problem · It Sneaks Up on You · Clear the Decks · Ready on the Right—Ready on the Left · Ready on the Firing Line · Fire! · A Man for Tomorrow

VIII. EXECUTIVE MOTIVATION THROUGH INCENTIVE COMPENSATION 101
The Well-Fed Executive · Up, Up—and Boom! · The New Incentive Picture · Unified Whole

IX. CANDOR, COURAGE, AND WARMTH 113
Spoiled or Sparkling? · A Keel of Candor · Humility and Obsequiousness · To Fill a Bigger Mold · Empathy, Insight, and Intuition · The Tap Roots of Warmth

X. VITALITY, SECURITY, AND DIGNITY 125
The Search for Inner Space · The Trim Silhouette · The Anxious Vice President · The Exploited Boss · Levels of Productivity

XI. INTEGRITY THAT LIVES AND BREATHES 137
Today—and Tomorrow · Managers Must Lead the Way! · The Contemporary "Con" Man · Integrity Is Good Business · Variance from Standard · The Futility of Deception

XII. WISDOM: THE STUFF OF MANAGEMENT 149
Only People Get Things Done · The Substance of Wisdom · The Development of Wisdom · The Identification of Wisdom · Hardness or Tough-Mindedness?

XIII. HOW TO BUILD ON STRENGTHS 161
Know—and Accept—Thyself · The Theory of Crutches · What Others Think · Inevitability of Mistakes · Getting to Know People · Matching the Strengths with the Tasks · For a Dynamic Organization · Personal—to Company Presidents

XIV. FACE UP TO COMPANY POLITICS! 175
A Matter of Climate · The Crisp Crackdown · Stacking the Deck Positively · Masters of Manipulation

CONTENTS

XV. PERSONAL ORGANIZATION FOR TOUGH-MINDED RESULTS   187

What Is New About Tough-Mindedness? · Cult? Fad? Doctrine? · What It Takes · What There Is in It for <u>Me</u> · How Do I Start? · Where Do I Stand Now?

XVI. COUNSEL, DON'T ADVISE   199

The Tools of Counseling · Expand the Whole Man · A Blend of Objectives · Principles Build Practices · The "Go-Giver" · Counseling's Emotional Context · Appraisal for Results · Praise the Man for His Strengths · What About the Problem Employee?

XVII. THE UNCOMMON MAN   215

Values and Voltage · The "Square" Executive · Basic Equipment · Standards Which Pull and Stretch · Positive Attitudes · The Abundant Life · The Fresh Wind of Individualism

XVIII. MANAGEMENT HORIZONS   227

The Coming Burden on Management · Enjoyment, Not Just Results · Motivation, Tired but Still Untapped · Self-Confidence and the Team · Gearing for the Space Age · Management and the Millennium

XIX. A REAFFIRMATION OF FAITH   237

The Tools of Enterprise · The Tools of Faith · The Tools of Humanity

GLOSSARY OF TOUGH-MINDED TERMS   247

THE AUTHOR   251

Also by J. D. Batten:

TOUGH-MINDED MANAGEMENT, *American Management Association*, 1963

Foreword

AS I OBSERVE, WITH BOTH SATISFACTION AND DISMAY, THE AVID HUNger shown for *Tough-Minded Management* by the business communities of the world, it becomes increasingly clear that a second volume dealing more definitively with its major principles is imperative. The truths of the first book have been eagerly grasped, but more how-to is needed.

Here I have tried to provide that "how-to," but—more important—I have sought to pinpoint and show how to use that elusive and vital something, the spirit that enlightens and energizes the ordinary corporation so that it may accomplish extraordinary things. There is no doubt that the true potential of our free enterprise system has scarcely been tapped. I am completely confident that the principles of tough-mindedness will ultimately win out over the cloying, gray encroachment of collectivism; so I have endeavored to write about much more than the orderly and efficient operation of a business. I have attempted, in short, to describe an entire business way of life, a way that promises abundance far beyond our past achievements. I hope sincerely that the approach described in these pages will open the gates to new wealth—financial, emotional, and spiritual.

Every major point advanced has been tested and proved in the marketplace and the executive suite. To insure this, I have called on the experience represented by 11 colleagues from my consulting firm—men who have applied the principles of tough-minded management to an infinite variety of problems and challenges. I am in fact indebted to the following men for the planning and preparation of specific chapters:

E. M. ANSON: Chapter VII, "Decision Making in the Space Age."
H. J. BATTEN: Chapter X, "Vitality, Security, and Dignity"; and Chapter XI, "Integrity That Lives and Breathes."
ROBERT L. CHASE: Chapter XV, "Personal Organization for Tough-Minded Results."

LEONARD C. HUDSON: Chapter VIII, "Executive Motivation Through Incentive Compensation"; and Chapter IX, "Candor, Courage, and Warmth."

NORMAN LOVETT: Chapter XVII, "The Uncommon Man."

JOE E. MCBRIDE: Chapter II, "The Ultimate Test Is Profit"; and Chapter XII, "Wisdom: The Stuff of Management."

JAMES MCMAHON: Chapter III, "Organization and the Taut Ship"; and Chapter XVI, "Counsel, Don't Advise."

CHARLES H. RICHARDS: Chapter VI, "Making Systemation Work."

DALE H. STOUDER: Chapter XIII, "How to Build on Strengths"; and Chapter XVIII, "Management Horizons."

JAMES L. SWAB: Chapter IV, "Tough-Minded Marketing Management"; and Chapter XIV, "Face Up to Company Politics!"

HARRY M. WILLITS: Chapter V, "The Production Executive Today and Tomorrow."

Our clients, for their part, have been the most invaluable resource of all. They have provided the opportunities to prove that the concepts of tough-minded management are valid and very practical principles for successful enterprise.

Business carried on in a tough-minded productivity climate need never be dull or deadly, gray or mediocre. It can—indeed, it must— become increasingly a series of positive challenges thrusting toward new dimensions of profit, new dimensions of individuality. It must develop, demand, settle for nothing less than men who walk tall with integrity.

—J. D. BATTEN

Developing a

TOUGH-MINDED CLIMATE

. . . for Results

CHAPTER I

The Winning Edge: Self-Discipline

A favorable environment in an organization reflects a leadership which one trusts and respects, an absence of restraints limiting individual development, assurance to the individual of recognition, opportunity, fair treatment. We start with the assumption that the employee who finds himself uncertain on these grounds will look elsewhere for opportunity and appropriate reward.

—CRAWFORD H. GREENEWALT
The Uncommon Man
McGraw Hill Book Co., Inc., New York, 1959

WHAT MAKES THE DIFFERENCE BETWEEN THE MEDIOCRE COMPANY and the good one? More importantly, what makes the difference between the good company and the excellent one?

This is probably the most important question being asked in business today. What are the criteria of excellence? What transforms the drifters into dynamic pacesetters in their industries and in national and international trade? There are old, respected companies that have slowly drifted into the graveyard of obsolescence and bankruptcy, while at the same time other companies—with less money, less reputation, and inferior physical facilities—have rapidly taken share of market, share of profit, and share of prominence in the industry right out of the hands of their fat and semicomplacent competitors. Again, why? Repeated studies have shown in many cases that there was little difference in quality of product, that each company possessed the same basic resources of men, money, materials, time, and space, and that these were "planned" and "controlled" in acceptable procedural fashion.

In the urgency of trying to discover why a company is floundering, we generally look first at profit indices, at individual performance indicators; then we seek to determine how well our methods and systems are working. But here is where we often make the greatest mistake. We look for evidences of inefficiency or lack of productivity and profits by "compartments." Just as we have long sought to solve management problems by crash programs, we also have a strong inclination to try to diagnose both total company success and failure on the basis of crash analysis.

The best companies are not the ones that have developed the best charts and graphs, the most sophisticated training programs, the biggest methods departments, the most elaborate array of market researchers, the most status symbols—in short, the greatest complexity. And yet there is a constantly increasing tendency to attempt to create business success through programs, projects, and prestidigitation.

What is needed is a *climate*. A climate in which every employee understands the basic beliefs and purposes which breathe life and meaning into glass and steel structures, into piles of brick and mortar, into rows of machinery and desks.

Much of this book is devoted to the discussion and application of the steps required to create such a climate. Our concern here in Chapter I, however, is with the top executive who sets the style and tone of the enterprise. This concern with him and his immediate team is vital, for without a disciplined, positive, and vigorous man at the helm the best plans and controls become a meaningless mumbo jumbo of papers and reports. Whether he heads a company, a division, or a major department, the resources under his direction will be only as effective as the foundation of basic attitudes and beliefs which he holds and communicates.

Obviously a potential skyscraper that is built on a weak and inferior foundation is handicapped in size and durability. It may crumble and collapse inopportunely in spite of elaborate and sophisticated efforts at maintenance. Thus the corporation that begins to falter must look closely at the underpinning of values and beliefs which of necessity permeates its entire atmosphere.

What of the top man, then? What can and should he do about this essential role of his in building the productivity climate?

A Profile of Self

Before the executive can set objectives, before he can measure the performance of subordinates, he has a basic obligation to his company to let his people know what he wants. Objectives, procedures, methods, tools may constantly be drained of real contribution unless they are developed and installed to accomplish the kind of objectives which fit the top man's master blueprint. To provide this master design, however, he must *know what he stands for as a man.*

A sound set of basic beliefs or values can be built firmly around a clear understanding of the following principles:

1. Free enterprise has produced more benefits, for more people, than any other economic system yet devised.
2. The dignity of the individual must be paramount.
3. Selling is honorable and essential.
4. Profit is American.
5. Integrity is the most essential quality in all human activity.
6. Every truly effective person needs a strong personal faith.
7. Excellence in every facet of the business is a constant and perpetual goal.

Some company president may comment sagely, "These are good things to believe. But everyone is already aware of them, so what?" The point is that everyone is *not* aware of them. Probably 90 per cent of nonmanagerial employees in business today cannot explain fully why profit is vital, why it is American, and what it takes to create it. Thus one of the most important reasons for the existence of a company—profit—makes very little contribution to employee motivation or enthusiasm. Workers see no reason to do more than meet the minimum requirements of their jobs. Why should they—except to be able to eat, sleep, and buy more material possessions? Moreover, probably 70 per cent of managerial personnel have just as little real knowledge of these beliefs and values. So the job must be attacked daily and weekly, in a grim, dogged sort of way, rather than welcomed with a lift of spirit and the feeling of being part of a great challenge and adventure.

The top executive must know what *he* is for before his subordinates can completely determine what *they* are for. And, until they know, they will make a less than excellent contribution to the quantitative objectives of the business.

Attitudes Are the Key

Overhauling attitudes, converting them from negative to positive, can and should be one of the manager's most exciting jobs, no matter what his level.

DEVELOPING A TOUGH-MINDED CLIMATE

Look in on the average company. There is a certain amount of internal politicking, a certain amount of diffidence and lassitude, a certain resentment of authority, a certain amount of belief that nothing new and vigorous can be accomplished until proved otherwise. It is these attitudes, essentially, that keep the company down. *Every* phase of the business is permeated with them. The top man's overriding objective is to make sure that his own thinking is clarified, that his subordinates are not held back by negative attitudes but are focused on dynamic, "stretching" goals which embody the basic beliefs and values of management.

Make no mistake about it—it takes self-discipline to study, revise, update, and clarify beliefs and attitudes. It is much easier simply to delegate another new program or project even when you know it is not the solution to the vexing, kaleidoscopic problems of today's and tomorrow's business world.

The tough-minded manager defines discipline as "training which corrects, molds, strengthens, or perfects." He must apply this discipline to his own mind, heart, and soul or he simply won't deserve—and can't command—the respect of his subordinates. He must, by directive and example, do all he can to insure that the disciplined approach to problems converts them instead into challenges.

The Profit Priority

In the tough-minded approach to business, we must not settle for less than a sound understanding of the profit motive on the part of every employee. Easy to say—but it takes guts and it takes work. Once we've achieved this understanding, though, look at what we have:

1. A greater feeling of individualism as opposed to collectivism.
2. Proof of how free enterprise operates.
3. Greater unity and oneness.
4. A lessening of union domination and control.
5. A recognition of individual dignity.

Sometimes the objection is heard, "If they know how much profit we make, they'll keep asking for more." This is based on the fundamental fallacy that people want something for nothing. Few do;

most accept the principle of a "fair day's work for a fair day's pay." It is therefore important that sound compensation procedures be developed which reward *extra* contribution to objectives with *extra* money. In many companies this alone is going to call for a painful reshaping of practices. But do it we must or miss out on much productivity that is currently dormant.

A leather goods manufacturer had scrupulously withheld every scrap of strategic information from his hourly employees: sales volume, costs, all types of operating data. His people didn't trust him and he didn't know why—he was benevolent and cordial whenever he talked to them. Union relations were strained to the breaking point. Sales went down and costs went up, and still the president opposed every suggestion. Hadn't he built the company? Wasn't he well-intentioned? Wasn't there a fundamental difference between "entrepreneurs" and "workers"?

The president did have the courage and vision in the end to revise his basic attitudes sharply and reflect them in new policies of a much more statesmanlike nature. In addition, specific courses in the basic economics of profit were developed; employees learned how the sales dollar was split: what portion went for fringe benefits, wages, new research, facilities enlargement. When they saw clearly *why* the company must make a profit, *how* it was done, and *what* would happen without it, things began to change.

The Practical Man

"Come on, let's be practical! Why talk about 'underpinning,' values, beliefs, self-discipline? That stuff is all right in theory, but I've got to get the product out the back door and to the customer." Here is a typically self-righteous statement of what is possibly the single attitude most responsible for keeping companies from advancing. It can serve as a very comforting crutch for avoiding vigorous brain twisting and necessary changes in management practices.

An old saying goes, "Show me the man who knows *how* and I will put him to work for the man who knows *why*." Many people in mediocre companies have a good knowledge of the *what, where, when, who,* and *how* of their jobs. The factor that's consistently lacking is the *why*. When an able executive in a job suited to his abilities consistently performs well, you can be sure he knows why he should. And when he consistently falls below standard, you can be sure he has not fully seen why he should do otherwise.

What is more practical than making one's effort yield greater returns to the company and to oneself? Let's take a look at IBM, a company that is uniformly rated as one of the most outstandingly successful in America. Its growth and dividends stamp it as very practical indeed. Yet Thomas J. Watson, Jr., president, states in *A Business and Its Beliefs:*

> Along with wages and job security, we have always thought it equally important that the company respect the dignity of its employees. People, as I have said, occupy more IBM management time than our products. As businessmen we think in terms of profits, but people continue to rank first. Occasionally our actions have been harsh. Sometimes a fair amount of dignity has been stripped from individual managers who were being ineffective, but great efforts were then made to rebuild their pride so they could carry on with self-respect.
>
> Our early emphasis on human relations was not motivated by altruism but by the simple belief that if we respected our people and helped them to respect themselves the company would make the most profit.*

Theory—for What?

I have heard Harold Koontz say, "Principles will always defeat practice."

Time after time we see struggling companies being governed by hunch, intuition, and fancy. Sometimes they have grown rapidly because of a product lead on their competitors. Sometimes a son has taken over from a father who practiced one-man rule in the days when competition was virtually nil. Such businesses seem to be up against constant crises. Sales campaigns, cost reduction campaigns, and rashes of union grievances keep both top and middle management in a state of chronic nervousness and anxiety.

Surprisingly, though, we also see struggling companies whose executives can glibly recite the "principles" of management. It's

---

* McGraw-Hill Book Company, Inc., 1963.

THE WINNING EDGE: SELF-DISCIPLINE

when you begin to ask penetrating questions about the substance and fiber of planning, for instance, that you often find a distinct lack of conceptual underpinning. *Why* and *how* does a company plan? *What* information is needed? *Who* should be involved?

It is safe to say that a smooth transition to excellence in management cannot be achieved by an abortive hodgepodge of borrowed programs and panaceas, of assorted tools and techniques. Really first-rate company success must derive from a top executive who can think. He should ideally relish the challenge of disciplining his mind and emotions to think through the basic purpose and goals of the business. He should rationally determine how best to blend his philosophy smoothly with that of well-selected subordinates. He should be able, from the wellspring of his inner resources, to provide the rest of the team with a feeling of some uniqueness, a desire to excel, and a distinct impatience with mediocrity.

As executives at all levels develop ever greater maturity and wisdom, this will likely be because of their skill in consistently shaping fundamental concepts, refining them into management theory and principles, and applying them so as to achieve the desired results. Thus:

CONCEPTS	THEORY	PRINCIPLES	RESULTS
Nature of business	Best blend of resources available to the enterprise: Men Money Materials Time Space	Planning Organization Coordination Execution Control	Profit Growth Excellence Psychic wage Other
Nature of society			
Nature of man			

The business executive looms increasingly as the true power figure in our society. Many top men have not only millions but billions of resources to employ for good or evil, for mediocrity or excellence. It must be clearly understood, however, that power carries not a corresponding but an even greater measure of obligation and accountability for management by integrity. And, stripped to its essence, management by integrity is impossible without the tough core of resolve called self-discipline which is central to every successful company, division, department, and individual.

DEVELOPING A TOUGH-MINDED CLIMATE

Prescription for Productivity

By all odds the two greatest deterrents to constructive, dynamic, tough-minded management are (1) insufficient self-confidence and (2) fear. Essentially the same, these foster the *status quo*. Together they add up to formidable roadblocks in the way of progress.

If the corporate climate could suddenly be drained of all negative, self-centered fear, the results would be wonderful to behold:

1. No "protective" memos, letters, or conversations.
2. Greater ebullience and enthusiasm.
3. Positive, goal-oriented action.
4. No more politics.
5. No destructive tensions.
6. Opportunity to examine the nature and requirements of the business; minimum preoccupation with self-protection.
7. Consistent and planned innovation—the lifeblood of a business.

It is of course utopian to believe that all this can be completely accomplished immediately. Significant improvements can be made, however, when a true productivity climate is encouraged and its structural elements are fused and knit into an operational whole by the application of tough-minded management.

SUMMARY AND ACTION STEPS

Every executive who truly wishes to achieve full success both as a whole man and as a business statesman, regardless of company, will set about creating a complete climate of productivity. This can and will come about only as a product of courageous and disciplined effort. The essential steps are these:

1. Develop and *communicate* a clear-cut statement of basic beliefs, values, and principles throughout the organization. (In the final analysis, your company or division *is* only as effective as the beliefs *you* hold and practice.)
   Questions to ask:
   · What media should be used?
   · What timing and approach are needed?

- What should a statement or series of statements encompass?
- Why take this step at all?
- What tools and techniques should be used? Handbooks, manuals, bulletin boards, house organs, meetings? Why?
- Will the top man's choice of personal friends and social activities have any bearing on the results he experiences within the company? In what way?

2. Lay out clear overall company objectives. (People talk about objectives, but too few do anything about them.) Examples: productivity, innovation, manager performance and development, physical and financial resources, public responsibility, worker performance and attitude, marketing, profitability.

   Questions to ask:
   - Who should be involved?
   - What methods of coordination should be used? What media, timing? How long should discussions be?
   - What type of research, analysis, and evaluation will be necessary? How should it be conducted?
   - Who should have primary responsibility? Why?
   - Who should be accountable?
   - What type of timetable will be needed?
   - What about controls?

3. Select the best and most appropriate people for clearly defined jobs; people whose values fit into a vigorous, positive, stretching environment; who are fit and tough-minded. Use orientation procedures which stress that here is a company which lives and personifies the values it professes.

   Questions to ask:
   - What types of selection tools are available?
   - How are values developed?
   - What other selection criteria should be used?
   - What will be the best orientation procedure?
   - What organizational relationships should be established? Why?

4. Define the results required in each job. Insure that *all* employees know the *what, where, when, who, how,* and *why* of their jobs.

   Questions to ask:
   - What research data are needed? How and where should the research be conducted?
   - Who should participate? To what extent?
   - Who should be accountable?
   - What techniques or tools should be used? Why?
   - How can job results be related to personal, departmental, and company objectives?

5. Evaluate the worth of every department, person, and job in the company in terms of contribution to the company's goals (not person-

ality factors). Develop departmental objectives which contribute directly to the greater purpose of the company; convert position descriptions from responsibility to results requirements; justify all resources on the basis of profit-center accounting; relate compensation directly to contribution.

Questions to ask:
- What general format should be followed in writing statements of objectives and position descriptions?
- What is profit-center accounting? How does it differ from cost accounting?
- What general sequential procedure should be developed to provide compensation for results rather than activity? Should it differ from point and factor systems? If so, how? How should it be installed? Who should be responsible and accountable?
- What type of coordination is needed to install profit-center accounting?

6. Hold all key personnel accountable for the results requirements of their positions. See that they receive all information and guidance necessary to high-level performance; develop and apply yardsticks for measuring their effectiveness; tell them they must produce the desired results or be subject to appropriate disciplinary action.

Questions to ask:
- Before accountability can be enforced, what type of information (operating and nonoperating) is needed by the chief financial executive? The chief production executive? The chief marketing executive?
- In what way should each key employee be informed of his accountability? What degree of counsel and guidance should he be given?
- What approach should be taken in applying disciplinary action? Transfer, demotion, termination, counsel, reprimanding?
- What yardsticks are needed?

7. Make sure all management personnel understand and apply the philosophy that management is the development of people, not the direction of things.

Questions to ask:
- What media should be used?
- Is a manifesto from the top executive needed?
- Does the philosophy need selling? Why? How?

8. Focus the energy, goals, and aspirations of everyone in the company on the achievement of clearly spelled out objectives or goals. Let each executive feel like a businessman in his own right.

Questions to ask:
- What should the starting point be? What media should be used?
- Can you distinguish between the aspirations of executives and other

THE WINNING EDGE: SELF-DISCIPLINE

people in your business? Do they all have the same basic needs and drives?
- Why should all employees know why the company is in business and why they must meet certain results requirements?
- What meetings are needed?

9. Teach all key personnel the substance and application of the five key elements of management: planning, organization, coordination, execution, and control.
   Questions to ask:
   - Who should be considered key personnel? Why?
   - What are the basic components of the five management elements?
   - How can the objectives of a management development course be stated?
   - How can the application of development sessions be measured?

10. Build an understanding of motivation, its components and application, into all key personnel. Understand and meet the basic needs of all personnel, consistent with company objectives; determine the personal objectives of all key people, relating these goals to departmental and company objectives. Emphasize strengths instead of focusing on weaknesses.
    Questions to ask:
    - What should be the first step?
    - Who should be involved?
    - What tools and techniques should be used? What media?
    - What controls should be developed and applied?

11. Establish the realization that work can and should be part of a life of total productivity.
    Questions to ask:
    - What type of information is needed? What type of program? Bulletin boards, handbooks, house organ, meetings, directives?
    - What department, person, or function should handle the program?
    - How can the impact on productivity be measured?

12. Incorporate in all activities the belief that applied integrity is the most important ingredient in life and on the job. (Conniving and dealing may seem stylish, but integrity pays off—not just in conscience but in real bread-and-butter considerations.)
    Questions to ask:
    - How can integrity be defined?
    - What are some examples of the dollars-and-cents impact of "management by integrity" on manufacturing, marketing, general administration, engineering, personnel, financial management?
    - How is management by integrity disseminated, interpreted, applied, and controlled throughout the company?
    - Do you really believe "phonies finish last"?

13. Measure every major function on the two main premises that (a) the

only reason for being on a payroll is to produce results; and (*b*) the use of men, money, materials, time, and space can be justified only on the basis of positive results.

Questions to ask:
- What kind of coordination must precede a program of results measurement?
- What kind of research is needed?
- How would you carry out the following five essential management steps in a program of results measurement: plan, organize, coordinate, execute, control?
- What are some key result indicators for manufacturing, marketing, general administration, engineering, personnel, financial management?

Finally, do you like to engage in bull sessions about tough-minded management? Cozy intellectual discourses? Or do you have the discipline and guts to perspire a little bit, to really get things done?

CHAPTER II

The Ultimate Test Is Profit

TO THE VAST MAJORITY OF PEOPLE—BUSINESSMEN, WORKERS, AND even economists—profit is the *raison d'être* for business. Our whole free enterprise system has been described and rationalized in terms of the God-given constitutional right of a man to employ his resources for maximum personal profit. This is wrong. Profit tells us nothing about a business's reason for existence and even less about our free enterprise system. It is a stale abstraction used by accountants and economists to quantify and oversimplify the operations of a business. As Peter F. Drucker states in *The Practice of Management*, "The profit motive and its offspring, maximization of profits, are . . . irrelevant to the function of a business, the purpose of a business, and the job of managing a business."* They are irrelevant because

1. Businesses are made up of people, and succeed or fail because of the efforts of people.
2. Businesses sell products or services to people.

In other words, businesses exist to meet human needs—to provide security, recognition, a feeling of belonging, and opportunity in all their many-faceted forms to all the people in the organization; and to fulfill (and, in some cases, even create) the needs of its customers.

What Profit Really Is

To say that a business exists to meet people's needs in no way negates the importance of profit. Profit is essential to the survival of the enterprise—which will meet no needs if it flounders into bankruptcy for lack of profit.

Fundamentally, profit is the residual or difference between the

* Harper & Row, Publishers, Inc., 1954.

total cost of producing and marketing the products or services of the enterprise and the income or revenue received for them. Although accountant's rules of thumb and burgeoning government regulations have muddled the profit-measurement problem considerably, the fact remains that profit serves to

1. Measure the productivity of the enterprise and its people's use of its resources: men, money, materials, time, and space.
2. Provide or attract new capital for developing new markets, new products, and new processes and for other expansion and innovation which will insure the company's perpetuation over the long run.

Since profit is the measure of how well a business meets its customer's needs or how much value it creates, it follows that the better the customers' needs are met, the higher the profit to the business. This idea is fundamental to our free enterprise system. Profit, when honestly earned in the open market, is something to be proud of—and the greater the profit, the greater the pride should be. But how often businessmen take an apologistic, insipid approach to the idea of profit, both inside and outside their companies. Too many so-called enlightened managers rely on pious platitudes and other nonsense in house organs, in office party speeches, and on bulletin boards to sell their employees on profit and free enterprise, while at the same time they

1. Keep the company's profit picture a closely guarded secret, to be discussed furtively among a select few in the inner sanctum of the executive suite.
2. Pay the same uninspiring wages and salaries to both outstanding and mediocre performers.
3. Promote on the basis of seniority, loyalty, appearance, glibness, and other equally ridiculous factors unrelated to performance and profit contribution.
4. Squash employees' ideas for profit improvement or appropriate them as their own.
5. Talk in terms of labor efficiency, material yields, and other abstract measures instead of in terms of cold, hard cash.

6. Invest heavily in unneeded company limousines, airplanes, plush offices, and other status-seeking trappings.

Is this selling free enterprise? Absolutely not! It's no wonder employees go away grumbling, "Why should I break my back so that s.o.b. can line his pockets?" To sell profits, to sell free enterprise, you must live it and demonstrate it in every nook and cranny of the business.

The chief engineer of a medium-size metal fabricator fought the installation of an improved production control system at every turn, through both active and passive resistance. "I don't see any need for it," he said sharply. "We've worked without this planning and control stuff for years and have gotten along. I think we should leave well enough alone." Incredibly he was unaware that his company had lost money for the past five years. When he learned this important fact, he began to put his full support behind the effort to improve profitability.

The profit picture and the concept of free enterprise should legitimately concern the people in a company. But neither will concern them unless it is related to their personal goals and needs. You must talk profit and live free enterprise in terms people understand. For example:

- *Security:* Perpetuation of the company—and of jobs, which only profit can insure. Compensation which is tied to results, contributions to profit.
- *Opportunities:* For promotion (increasing as a company grows and prospers). For making full use of one's abilities. For improving one's skills and capabilities. For enriched recreational and social life.
- *Recognition:* Oustanding compensation for outstanding results. Recognition and reward for ideas.
- *A feeling of belonging:* The pride which comes from being a part of a successful, progressive, profitable company. The sense of achievement and confidence which comes from accomplishing something worthwhile with other, like-minded individuals.

DEVELOPING A TOUGH-MINDED CLIMATE

Tooling for Profit

The most sterile, frustrating company environments are created by managers who believe that business operations can be programed and proceduralized so that the company inexorably marches on to achieve some predetermined return on investment or other profit goal each year. Such men view business as the manipulation of economic variables—inventories, sales, labor costs, capital expenditures—and put great stock in a complex of techniques, formulas, and procedures to accomplish this manipulation. They view management not as the development of people but as the direction of things. Their personal utopia is a large desk in a paneled office where they need do nothing more than read control reports, make decisions, and issue memoranda. They yearn for the day when they can computerize the whole business and eliminate all those unpredictable and irritating human variables.

These men are striving not for excellence but for arid mediocrity and ultimate extinction. They are crushing the insight and imagination which enable a business to create new markets and new products, to adapt and change to meet new needs, to score real breakthroughs in productivity. For all the tools and techniques in the world will not provide that which only people possess: judgment and wisdom.

Tooling for profit involves a continuous, creative effort to provide information for people so that they can achieve—and exceed—the results expected of them. This information must be geared to (1) decision making and (2) measuring the results of those decisions, both in terms of contribution to profit. But information alone is not enough. No matter how lucid, how timely, or how relevant, information accomplishes nothing. *People* get things done, not reports; and, if properly motivated, they will *demand* the kind of information they need for accomplishment.

A lot of useless reporting can be stripped out of most companies if one simple test is applied: Does this piece of paper contribute directly to the accomplishment of company objectives by people? If not, throw it out. There are probably millions of systems, methods, and techniques in use for gathering and communicating business data, but one thing is certain—the typical company needs a lot better tools than it has, and a lot fewer. The key here is simplicity. The overzealous controller or the insecure marketing manager trying to justify his overstaffed department can turn out a whole raft of expensive and oppressive reports—most of which, once started, go on forever.

The way to achieve simplicity is to concentrate on results, and the logical approach to tooling for profit is simplicity itself:

1. Determine, as specifically as possible, the results required of every key job in the company.
2. Develop plans for the achievement of these results.
3. Develop relevant measures of performance which will show whether the results are achieved.
4. Design management reports which will portray actual performance versus planned performance. These reports should be
    a. Simple, providing only essential, summarized, easily read information. Highly detailed information should be kept out but should be available upon request for further analysis.
    b. Comparative, providing both current and past information as well as actual versus planned. This will help to spot trends and significant variations.
    c. Analytical, providing reasons for significant trends and variations from planned results. The analysis should be in narrative form, oriented toward what needs to be done, and it should be a primary result required of your controller or chief financial officer.
5. Develop systems throughout the company which will produce the needed financial information as simply, as quickly, and as inexpensively as possible.

Because management reports must emphasize results, the results expected must be defined before management tools to measure those results are developed. Sounds simple, doesn't it? But the fact is that most managers, controllers, and systems men begin by designing the systems—usually involving highly routine functions such as payroll, billing, and inventory control—and end with designing the reports (as byproducts of the routine administrative system). They never get around to considering the results expected of the key people in the company!

DEVELOPING A TOUGH-MINDED CLIMATE

What about machines—electronic data processing? There is no doubt that EDP has had a tremendous impact on business and that the potential for its use has barely been scratched. But, while many companies in the forefront of American industry have been very successful in mastering it, many others have become slaves to their own machines. For example, the president of a building products distributor confided in a business discussion that installing a computer was the worst mistake he had ever made; he was even in doubt as to his own future with the company. Why had he leased the equipment? He ticked off the reasons:

- "To reduce our overhead. It didn't. Oh, we saved a few clerks, but rental costs, site-preparation costs, additional higher-paid people, and the like have increased our overhead by a net of $2,600 per month."
- "To improve our accuracy in inventory control, billing, and so on. But now we have more errors than ever and I suspect it's the sloppy clerical procedures that precede input to the computer. My theory is that the relative accuracy we achieved in the past was built on continuous human checks of the data as it was processed manually but that, with the machine, we have lost even that capability."
- "To provide more current management reports—but all we are getting is fresher history."
- "I suppose for prestige. But with the billing errors and other problems we have had, we have lost much more than we have gained in that respect."

Eventually the computer was taken out in favor of a well-managed, results-oriented, punched-card equipment installation. The point is that too many companies, like this one, install electronic data processing for the wrong reason: to do what they are now doing cheaper, faster, and quicker. The only sound justification for a computer is that it allows managers to do things that they couldn't do before; to continuously summarize, analyze, and report data from the guts of the business, to predict the effects of alternative employment of resources (simulation), to assimilate feedback on shifts and trends in markets, and so on. The computer should serve as an extension of people's ability to grasp information, to draw conclusions from it for decision making, and to foresee the results of those decisions. But computers cannot make decisions—only people can.

Costs Planning Versus Profit Planning

The haggard executive with the littered desk was obviously a tired, perplexed victim of the gray sickness which permeates the very roots of an unprofitable company. "I can't understand it," he said. "Since I took over this outfit three years ago, I have done everything I knew how to put us into the black. Yet we are teetering even nearer to bankruptcy. I'm ready to chuck it all and sell out."

What kinds of things had he done to make the company profitable? He had installed strict expense budgets in all areas; reduced salary costs by 20 per cent through reductions in manpower, primarily among management and clerical people; reduced the ratio of indirect to direct labor by 18 per cent; applied continuous pressure to reduce inventory levels; and put a tight lid on all capital expenditures. In short, he had established a pattern of nickel nursing which had obviously created a climate of fear and defensiveness throughout the organization.

And what about sales? "Oh, I let the Sales Department worry about that. I'm a finance man. I keep after them to get their selling expenses down."

Farfetched? Yet it's amazing how many companies today equate profit improvement with cost reduction—a myopic approach that produces some highly predictable reactions to adverse profit situations: Reduce costs, save money. Many enterprises save themselves right out of business. A pump manufacturer, for example, in a lean year cut back severely on product research and development "until business picks up." When it didn't, market studies were finally initiated to find out why. The results showed a definite shift in customer preference to a more efficient type of pump which competitors had developed. Needless to say, it took a few more lean years for the company to close the product gap after reconstructing its research and development function from the ground up.

Planning must be oriented to planning profits, not just planning costs. Unfortunately, it's easier to plan costs than to plan profits, so that's what most companies do. The total effort may revolve around preparing an annual budget, carefully laying out expenses and capital expenditures for each department, but giving almost no thought to expected sales except perhaps in the form of a simple sales projection or forecast. This is ridiculous! How can expense and capital expenditure plans possibly have meaning except in terms of sales and profit? To achieve any results through planning, we must look at both sides of the picture.

Profit planning requires, first and foremost, knowledge. We need information, intelligence, upon which to base our planning decisions. We need to know (1) the environment in which the business operates—economy, markets, competition, suppliers—and (2) the costs of doing business: product costs, breakeven points or cost-volume relationships, costs of replacement, obsolescence, and so forth. Costs within the business must be related to factors outside it to have any meaning. Cost control or cost reduction by itself is essentially negative and self-defeating. Profit planning, on the other hand, aims at the best possible use of the company's resources to achieve its objectives through roughly these steps:

1. Define the markets for the company's products in terms of geographic location, market potentials, market dynamics, and the like.
2. Appraise the company's position in the market; that is, with respect to share of market, price standing, product trends.
3. Develop company marketing objectives and a thorough marketing plan to meet those objectives.
4. On the basis of these marketing objectives, break out objectives for the other major functions of the business: manufacturing, finance, engineering. Lay out plans within each function specifying the resources needed to meet the objectives.
5. Resolve inconsistencies among the various functions' objectives and tie the entire profit plan together.

Note that this approach begins with the complete development of marketing objectives and plans and relates all other objectives and plans to the market. This, the essence of effective planning, controls the progress of the business and will do much to pare down an organization for taut, lean performance.

Innovation: Charting for Profit

Recent years have seen the beginnings of a shift in management thinking to a strong emphasis, not on doing, but on *getting things done.* Thus management is increasingly concerned with the development of people who achieve results through a continuous process of change, innovation, and improvement—this in contrast to the traditional approach in which administrative smoothness, the *status quo,* and highly programed, repetitive operations were the order of the day.

Amid this shifting of management thought and practice, new planning and control techniques have emerged. Probably no other innovation in management has received so much publicity, and has progressed in so short a period of time from the status of a novelty to that of a tested tool, as PERT (Program Evaluation and Review Technique), CPM (Critical Path Method), and related procedures. Yet, even though hundreds of companies have added PERT to their bag of tools with which to get things done, thousands of others have shied away from it or have tried to use it and failed. Among this latter group, the following reactions are typical:

- "All that I read and heard about PERT led me to expect miracles from it. I assumed that if we weren't using it, we weren't managing. Needless to say, we were quite disillusioned, and we scrapped the whole program."
- "Frankly, I'm frightened away by all the esoteric terminology, the talk about computers, and the mathematical controversies those people engage in. I figure this PERT stuff is for the big companies, not for us."

Actually, PERT involves nothing more than a series of concepts: the representation of a plan by means of a network that defines which activities must precede others and which can be carried out con-

DEVELOPING A TOUGH-MINDED CLIMATE

currently; the prediction of a time schedule; the recognition and measurement of uncertainty; and the ability to adapt the plan continuously to environment and circumstances. It is this simple set of concepts—not the methods, forms, reports, procedures, or hardware used—which is the essence of PERT. The application of these concepts can dramatically improve the quality of planning in an organization, for the procedure is simple and understandable, its logic and discipline are inescapable, and it focuses clearly upon the results to be achieved.

At least 80 per cent of the value of PERT or any such advanced management tool is that it makes systematic planning possible. But it is not planning! Planning is decision making about the future—and, to repeat, only people make decisions. Special tools and techniques will provide valuable planning know-how, but they will not supply the imagination, initiative, and guts required to make things happen.

The PERT diagram is an excellent device for communication, coordination, and control. With it, each responsible manager has a good grasp of the complete graphic plan and how he fits into it, rather than a dissociated, fragmentary picture of the project from his own restricted viewpoint. In addition, through thorough planning the groundwork is laid for dynamic, stretching management control, since each event or subobjective in the PERT network represents specific results which are to occur at a specific time. Management is thus able to concentrate on the most important results, and specific information on deviations from planned performance and what to do about them is continuously available.

A final point is that PERT or any other management technique is a tool of, by, and for managers. Planning, for example, cannot be relegated to a bunch of specialists in some staff department; if it is to be effective, each manager must do the planning for his own area of responsibility and must be held accountable for his progress against that plan. Planning techniques must be applied with a liberal dose of wisdom and practical judgment. They must be *working* tools, providing managers with a common planning denominator for use inside and outside the company, a logical and systematic approach to planning, and a means of focusing on results rather than activity.

SUMMARY AND ACTION STEPS

A business enterprise exists to meet people's needs: financial, social, psychological. To meet those needs, it must make a profit; and the greater the profit the better for customers, employees, stockholders, and community alike. But profits don't just happen; they are earned by wise planning, by tough-minded follow-through, and above all by living free enterprise and awakening the entire organization to its precepts.

The specific steps needed to gear your operation to profitability are as follows:

1. As the top man, communicate your basic philosophy and beliefs to everyone in the organization.
2. Establish a continuous program for educating people at all levels in the value of the free enterprise system. Relate free enterprise to practicality and human needs through all available channels.
3. Define clearly the organization's objectives, both short- and long-range, and the results expected of each person. Spell out specific contributions to profit.
4. Review all management policies and practices thoroughly. Revise them to recognize and reward individual free enterprise and contribution to profit.
    a. Insure that compensation practices provide outstanding pay for outstanding contribution.
    b. Insure that promotion and advancement are based on demonstrated results, long-run contribution, and the personal strengths of the individual.
    c. Provide for recognition of excellence through all available media.
5. Orient all planning and results requirements to profit, not cost.
    a. Define the markets for the company's products and services.
    b. Appraise the company's present market position. Develop marketing, profitability, and allied objectives.
    c. Develop company marketing plans to meet marketing objectives.
    d. Develop objectives for all major functions based on marketing objectives. Lay out plans for meeting those objectives.
    e. Tie in all planned expenditures for men, equipment, materials, and space to the expected contribution to company profit.
6. Design management reports which show actual versus *planned* results, with emphasis on simplicity and analysis.
7. Develop systems throughout the organization which will produce the needed information as efficiently and as quickly as possible. Evaluate the use of electronic data processing in terms of breakthroughs in new information, not in terms of getting present information electronically.

DEVELOPING A TOUGH-MINDED CLIMATE

8. If you decide to introduce PERT or any similarly advanced management technique, train all key personnel in its concepts and application. See that it is viewed as a working tool for all managers.
   a. Select a pilot project.
   b. Have a meeting of all key managers involved in the project.
   c. Obtain each man's best thinking on the results required to achieve the project's objectives. Distill the combined wisdom of the group.
   d. Prepare the final plans together and put them into operation, making provision for progress review sessions and reports and other appropriate measures.

CHAPTER III

Organization and the Taut Ship

ORGANIZATION IS ONE OF THE FIVE FUNCTIONS WHICH ARE COMMONLY referred to as the management process. Like the other four—planning, coordination, execution, and control—it defies categorical description. Frequently it is combined with one of the others—for example, in the phrase "organization planning." In fact, organization is a tool of the rest, just as each in turn is a tool of organization. In order to organize, it is necessary to plan, to coordinate, to execute, to control.

Organization also supplies the vital communication network—the nervous system of the company—by providing for the flow of directives downward and feedback on the results of the action taken. The greatest single reason for lack of results in most businesses is the lack of effective communication, especially when someone simply did not get the word. Organization helps to build a climate that minimizes communication problems.

Formal Versus Informal Organization

There are two kinds of organization within any company: the one that is formally recognized and acknowledged and the informal one. Should a manager fail in his responsibility for organizing the activity within his unit, the people will group themselves naturally in an informal organization.

If a manager is to run a taut ship, he must delicately balance formal and informal organizational relationships so that no single individual or group has undue influence. It is essential that the manager maintain control and himself be the guiding influence. To allow the organization to take the lead can be a major mistake, especially when a new man assumes the presidency of a company or heads up a particular unit. While he should get the feel of his new responsibilities before he acts, he must time changes in the organization so that these occur before the informal organization "jells." Up to that point people will expect change and be receptive to it; once they have grown comfortable, they may resent it and the man who brings it about.

In one diversified company, rife with paternalism and politics, a young man in his late thirties was vaulted into the presidency. Afraid of widening any schisms that his promotion over a number of highly qualified men might have created, he made no immediate changes in his organizational structure; he failed to cut out the deadwood. The irony of the situation was that his very lack of action came between him and his subordinates. The men he had passed on the way up recognized his leadership abilities and looked with enthusiasm for him to straighten out the organization's obvious inadequacies. As soon as it became apparent that he was not going to act decisively, their enthusiasm cooled. The older members of the group merely shrugged and went on as before. Many of the younger, more energetic men, feeling that their champion had sold out to the "system," chose this opportunity to resign and seek a better climate.

Change and Its Uses

The aggressive manager is never satisfied with his organization. He realizes the need for flexibility, innovation, and fluidity. He cannot countenance the stereotyped, hackneyed, inflexible organization that chains people to sterility and mediocrity. He recognizes the need for change and uses change constantly as a tool to strengthen his group, to stimulate the growth of individuals, to meet changing objectives, to keep the fat out.

Reorganization can often be utilized to bring about a vast number of changes concurrently that would be impossible if attempted on a piece-by-piece basis. Properly handled, it can breathe new life into a tired company, whether the reorganization is designed to increase centralization or decentralization. Basically, the same results will be achieved. The decision to centralize or decentralize, in other words, is not nearly so important as the decision to reorganize.

Unfortunately, many subordinate managers seem to feel that organization is a tool for top management alone. They are wrong—it is a tool for anyone who wants to get things done through people. Men in middle management sometimes say, "I'll organize my unit if someone will only tell me the company objectives and what is expected of my unit." This is buck passing, pure and simple, even though it may point to the inadequacies of the company. If no one provides you with proper objectives, decide what you think they should be and communicate them to the next higher level of management. If they encounter no opposition, proceed to organize accordingly. This type of action has often motivated others and triggered a chain reaction—eventually the whole company is reorganized. It is also the type of action that earns promotions.

But remember: Change should never be instituted for its own sake. Change is justified only when it advances the objectives of the business.

Why Organize?

Under the marketing concept of management, as we have seen, a business exists to meet the needs of the customer; thus there is only one valid business purpose—to create and keep customers. But a business organization meets the needs of a customer or creates a customer for the simple reason that through these actions the needs of the people in the organization are better met than through some other means. "The only reason for an organization to exist is to meet the needs of the people within the organization." So says Victor Pomper, executive vice president of H. H. Scott and Company.

Foremost among the people within the organization whose needs must be met is the top man. People come together voluntarily because they know more can be achieved through group action than by individuals working separately. This is basic to the American free enterprise system. Yet serving the needs of all the people in the company seems to elude many in top management positions. Hence employees sever their employment, strike for what they want, or—saddest of all—stay with the organization but withhold their productive talents. The alert, more successful manager will, however, in developing his organization recognize the personal goals of individuals and, insofar as possible, see that they are in harmony with company objectives. This is how he builds a dedicated, hard-working staff of people who are able to identify almost completely with the organization and its objectives.

Just what are these personal needs and goals? Are they limited to the security, recognition, opportunity, belonging, and self-achievement of the psychologists? Certainly we all want these in varying degree, but there are wide variations among individuals. One man may want freedom to work on a pet research project; another may need to know he can continue to have a job with the company until he retires. Still another—the dynamic type—yearns to be president.

How the Principle Works

How does this principle of need fulfillment function in practice? The best example can be found in the formation and growth of a new business.

A man with personal needs to meet has an idea for applying his talents to meet the needs of other people. He begins a business. As it prospers and grows, he finds it is making excessive demands on his time; therefore, he decides he can better meet his needs by hiring an assistant to help him.

This is a crucial point in the life of an organization. A nonmanagerial person might decide to limit the amount of business he accepts and let someone else meet the excess demand. Our man, however, comes to the conclusion that by combining his effort with another person's more can be accomplished than by the two of them working separately. The man hired must concur in this decision. No matter how many facts are available, it requires an act of faith on the part of each.

Shortly the head of the business discovers that his personal objectives are no longer exactly the same as those of his business. The difference isn't large, but the modified objectives of the business must take into consideration the personal needs of the second man if he is to meet his needs and make his maximum contribution to the business's growth. This is when the leader begins to mature as a manager. He begins to understand the wisdom of Lawrence A. Appley's statement that "management is the art of getting things done through people." Each time he makes a decision he must keep in mind the impact on the other person's needs. At the same time, the second man accepts the fact that his actions will have an impact on the founder's needs.

Some men react to this new relationship with, "I'll make the decisions, and if he doesn't like them he can quit." In such a case, that is exactly what the subordinate should do. If he lacks the guts to quit, the manager should bring matters to a head. This is sound business practice; both parties will benefit in the long run. If the occasion arises too frequently, the manager will soon discover that more moderate decisions will serve better to meet both his own needs and the needs of others in the organization. If he doesn't learn this, the business may fail. A pattern of action, without self-discipline, which takes into account only the requirements of the top man smacks of irresponsibility.

Even though the business fails to grow appreciably, the needs of its people are bound to change, and the leader must be alert to these changes. And, should the business prosper, the needs of new people will augment those of the existing group, calling for further and further modification of objectives. In more than one instance a man has discovered that the company he founded no longer meets his needs and, rather than disrupt the whole organization, has sold out and formed an entirely new group.

Since an organization of any size must meet the needs of all its people, its objectives must be a statement of their conglomerate needs. They will never be completely inclusive, but they will serve as a guide by which individuals may identify their personal objectives with those of the company.

A Climate for Results

The better the climate within an organization, the less the need for an overly formal organization structure. In such a climate people tend to be perceptive; they sense what needs to be done and take action to solve problems rapidly. They seem to call upon hidden strengths to meet challenges that appear insurmountable to outsiders.

Mutual faith and common cause are at the core of such success. The common cause or objective may be written down, but in all probability the organization has grown so rapidly that no one would know where to find it or, if anybody did, it would be out of date. People in this kind of dynamic "growth" organization apparently keep in tune with its objectives through continuous communication with each other and with the leaders of the group.

We have said that the creation of the productivity climate—or a climate for results—within the organization is the leader's responsibility. If it is to motivate people to dynamic action, it must be based on deep conviction—conveyable only when the head of the organization communicates his personal objectives into soundly conceived company objectives. Any problem can be solved, any challenges can be met, when the top executive begins to exercise real leadership and states his beliefs in inspiring words. Soon he will find himself surrounded by bright-eyed associates who are eager to prove that it can be done and want to be judged by actual achievement. This is the beginning of the sort of climate that is essential if any combination of people in an organization structure is to realize its maximum potential.

The Organization Chart—Results or Esthetics?

We have said, too, that the better the climate within the organization, the less the need for an excessively formal organization structure. Many organizations do not have an organization chart. Does this mean that they have a climate for results? Not at all. In most cases it means that they have been lax in using one of the tools of organization.

The only reason for using any organization or management tool is that it contributes to the effective achievement of results. A company may have an organization manual luxuriously bound in leather and stamped in gold, with each chart artistically drawn to fill one page precisely. Yet, for all the good it does, the company might never have had a formal organization structure. At the opposite extreme is the company where an employee can comment (with the type of pride that any president would be pleased to hear): "We don't have an organization chart. If we did have one, it wouldn't mean much because we're growing so fast it would be obsolete by the time it was duplicated and distributed."

The organization chart should be used only when it will be more effective than other tools. For example:

- To clarify graphically the reporting relationships that exist between positions within an existing organization.
- As a tool for planning changes in the existing organization.
- To help people outside the organization make decisions on whom to contact.
- To help new employees find their way around the organization.

The value of organization charts and manuals must be constantly weighed in terms of contribution to profits. There is no need to revise them each time a man or a function is changed; many companies simply announce the change, letting people pencil it in until such time as the chart or manual may be reissued. This tends to keep everyone alert and to insure that when a new edition appears it will be reviewed carefully instead of being filed with no thought of what its implications may be.

In short, let the technicians and chartmakers worry about the esthetics. As a manager, you should be concerned with whether or not the chart you issue—or receive—will be of any value in terms of actual job performance.

Creativity and the Organization

Cut off creativity and an organization will wither on the vine and die. Without creativity it cannot perpetuate itself.

A rigid, inflexible organization structure often stymies rather than encourages creativity. This is especially true when job descriptions are allowed to box in a position so tightly that the person who fills it doesn't feel he is expected to use initiative, individuality, judgment, and wisdom on the job.

In such organizations it isn't uncommon for an employee to lapse into the habit of escaping accountability by merely stating: "It wasn't in my job description, so I didn't do it. I assumed someone else was accountable." Such a man is myopic, destined to shape up or ship out. If he is lucky, he will reach retirement before the company collapses or new management pumps energy into it and casts him aside. Less fortunately, he may be turned out to wander aimlessly from job to job—all, quite possibly, because he has in good faith accepted the dictates of an overly restrictive organization and lost contact with his ability to be creative.

DEVELOPING A TOUGH-MINDED CLIMATE

An organization, to continue in business, must balance organized effort with encouragement of creativity. There is really no dichotomy between the two. "Organized" creativity is quite attainable within a climate of stretch, accountability, and targeted innovation.

Results-Oriented Job Descriptions

Like organization charts, job descriptions in their simplest form are merely tools of organization and management. They are guides, and guides only, to organized action and should never contribute toward stifling individual creativity. They were never meant to pinpoint each and every action expected from a job, nor were they meant to replace judgment and wisdom. Hence they should be kept simple.

Job descriptions should make a valid contribution to increased profits or be eliminated as excess baggage. Their major faults, as they are currently used in business, are that they

1. Focus on activity instead of results.
2. Do not provide for measuring performance.
3. Do not provide for stretch and growth.

The typical description of a job outlines in general terms what the person who is on the job does—that is, *activity*. What he accomplishes, on the other hand, is *results*. Activity may or may not be converted into profit, but results are specifics that can be measured in terms of their contribution to profit.

What does the president expect from, say, the vice president of marketing? Does he expect him merely to develop a sales organization, or does he expect him to develop an organization that will increase yearly sales to $50 million, with a ratio of salary and direct selling expense amounting to no more than 10 per cent of sales, while maintaining a profit contribution, before overhead, equal to 30 per cent of sales? Obviously he wants a sales organization which will accomplish specific results. Some results, admittedly, will be less specific than others, and performance may be more difficult to measure. Here, for example, is a representative list—a mixture of the general and the specific—for our vice president of marketing:

- Initiation of a formal sales promotion and advertising program that will promote products on a year-round basis. (Plans due January 1.)
- Reduction of the ratio of direct sales expense to sales from 8 to 5 per cent.
- Increase in dollar sales per salesman to 150 per cent of the average salesman's goal in similar companies. Yearly average per salesman to be as follows: rural, $1.5 million; metropolitan, $2 million.
- A candid personal review of each salesman's strengths and weaknesses. (Prior to July 1.)
- Initiation of a proceduralized reporting system to provide the general manager with information on significant sales trends and sales activity on a monthly basis. (By February 1.)
- Development of a measure for determining the company's share of market by product and geographic area.
- Establishment of a system for providing the sales manager with a weekly summary of significant sales activity and results: calls made, work estimated, and so forth.
- Specific recommendations on how to increase profitable sales based upon market analysis of customers' and potential customers' attitudes toward the company's products, policies, sales, and service.

The president does not tell the vice president of marketing how he is to bring these results about. He leaves this up to the vice president's judgment and wisdom. Once the vice president has developed the necessary plans and the president has approved them, the resulting commitments become the basis for measuring performance. Thus the vice president has ample scope for stretch and growth, especially if guidelines are kept to a minimum.

The following guides were developed to provide maximum freedom of action within one company:

1. Your job description outlines only the most significant aspects of your position, those aspects that distinguish it from other positions. It is not meant to pinpoint all the responsibilities of your position, and you are to use mature judgment in interpreting its full scope.

DEVELOPING A TOUGH-MINDED CLIMATE

2. The phrase "full managerial authority" as stated in your position description is to be interpreted liberally. At the same time you are expected to use good common sense. You should assume that you have authority commensurate with the responsibilities of your position unless otherwise specified. When doubt exists, you should ask your immediate manager for clarification, but this should not be used as a crutch to justify lack of action on your part.
3. You are expected to indicate in the last section of your position description how the specific results expected will be achieved. List the major steps you will undertake toward the accomplishment of the results expected and assign priority for accomplishment of each.
4. You are expected not to fail on a commitment, but from time to time it may be impossible to meet a deadline. In these cases, you should discuss matters with your supervisor; whenever possible, commitments will then be retargeted. *Failure to meet a commitment without discussing it prior to the deadline is more serious than changing a commitment in advance because such failure may upset the intricate pattern of other commitments that mean success or failure for the company.*
5. Coordination and cooperation between equal management team members are essential to the organization. When two members of a team coordinate and cooperate, they assist each other to achieve the results expected of their positions. You are encouraged to coordinate and cooperate as thoroughly as possible. Should differences of opinion occur, each party has an obligation to present his views to his manager.
6. You will be able to further clarify the results expected of your position by relating them to the results expected of other positions reporting to your manager, your manager's job description, and so forth.

The sum total of the results expected of all positions in a profit-making concern is reflected in the profitability of the company. Should management fail to make the targeted profit, the reason will be apparent from a review of the results that were not achieved. This will point out where decisive action must be taken to overcome weaknesses.

SUMMARY AND ACTION STEPS

1. Determine whether your organization is meeting the needs of all its people.
   a. Develop a list of the needs you personally expect to satisfy through the organization.
   b. Ask members of your immediate staff what needs they expect to satisfy through your organization.
   c. Have a needs survey conducted among people at all levels within your organization.
   d. Personally, and in conjunction with your staff, determine what results the company wants to achieve.
   e. Initiate a termination procedure with specific emphasis on depth interviews and post-exit questionnaires to determine what needs were not met by the company.
   f. Personally determine what needs present company objectives are designed to meet.
2. Create a climate for results.
   a. Restate company objectives which provide for the needs of the people within the organization. Be specific.
   b. Communicate and sell these objectives throughout the organization with specific emphasis on what accomplishment of each one means to all concerned. This will give people a reason for working toward them.
   c. Encourage everyone to determine what accomplishment of the objectives means to him as an individual.
3. Develop an organization structure designed to achieve the desired results.
   a. Specify what has to be done to achieve each objective.
   b. Lay out the work on an organizational chart by function.
4. Combine functional organization with staff strengths for maximum results.
   a. Evaluate the strengths of your staff—if feasible, by the use of psychological tests and the like.
   b. Modify the functional organization to take advantage of these strengths.
5. State in writing the results required of each position in the organization.
   a. Encourage participation on the part of each staff member.
   b. Provide flexibility and encourage creativity.
   c. Provide opportunity for each man to exercise maximum authority.
   d. Be specific as to what is expected, when it is to be accomplished, and how much is required.

DEVELOPING A TOUGH-MINDED CLIMATE

    e. Pinpoint the action that will be taken if the results are not achieved.
    f. Determine the actual profit contribution expected of each major function.
6. Insist that each staff member make personal commitments as to how the expected results will be accomplished.
    a. Set a target date for discussing each man's plans.
    b. Modify his plans only when it is clearly apparent that they will conflict with accomplishment of the expected results.
    c. Establish dates on which to follow up the major steps toward accomplishment of the results.
7. Have each staff member repeat this process with each member of his staff—and so on down through the organization.
8. Follow up on commitments and take disciplinary action when commitments are not met.
9. Make sure that the need for profit is thoroughly understood. Talk about profit and its components.
10. Make sure every executive knows the profit contribution to which he is committed. In short, *organize to make profit happen.*

CHAPTER IV

Tough-Minded Marketing Management

DESPITE THE NEW ELECTRONIC TOOLS AND THE EVOLUTION OF "scientific" marketing, nothing has as yet replaced marketing management. The marketing manager is here to stay at least until computers can be programed to supply wisdom, judgment, reason, intuition, and an occasional hunch.

Certainly nothing is likely in the foreseeable future to replace the exceptional management needed to meet the challenges and complexities of tomorrow's marketplace. New market segments will constantly be developing and requiring identification as old markets splinter and become less definable. Improved technology will continually be increasing production capacity faster than population growth can absorb it, thus requiring companies to be alert to new consumer needs and new products to meet them. Computers will enable competitors to discover marketing strategies before a comfortable sales lead can be gained. Revolutionized distribution requirements, with emphasis on better service and lower costs, will demand new and improved methods; increased advertising, coupled with higher advertising costs, will force more careful spending of the advertising dollar.

While it is probable that the average marketing executive would be quite ineffective if he were suddenly transported 15 years into the future, he will be extremely effective 15 years hence if he meets each of those 15 years one at a time, solving the problems of today and anticipating those of tomorrow. The challenges ahead are going to be met, not by supermen, but rather by ordinary executives motivated to develop outstanding management ability, to settle for nothing less than excellence.

What can today's marketing manager do to insure that he and his company can confidently grasp tomorrow's opportunities? Four things:

1. Prepare himself for the future.
2. Create a marketing orientation throughout the company.

3. Develop a marketing plan.
4. Organize the marketing job.

Preparing Oneself for the Future

Good managers in all company areas realize that personal development is a continuing process. Just keeping up to date with the body of management knowledge is time-consuming and will become more so. The greatest personal problem facing the individual manager, however, is the need to develop or possibly change those abilities, traits, and attitudes which are the components of total personality. For some very distinct characteristics, evident in few marketing managers today, seem certain to become the pattern for tomorrow. The emerging executive will have to demonstrate these specific, tough-minded attributes if his job of managing is to be made easier and more effective.

1. *Ability to make things happen.* This marketing manager is not content with letting things happen; he attempts to control the future rather than let the future control him. He is able to separate the reality from the dream, the attainable from the unattainable. He is a goal setter, adept at recognizing opportunities, at defining problems and translating them into specific objectives. His positive attitude toward the attainment of established objectives inspires the belief that the impossible is possible and the impractical can be made practical.

2. *Ability to think intuitively.* The art of intuitive thinking can be developed, but few men consciously attempt it. Particularly evident in successful marketing men, it is the ability to know immediately, without conscious measuring, the correct decision or course of action to be taken. This does not mean basing decisions on hunch or guesswork; instead, it results from an accurate "feel" of the market, a complete knowledge of the situation, and a full understanding of available resources and their capabilities. The intuitive thinker probably makes greater use of market research and other sources of facts than his less gifted and less successful counterpart; by obtaining and absorbing as many facts as possible he can let his subconscious go to work and develop his intuition. Thus, as the years go by, he steadily builds his decision-making skill.

3. *Willingness to accept change.* One of the most essential quali-

ties of the effective marketer is the knack of being flexible, realizing that change is not only inevitable but necessary. Marketing is probably more susceptible to changing conditions than any other area of management; change must be not only accepted but anticipated and made to work *for* the organization rather than against it. This calls for a staff that is open-minded, curious, hungry for innovation, suspicious of conformity, and dissatisfied with any situation that has become habitual. An idea needs encouragement; the premise that it is worthless until someone sells it or makes it a reality must be constantly emphasized.

4. *Skill in developing people.* The effective marketing man firmly believes and faithfully practices the precept that "management is the development of people." He knows that the profit contribution of the marketing function will be no better than its people's ability and desire to contribute. He develops his subordinates by creating an environment in which they are constantly challenged and mediocrity is not accepted, one in which people *want* to work and contribute. He is adamant in requiring that primary psychological needs be provided for. He recognizes strengths and submerged talents, brings them to the surface, and channels them toward achieving company objectives.

5. *Background as a generalist.* Although a student of his specialty, the marketing manager realizes that this is only one of several important functions within the organization. He constantly endeavors to expand his knowledge of production, finance, personnel, and engineering so as to discover and utilize new ideas that will strengthen the marketing effort. He establishes friendly relations with these other departments so as to increase their awareness of marketing problems and to add their strengths to the total marketing function. He has at least a cursory interest in history, the social sciences, and art. He realizes that psychology, sociology, and anthropology all have definite contributions to make to marketing, particularly market evaluation.

Creating a Marketing Orientation

Few companies, if questioned, would concede the possibility that they might not be marketing-oriented. Most endorse the concept and contend they are practicing it enthusiastically. Yet engineers are still designing components with a probable life of 20 years for equipment with a maximum useful life of 10 years, packages are still being designed to utilize special machinery rather than suit the convenience of the consumer, and credit departments are still refusing new accounts instead of determining how to help an account become a better credit risk and a good customer. Employees don't know who customers are or the important role they themselves play in satisfying customer wants. Market researchers are more concerned with methods than with the practical application of facts to the solution of marketing problems. Advertising managers care more about impressing management and other advertising people than about selling products.

Some companies have embraced the marketing concept only to the extent that they have placed the sales and marketing functions under the direction of one man with responsibility for planning, directing, controlling, and coordinating them all. This, however, is just the beginning. For a company to be truly marketing-oriented, every individual in it should understand and believe that *a satisfied customer is the primary source of profit*. Every decision that is reached should be made only after considering in full its possible implications for that customer.

Unless the president has come up through marketing, the job of selling the marketing concept will almost always be the sole responsibility of the marketing manager—a task requiring the utmost in ingenuity, patience, tact, and salesmanship. If he is sufficiently mature, he will accept the fact that, while *he* believes he has the most important job in the company, he is probably the only one who thinks so. He will also realize that the marketing department does not necessarily have to be the most important or most powerful function in the company nor does the marketing manager have to be the highest-ranking or most influential executive. Building the marketing concept strengthens the whole organization by increasing the effectiveness and profit contribution of every department.

Here is how the marketing concept was developed by a medium-size farm implement manufacturer whose vice president of marketing had been fighting an uphill battle to keep his distributor organization happy and intact and to meet customer demands. He knew the potential profits that could be realized with a change in company attitude and the development of a truly marketing-oriented organization, and he planned his strategy well.

The Marketing Department

1. The concept, now called the *customer-awareness program,* was presented to the sales and marketing staff, who were required to submit
   a. The benefits that would occur in their departments or jobs if such a program were adopted.
   b. Specific instances in which negative or apathetic attitudes toward customers hurt the company.
   c. Suggested ways of obtaining better cooperation from other company departments.
   d. Suggested ways in which marketing could cooperate more closely with other departments to improve effectiveness or lower costs.
2. Objective evaluation of the sales and marketing functions indicated a need for development and adoption of an internal consumer-awareness program. It was discovered that the final consumer—the farmer—had received little attention.
3. Marketing objectives were revised and department plans and programs were changed to provide more emphasis on all three classes of customers: distributor, dealer, consumer.
4. Marketing objectives were communicated throughout the department and constantly referred to. Complete knowledge of them was made a strict requirement for all marketing staff people.
5. A market research study was made of the company's image and those of competitors among distributors, dealers, and consumers.

The President

1. Figures for the past ten years were analyzed to show trends in company sales (up), share of market (down), competitors' share (up), market potentials (up), and profit (up slightly).
2. A five-year projection of profits showed an anticipated 50 per cent increase would be possible if the marketing concept were adopted—as compared with a 22 per cent increase if present policies and practices were continued.
3. Specific situations involving poor customer relations were described along with the actual or probable effect of faulty attitudes on sales and profits.

DEVELOPING A TOUGH-MINDED CLIMATE

4. The results of the market research study indicated that while the company's image was still very good, there was a marked increase in the acceptance, by all segments of the market, of two competitors.
5. The role the president would play in selling and installing the program throughout the company was outlined.
6. It was planned that the president would accompany the marketing manager on a two-week field trip to meet salesmen, distributors, and dealers, visit with customers, and see the company's equipment in operation.
7. The programs for selling the marketing concept to the executive staff and the organization as a whole were submitted in outline form.

This carefully planned approach changed the president's attitude from one of polite interest to an excited, enthusiastic desire to get the program under way. He realized the importance of his role and agreed to assume titular responsibility for customer-awareness.

Executive Staff and Department Heads

It is not very difficult to obtain staff agreement that the customer is "king." It is oddly difficult, however, to get intelligent, logical executives to remember this in their day-to-day decisions. Thus the objective in the following steps was not so much to obtain acceptance as to obtain action.

1. A staff meeting was held for all department heads, with the president in the chair, to show why the customer-awareness program was necessary and explain the benefits that would accrue to both the company and the individual.
2. The president held individual conferences with each department head to determine his attitude toward the program, motivate him personally, and discuss implementation within the department.
3. Each department head was required to submit an outline of action steps and time commitments for carrying out the program in his department.
4. Field trips were scheduled to enable each department head to attend sales meetings and get to know customers and consumers.

The immediate effects of departmental action included:

- A value analysis program adopted by purchasing and engineering.
- Simplified billing procedures developed by accounting.
- Increased use of computer time for sales and customer analysis.

- Revision of the employee indoctrination program by personnel.
- Re-evaluation of quality control by production.
- Development of new pricing policies by marketing.
- A customer service program planned by sales.
- Motivation research study by advertising.
- The addition of sales and marketing indoctrination to supervisory development by the training director.
- Re-evaluation of shipping methods by traffic.
- Packaging studies by shipping.

The Employees

The final stage of implementation called for creating an awareness of the customer among all the people in the organization.

1. Every employee, not in sales, who had any direct contract with customers—whether personally, by phone, or through correspondence—was given the same basic indoctrination as a department head.
2. Correspondence and telephone techniques were evaluated with a view toward increased customer empathy.
3. The regular suggestion system was augmented to provide special awards for ideas leading to improved customer relations, improved customer service, or savings of customers' money.
4. All in-plant programs were revised to include information on sales, service, and customer relations. At least one member of the marketing department attended every meeting and participated in at least a portion of it.
5. A new "pride in workmanship" theme was promoted throughout the plant, stressing the customer as beneficiary.
6. The company paper was used extensively to publicize the whole program. A monthly feature column was devoted to customer reactions, with emphasis on any situation that could be tied directly to workmanship.
7. Special bulletin boards were installed to display complimentary letters and complaints from customers.
8. Each employee received company sales literature on products for which he had any responsibility. Particular emphasis was placed on sales claims requiring careful workmanship.
9. Special mailings to employees' homes included a letter from the president explaining the importance of the customer-awareness program.
10. Special displays highlighted company and competitive products. Differences in workmanship were pointed up graphically, and prices were posted.

DEVELOPING A TOUGH-MINDED CLIMATE

Two years have elapsed since this program was first started. Although it is still not complete and will require continuous effort, the results have been dramatic. Sales and profits have exceeded the most optimistic projections. People are enthusiastic about their work, there is a new climate of cooperation, costs are down, and production is up.

Developing a Marketing Plan

Once a company has adopted the marketing concept and it is operating well, real diligence must be displayed by the marketing manager in developing long-range objectives and an overall plan which will insure that the increased sales made possible by the new climate are realized. At the same time he must develop a short-range strategy for getting business *today*. The development of this marketing plan, usually for at least 12 months into the future, not only will insure maximum results but will become the primary vehicle for organizing, coordinating, directing, and controlling the entire marketing function.

Developing a marketing plan requires, first, a comprehensive, objective evaluation of (1) the market and (2) the company and its place in that market. The value of this process lies in the honest attempt to obtain all the pertinent facts, even if they point to weaknesses or failures. Too often there is a tendency to recognize only those facts that verify the astuteness of past decisions or that validate a proposed recommendation. This is not enough; you must determine precisely where you have been, where you are, where you are going. Thus:

- Where are present and prospective customers located? Are there any holes in our distribution?
- What about trends in market potential? Is general demand for our product dying or increasing? Where? Why?
- Who are our competitors and where are they located? What convenience advantages have they?
- Are we selling to the whole or a fragmentized market?
- What are the channels of distribution, past and present, used to serve this market? Are there other, possibly better ways to reach the consumer?

- How is the product used? Can we discover and promote new uses for it?
- What is our advertising history? Has it actually been effective?
- What are our competitors doing in the way of sales, advertising, distribution, sales promotion?
- What are the buying and selling habits of each segment of our distribution network? Are there weak links or unknown quantities?
- What are the sources of our sales dollar? Are significant trends developing?
- What are the sources of sales by geographic area, distribution outlet, product, and the like? What are our sales strengths and weaknesses?
- What is the profit history of each product line? Which ones need replacing or strengthening?
- What is the share-of-market trend by product and geographic area? What kind of a sales job are we actually doing?
- What are the major strengths of the company's marketing function? Are we building on them?

As you answer these questions, a new perspective will begin to form and specific problems and opportunities will emerge. For example, a food-processing firm identified a high percentage of its customers as being over 45 years of age; it was reaching only a small part of its market. Changes in advertising and sales promotion specifically aimed at the younger housewife increased overall market penetration and yielded a substantial sales increase. Similarly, a manufacturer of fabricating machinery discovered that a history of product reliability and service had maintained sales, but that the firm was being outclassed in product design by its hungry competition. This company was able to institute design improvements before the competition made too great inroads into its market.

When the problems and opportunities have been defined, the list should be submitted to each marketing staff member for his best thinking as to the goals that should be set for (1) the marketing division as a whole and (2) his individual department. With this help the marketing manager can develop short-range marketing objectives for the division and the specific results that will be required from each department. He must then sit down with each department head to review these results requirements and secure agreement that they can and will be met or exceeded. The department head is responsible for developing the plans his group will need to contribute to divisional objectives and to meet each of his results requirements.

A metal-fabricating company discovered through market evaluation and analysis that the potential for its heating-equipment division was increasing and that this division could logically be expected to achieve an 8 per cent increase in sales. With this information, the marketing manager made it one of his divisional objectives to "increase the sales of the heating-equipment division to $3,750,000 in the next fiscal year." Each department—sales, advertising, sales promotion, market research, and distribution—was required to submit a plan of action that would be taken to insure this objective was met.

The sales department, for example, listed these major steps:

1. Determine and add necessary number of manufacturers' representatives to sales staff.
2. Determine and appoint necessary number of full-time salesmen to sales force.
3. Increase the effectiveness of present sales force.
4. Determine new markets for present products.

The action necessary to accomplish these steps was determined; and, as each was further broken down into substeps, still more recommendations were accumulated for preliminary approval by the marketing managers and the determination of resource requirements, each action or program outlined being evaluated in terms of cost, personnel requirements (tentative delegation of assignments was made), special material and facility requirements, and time requirements (including target dates). With this information a realistic budget could be developed—a budget based upon resources needed to obtain results rather than, as is so often the case, upon past spending.

The completed plan was given to the marketing manager for approval. After the necessary modifications it was placed with the plans of the other departments to become part of the company's marketing plan that would be guiding the operation of the marketing division for the next 12 months. The marketing manager would know specifically what was being done; and his people would know, not only what they were expected to do, but how they were going to do it. The manager would be able to exercise much closer control more simply. Periodic review of the plan with his department heads would determine the progress being made and indicate whether target dates were being met. In addition, the plan would be an excellent tool for measuring management performance, providing a sound basis for determining individual contributions to divisional and company objectives.

Planning will and does solve many management problems. It will not of itself insure success; for, once formulated, plans must be followed—and there are too many cases where extensive plans have ended up in the files. When, however, planning becomes a management way of life, the results can be spectacular. If you can't decide whether or not you can afford to stop putting out fires long enough to install a planning progam in your company, ask yourself one question: "Would it concern me if my competition did?"

Organizing the Marketing Job

Marketing organizations are like any others—they have a tendency to grow complacent. Sales managers write bulletins simply because one is due every week. Sales promotion men run contests because "we have three every year." Advertising men write ads because a new one is needed next month. Market research people make a survey because the department has to be kept busy.

These are not unusual situations; they occur every day in every company. The accumulation of "fat" must be stopped periodically, however, or profits will disappear entirely. To insure that a taut, disciplined, results-oriented organization is created and maintained, the marketing manager must re-evaluate his entire organization at least once every two years. Everyone's talents must be reconsidered in relation to the duties assigned him. Everyone must face the test of one question: "Would I hire this man for this job if the position were vacant, knowing the man as I do?" If the answer is no, there are three alternatives:

1. Keep him in his present job on probation if he has the basic abilities and can be motivated to perform. He must be completely informed of the results expected of him; what changes he must make, if any; and the action that will be taken if satisfactory performance does not materialize.
2. Assign him to a job that matches his abilities more closely—but only if he can make a substantial contribution to marketing objectives in the new position.
3. Replace him.

In addition, every marketing function should be isolated, defined, and evaluated in terms of its contribution to marketing objectives. The relative importance of functions is constantly changing. Pricing may have been highly critical two years ago when there was a need for new formulas, but its importance may have waned if present policies and procedures seem satisfactory and require only periodic study. On the other hand, advertising may be much more important this year because a new consumer product will triple the advertising budget. All such factors should have a pronounced effect upon the assignment of responsibility.

In re-evaluating and rebuilding its management team, a medium-size manfacturing concern took these steps:

1. Marketing and marketing department objectives were carefully reviewed to be sure they were logical and attainable, provided sufficient stretch, and would result in maximum contribution to company objectives.
2. Since this was the first time the marketing organization had been completely evaluated, all key personnel were tested and appraised to identify any hidden talents.
3. All key personnel were evaluated by their immediate superiors to identify strengths in experience, knowledge, and ability to get things done.
4. All major functions and tasks currently being performed by marketing were listed.
5. Each function and task was evaluated in terms of its importance in meeting present objectives, the logicalness of its present assignment, and the department and person to which it should be assigned.

TOUGH-MINDED MARKETING MANAGEMENT

6. The results necessary to meet department and division objectives were specifically defined for each function and task. For example:
   Sales compensation: Develop a plan that will provide optimum incentive without increasing unit sales costs.
   Sales operations: Develop minimum performance standards for dealers.
   Forecasting: Determine market potentials by county.
   Order service: Reduce time for order processing half a day without increasing costs.
   Media evaluation: Develop method and measure contribution of individual media to overall advertising results.
   Consumer research: Determine specific consumer wants, features, service, convenience, and the like for Product Line A.
   Market research: Design market test program for new Product X.
   Sales catalogue: Condense catalogue for direct mail program.
7. Functions and tasks were assigned to individuals on the basis of their strengths and ability to perform them.
8. Job descriptions were written to stress results requirements and responsibility.

SUMMARY AND ACTION STEPS

The need for good marketing managers has never been so great as it is right now, and the need is going to be even greater in the future for men with the ability to manage—to plan, organize, coordinate, direct, and control the marketing and sales functions—men with the ability to get things done through other people—men who will

- Make things happen, not just talk.
- Think intuitively, not in a sterile, overly structured sequence.
- Accept change; be impatient with "abominable no men."
- Develop people, converting laissez-faire negativism to vibrant positivism.
- Be broad-gauge; know the *what, where, when, how,* and *why* of the entire company.

To insure that the marketing department develops its full potential, it must operate within a total marketing climate which embraces the whole

DEVELOPING A TOUGH-MINDED CLIMATE

company. To develop such a climate, it is the marketing manager's responsibility to sell the marketing concept to his own people, to the president, to the department heads, and to the employees. While the adoption of this concept should ease the problems of marketing, it will place greater responsibility on the marketing manager to take full advantage of the increased opportunity for sales. The best insurance for achieving full benefit from the new climate is a comprehensive marketing plan. Such a plan will require:

1. An objective evaluation of the company's situation, market, distribution, and competition.
2. The recognition of opportunities and the definition of problems.
3. The conversion of problems and opportunities into specific objectives.
4. The development of action steps necessary to meet these objectives.
5. The determination of resource requirements in terms of men, money, materials, time, and space.
6. The establishment of controls to insure that the plan is followed.
7. Determination of the organization needed to carry out this comprehensive plan. This will require:
   a. Evaluation of present personnel.
   b. Definition of all necessary functions.
   c. Assignment of these functions to appropriate personnel.
   d. Definition of the results expected.

CHAPTER V

The Production Executive Today and Tomorrow

THE ABILITY TO MEET SCHEDULE WITH A HIGH-QUALITY, LOW-COST item is the key objective of every conscientious production manager. Certainly there are few who are not striving for just this. In too many cases, however, the good intentions are smothered in "activity" and the end result (on shipping day) is mass confusion, overtime, hot tempers, and unkept promises. There may even be an occasional grievance if the union is involved.

Why does this happen? How *can* it happen in this day of production schedules, forecasts, quality control devices, flow charts, PERT, and all the other scientific aids to management? It happens because the production manager does not practice the simple fundamentals of managing people and using them to his advantage in getting the work out the back door.

Management Know-how and the Production Man

There are few jobs in a manufacturing organization today that make so many and such varied demands on any one individual as that of the production executive. Probably he began as a plant worker and, because of his outstanding production record, was made a foreman—even though he had no real idea how to manage. Then, in time, he was promoted to higher and higher levels, still with little or no understanding of people or how to make the most of their abilities. No wonder he is so often out of his depth and, frequently, develops a "bull of the woods" attitude.

In one company whose sales were phenomenal, manufacturing couldn't seem to keep up. As one walked through the production area, it was obvious that equipment and facilities were adequate; the ingredient that appeared to be lacking was the bustle that is characteristic of a truly productive shop. Could this probably be a clue to the problem? It was.

DEVELOPING A TOUGH-MINDED CLIMATE

The company had been founded by two partners. One, an outgoing, cheerful person, handled sales; the other, who preferred to work alone, had seemed the logical man to stay at home and run the shop.

Here was a man with little management know-how, who did not enjoy working with people, attempting to head up a growing production organization. His intentions were good, but his approach was not dynamic. He zeroed in on weaknesses and ignored strengths. His production people were not happy because he seldom spoke to them; when he did, it was only to reprimand them for poor quality. Turnover was high, and much valuable time went into training replacements. Moreover, word had spread through the community that the company was not a desirable place to work.

This was clearly a case of inappropriate assignment of managerial talent. Fortunately, even with this burden, the company had grown to a point where the one partner could be placed in a position of responsibility outside the manufacturing area. He was replaced by a seasoned, tough-minded manager who enjoyed working with people and understood their requirements. He stressed individual contribution and growth, provided opportunities for advancement, and encouraged recognition, teamwork, security, and a sense of belonging.

Steps Toward the Productivity Climate

Here are the major steps he took initially to meet his people's needs:

1. He sat down with each of his foremen to explain what he planned to accomplish. At the same time he made it clear he would welcome suggestions for increasing productivity. These sessions led to regularly scheduled informational staff meetings. (Recognition and sense of belonging.)
2. He established a suggestion system to encourage ideas from production employees. All were considered, and those with merit received a fair monetary reward. (Recognition and sense of belonging.)
3. He helped establish a companywide monthly newsletter which was distributed to all employees and was designed to pass along general information of concern to company employees as well

as to provide recognition for outstanding performance. Bulletin boards were installed to supplement it. (Recognition and sense of belonging.)
4. He established an annual performance appraisal system, a more equitable salary structure and a bonus plan based on performance, and a fair and impartial bidding system for jobs in all classifications. (Security and opportunity.)
5. In conjunction with a local trade school, he established a program whereby the company paid the tuition of any employee who successfully completed a night course in any job-related field. (Recognition, opportunity, security, sense of belonging.)
6. He installed information boards in each department and posted data on backlogs, shipments, and departmental efficiency on them regularly. (Recognition, security, sense of belonging.)
7. He launched an effective and well-policed safety program. (Recognition and security.)
8. He established and directed a program of management development for all supervisory personnel and for carefully selected hourly-paid employees who showed interest in becoming members of management. (Recognition, security, opportunity, sense of belonging.)
9. At *every* opportunity he stressed quality and profit and the resulting benefits to all. (Security and opportunity.)
10. He weeded out the incompetents and insisted that everyone understand that the only reason for being on the payroll was to produce profitable results. (Opportunity.)

Within three months production was creeping up toward standard and meeting sales demands—all because this man could manage, because he understood people and knew that, basically, people *want* to work but must have a climate that requires much of them and rewards them in proportion.

Acting like a Top Executive

The tough-minded production executive of tomorrow, of next year, of the future, will be the man who thinks, acts, and responds like a top executive. He will find out all he can about the principles which guide his chief executive and then proceed to direct his own area in a manner consistent with the same basic principles of sound management. He will have prepared himself to exercise the same managerial functions. As a dynamic leader he will be able to organize his subordinates effectively, interpret company objectives to them in terms of production requirements, and guide them in achieving the established goals.

Production control. The production executive not only must think in terms of immediate planning, scheduling, and control but must be able to visualize the impact that these can and will have on overall accomplishment in terms of company growth and profit. Effort cannot be sporadic, with alternate periods of action and inaction. Planning must be a continuing, unfolding process with objectives set further and further ahead.

The tough-minded production executive knows that maximum accomplishment is achieved only when individual members of the management team have established the proper rapport and are thoroughly familiar with overall company goals. One of these, for example, is to convert raw materials to finished products in the most economical way. If inventories eat up the major share of available working capital, there will be no cash with which to meet payrolls, buy raw materials, pay advertising bills, and underwrite sales promotions. Therefore, the optimum balance of inventories by effective scheduling will aid greatly in reducing cash investment.

The production executive who is managing as though he were the chief executive also realizes that top management looks to the production planning and control function as a major means for attaining its goal of increased sales with greater profit and less investment. He and his department can make a major contribution toward this end by insuring that

1. Raw materials, standard finished parts, and semifinished products are available to the foreman and workers when required so that each production operation can be started on time.
2. All possible methods of manufacture are analyzed to determine the very best one compatible with a given set of circumstances, facilities, and requirements.
3. Methods of manufacture are realistically related to available production facilities, and replacement requirements are con-

tinually evaluated. Effective policies relating to tools, jigs, and fixtures are established and complied with.
4. Efficient materials routing has been achieved through careful study of operational sequence, machine layout, and materials handling requirements.
5. Realistic and meaningful estimates of manufacturing requirements are achieved by progressive industrial engineering. Machine loading requirements are carefully evaluated to permit optimum utilization of facilities, equipment, and manpower.
6. Dispatching, followed by timely follow-up to provide efficient feedback and prompt review of schedule requirements and target dates, receives the emphasis it deserves.
7. Data relating to past experience are carefully evaluated in order that methods, facilities, and processes may be improved where possible.

If, as a result, the production executive can increase output 10 per cent with plant and equipment worth $5 million, he has in effect increased the worth of these assets by 10 per cent, or $500,000, a sizable contribution to the company's financial position.

Cost control. When the tough-minded production man is managing like the top executive, he is constantly aware of the need for reducing or minimizing costs. One of his objectives must be to manufacture the company's products at costs lower than those of its nearest competitor possessing equivalent equipment. This he will accomplish by means of continuing innovation in production methods, vigorous cost reduction efforts of all kinds, and improved relationships with his people.

First and foremost, he is expected to develop an efficient production organization on which quality, costs, maintenance, and innovation will depend. But he himself must depend upon people to do the observing and the thinking that will result in more efficient and economical production. The degree to which he practices tough-minded management will largely determine the knowledge his people have of their costs and the extent to which they will try to control those costs. For his part, the tough-minded production executive will be aware that all operating decisions must be based on costs and that the success of his operation will be determined by how wisely the decisions are made. He will therefore maintain a good working knowledge of his overall function in terms of

- Material costs per unit of production.
- Man-hours per unit of production.
- Investment in equipment and machines per unit of production.
- Total cost per unit produced.
- Ratio of supervision to labor.
- Variation from established production schedules.
- Variation from standard costs.
- Raw materials inventory costs.
- Utilization of production facilities, machines, and equipment (per cent).
- Customer delivery dates not met (per cent).
- Customer complaints about product quality or performance.
- Percentage of substandard units and scrap.
- Number of overtime hours per period.
- Down time due to machine breakdown, illness, accidents, slow-downs, strikes.
- Maintenance repair costs.

The production executive will work closely with his subordinates, and they in turn will be expected to coordinate their work with his. Very often he will be in a position to advise them on a course of action which will greatly minimize operating costs due to unforeseen delays or expense. He will doggedly impress upon them the fact that communication and cooperation are indivisible.

Quality control. The topnotch production executive will also recognize the value of working closely with people in such other areas as research and development. He will find out what they are doing and offer his assistance wherever possible. His valuable experience and know-how may go a long way toward helping to solve technical problems involving quality and performance.

At the same time the production executive will make sure his own people are fully aware of their responsibility for turning out a quality product. Each worker should take personal pride in the part he plays in creating it; quality cannot be inspected into the product, *it must be built in.* Quality control requires constant follow-up, continuous emphasis, and careful programing; it must become a way of life for the organization that is to win out over its competitors. It must influence every function of the business which can affect the product; research and development, purchasing, manufacturing, stores, materials handling, shipping. Production employees will regard inspectors not as bogeymen but as members of a total organization dedicated to overall excellence.

When the quality control program is effectively administered, certain very tangible benefits will result.

1. Increased production:
    a. Identification and development of the one best method.
    b. Greater worker confidence in the operation.
    c. Marked reduction in rejected units.
2. Lower unit costs:
    a. Minimization of the unit rejection rate.
    b. Minimal reworking and scrapping of defective parts.
3. Improved employee morale:
    a. Less tension between the foreman and the workers or inspectors and between the foreman and the quality control department.
    b. Greater unity of effort.
4. Better quality:
    a. Lower rejection rates and, consequently, lower inspection costs.
    b. Fewer customer complaints.

Methods improvement. The production executive who prizes excellence recognizes the full value of the industrial engineering function. He also accepts the philosophy that responsibility for its proper utilization rests squarely with him and other members of top management.

Here again the impact of close coordination and cooperation with other groups is impressive. Sound relationships must exist among industrial engineering, finance, and research and development. It is extremely important that industrial engineering in particular be staffed with men who have that well-developed understanding of people—empathy, if you will—which is such a factor in the productivity climate.

DEVELOPING A TOUGH-MINDED CLIMATE

The end result of the industrial engineering function must be profit improvement. The production executive will expect, with the aid of continuing industrial engineering and methods improvement effort, to accomplish the following:

1. Development of a sound layout for the manufacturing operation—one which anticipates needs long before they become urgent.
2. Establishment of the simplest and most economical work methods and processes.
3. Determination of the most desirable lot sizes and work-in-process requirements for all phases of the operation.
4. Material and quality specifications and standard practice instructions covering all production operations.
5. Training programs to aid in the development of supervisors and workers.
6. Sound cost controls, budget controls, and performance requirements.
7. Performance standards, for every phase of the production function, which take into account quality and utilization of resources and materials.
8. Position descriptions and specifications, for each production job, stressing results desired and insuring that each makes a direct contribution to the overall manufacturing function.

Innovation. The tough-minded production executive is a broad-gauge manager well informed on matters outside his own area, able to see how functions must integrate to form the efficient, organized, effective machine that provides the end result. He will see the wisdom of providing his people with facilities which will encourage them to perform with increasing vigor; he will search for new machines with which to do a better job without sacrificing human dignity but, instead, permitting the worker to exercise his talents with the feeling that he is participating in positive, worthwhile accomplishment.

This superior executive will at every opportunity seek to foresee the needs of tomorrow and, when that day comes, will be providing products with which his company can lead the field. Concurrently he will have taken action to insure that facilities, machines, and equipment are under development with which to turn out the products which will succeed them.

Conscientiousness Properly Applied

We have spoken of the "conscientious" production manager. Most of his problems will, in fact, grow out of the way he applies this conscientiousness to getting things done through people. Conscientiousness can be a desirable attribute only if it is used as a motivating drive to satisfy a hunger for knowledge, achievement, and the desire to do an outstanding job as a production leader. If used in any other way, it is nothing more than bluff and good intentions and will never produce measurable results. In short, good intentions as reflected by a corrugated brow mean nothing.

In most types of management, some knowledge can be gained academically by younger men preparing for executive responsibilities. For example, accounting, marketing, and purchasing fall in this category. But, with the exception of a few graduate school courses spanning the broad spectrum of industrial management, there is little being offered in the mechanics of production management. Far too often, current academic offerings are entrusted to individuals who must temper with theory the knowledge they share with their students.

The logical way to prepare young supervisors for advancement in production management is by practical experience prior to assuming greater responsibility. Some grease under the fingernails can be a real asset to the academically qualified young man, and there are a number of methods by which this can be accomplished. Perhaps the best is an understudy program coupled with a series of participative classroom sessions on all facets of management. Well planned and professionally handled, such a program is a real shot in the arm for the production management team—provided great care is taken in the selection of participants. Inclusion in the program must be based on the individual's potential for learning and becoming an important part of the production organization. Candidates must have energy, courage, and a strong desire for achievement.

Much too frequently today, the production man is referred to as the "big hard guy with little ideas," or the production area is considered to be a wasteland of narrow-mindedness. This image has been brought about by production people themselves, and in most cases it is a sure description.

Take Pete, production manager for a firm manufacturing a high-quality line of durable goods, who was embroiled in a series of fiery arguments with his president. Pete had come up "the hard way." There was no machine in the plant that he couldn't operate better or faster than any of his men, and he was always quick to prove this if there was the slightest doubt of it.

In recent months, he had become disagreeable. He accepted suggestions only grudgingly, no matter what their source, and sometimes only after violent outbursts. His subordinates hesitated to approach him with problems because his answers were blunt to the point of rudeness. His relations with other departments had collapsed; sales, for example, had issued an ultimatum to the president and would communicate with Pete only by written memo.

Certainly, the easy way out of this situation was termination, but Pete did have strengths which were well worth saving. After 20 years he knew the mechanics of production far better than anyone else in the company. He was energetic, hard-working, and loyal. His problem, simply stated, was not much different from that of many production managers: He had confused tough-mindedness with two-fisted roughness and sincerely believed that this was the only way to run a taut ship. He knew something was wrong but couldn't identify it. The harder he tried to "pound sense" into people, the more they avoided him.

What was the basic difficulty here? Pete did not have a college degree and had taken to reacting resentfully each time a graduate was added to the staff. It was obvious to him that the newcomer was after his job. He had vowed that whenever a new idea or suggestion was put forward he would better it—just to prove to top management that he should always be the production manager.

Attitudes—Performance—Balance—Stability

The development program set up for Pete was not lengthy. The objective was to change certain of his attitudes, to encourage a positive instead of a negative, obstructionist approach to his daily activities, both inside and outside the plant.

He now knows that every man who aspires to be a success or to move on to a higher position will be helped or hindered by the effect that his attitudes have on his performance—and he knows that his performance affects everyone around him. He knows, too, that there are five resources which the production manager—like all managers—must utilize effectively: time, space, materials, money, and men. All five, he realizes, can be used to his advantage provided he will plan rather than operate by the seat of his pants; but, of them, manpower is the most important.

In short, Pete knows that to provide balance and assure stability, the production manager must make certain that he carefully plans, organizes, coordinates, directs, and controls all the resources and facilities available to him but, above all, his people's efforts.

SUMMARY AND ACTION STEPS

The big man of tomorrow in any field recognizes that the most precious asset he can inculcate in his people is clearly understood and applied principles—plus those all-important attitudes. What are some of the principles? Here are a few that every production executive should believe in:

- Free enterprise applies to all, not just a select few.
- The potential for new product innovation is still limitless. We are just beginning.
- Quality is paramount. No one need apologize for demanding it.

With attitudes, the problem is of course to change one's own thinking and—by the force of example—influence that of others. The areas toward which Pete was first counseled to direct his concern may be summarized as follows:

1. *Be courteous.* The position of production manager is a position of power. There will always be a temptation to be rude when dealing with subordinates because their questions and problems are in effect interrupting a planned schedule of activities. If this temptation is not checked, the rudeness becomes a substitute for good management. *Always plan your time to include interruptions.*
2. *Be willing to learn from others.* You will probably not always agree with others, but at least hear them out. It may surprise you to find out how much you can learn from listening. It will also encourage your subordinates to bring their ideas to you, and as a result you will actually be able to manage with less effort.

DEVELOPING A TOUGH-MINDED CLIMATE

3. *Approach problems positively.* It would not be wise to accept every suggestion at face value or to think that you can solve completely every problem which is handed to you; however, your chances for success will be greater if you adopt a positive approach. Constantly complaining about the obstacles in your way will only make the task more difficult.
4. *Never subjugate yourself.* You are as important as anyone else you work with. The respect you have for yourself is largely a reflection of the respect you have for others. You must know you *have* something before you can *give* something.
5. *Give credit where credit is due.* We all seek recognition—but don't try to take all the credit for a job well done or you may find you're working by yourself. Others will be reluctant to cooperate with you.
6. *Practice empathy.* Listen to problems from the other fellow's point of view. This involves more than understanding what he may be saying or doing. It means an honest attempt to understand *why* he is saying or doing it.
7. *Be flexible.* Tenacity—to a point—is necessary in your position, but flexibility is a "must." Remember that you can't be right all the time and that, if you attempt never to be swayed by changes, you probably will meet equally stubborn resistance.
8. *Be constructive with others.* Be certain that you recognize your shortcomings and have undertaken to correct those shortcomings before you dare to be critical of your associates.

Members of production management today are confronted with two paths to the future. One path will lead to failure, for it is directed toward doing nothing except in the same old tyrannical way. The other calls for rising above the fraternity of stereotyped roughnecks and becoming a believer in the productivity approach to management.

When the going gets tough, the tough get going.

CHAPTER VI

Making Systemation Work

TODAY'S COMPLEX PATTERN OF BUSINESS ACTIVITY IS FORCING THE progressive top manager to appraise his company's efforts realistically in terms of systems, procedures, electronic data processing, automation, and all the modern innovations and techniques required to stay in the competitive race. It is no longer a game of "wait and see"; the company that takes such an approach is doomed from the start.

To insure both direction and force for the systems effort, management must state in clearly defined terms the policies and objectives which will serve as guideposts for a sound, profitable program. It is surprising how few companies do so—in view of the great impact that data processing can have on the organization and, too, the investment required to support an installation. The failure to formalize objectives and establish definitive policies has many times created problems of communication and liaison between the various levels of management and the groups charged with systems/data processing. Wherever most success has been achieved, the information requirements of the organization were determined first in terms of desired results. Then equipment was obtained and used to fulfill the requirements as efficiently as possible.

Systemation can make a distinct contribution to any company willing to undertake it in a positive manner. It involves no dark secrets, no highly confidential formulas. First, the desire to make it work must be present. Second, there must be a thorough understanding of the basic processes of management—planning, organization, coordination, execution, and control—as these are employed to utilize men, money, materials, time, and space most effectively. Those directly responsible for the implementation and success of the program must be more profound and dedicated students of management than they have ever been in the past. They must be able to perceive management's information needs and have the capacity and vision to translate these needs into a management information system that will produce the desired results.

The response to overall policies and objectives will be determined largely by the man at the top. He is the one who sets the tone for the entire organization. It is therefore important that communication be kept open at all times with him and with all levels of management. Conflicting personal opinions and interests must be resolved in favor of the total effort, and a clear understanding of the use to be made of the data is essential.

Good management puts great stress on reducing the complex to the simple. This is vital when setting out to make systemation work. Also required is a strong, vigorous application of tough-mindedness.

Work Standards/Standard Work?

Today, more than ever before, the executive must know within a minimum length of time that the performance of every function is up to standard. If it is not, he must be aware of the situation early enough to take remedial action. For example, if inferior parts are being machined for installation in an aircraft engine, this should certainly be discovered as soon as possible. If the error is not detected until engines begin to fail and loss of life occurs, that is too late.

If the management information system is meeting the performance requirements that have been set for it, the flow of data to and from management will be accurate, timely, and meaningful. In untold numbers of companies, however, these requirements are not being met. Why? Because *who, what, when, where, how,* and *why* are being ignored as an organized approach. Because tough-mindedness is not being practiced and the productivity climate does not exist.

In systemation work the need for performance standards is real. The process of setting them establishes an understanding between superior and subordinate which is essential to proper control. Unless the subordinate—and in this case it might very well be the entire data processing division—knows exactly what is expected, what constitutes excellence of performance, no sound basis exists for assuming that the functions delegated will be carried out in precise compliance with the standards which the delegating authority has in mind. Almost without exception, in the absence of agreed-upon standards, subordinates will form their own opinion of what is "satisfactory."

Within the productivity climate, however, it is not possible to look upon the work being performed simply as standard work. Standards are determined for the explicit purpose of achieving excellence; therefore, they should be improved upon whenever possible in order to achieve an increasingly higher degree of excellence. Work which was considered standard last month, last week, or yesterday may no longer be standard today. Employees are constantly endeavoring to turn out more and better work, to increase their own effectiveness and that of their fellow workers.

Note what appears to be duplication of effort in almost any organization and ask one of the employees involved why he is performing a particular operation. "I really don't know," is likely to be the answer. "It's just the way we've always done it." This is an example of work being performed by old and obsolete standards, of a management which ignores progress, refusing to accept change.

The tough-minded administrator never ignores the influence of a changing, dynamic society which inflicts its whimsical yet stringent demands upon business. To keep pace, systems and procedures must undergo constant change—change reflected in standards which are reviewed continuously in terms of

What we want it to accomplish.
Where it should be applied.
When revision should be considered.
Who should be responsible for its application.
How it affects the end result.
Why it is important to maintain it.

Information Systems—for What?

Business has much to learn about management information systems and their application. As for electronic computers, they are essentially tools—and extremely valuable in system operation—but as tools they certainly are not capable of making decisions. They are, however, capable of helping men to make better decisions. To quote Andrew M. deVoursney, executive vice president, economic planning, for United Airlines, "The value of electronic data processing equipment lies in its use to extend man's mental skills in the same way that other machines augment his physical abilities."

Although computers are in wide use and integrated data processing systems have been applied to varying types of operations, not many firms have developed a truly effective management information system using modern forms of data processing. The difficulty lies in constructing the data processing system in such a manner that it can speedily produce the information needed by top and middle management to implement responsive forward planning and control. To do this, the systems design people and those actually in charge of data processing must be intimately acquainted with what is wanted; yet, despite all the advances in data processing, a breakdown tends to occur in this area: the preparation of managerial planning and control reports and their proper utilization. Communication has failed somewhere along the line, quite possibly at the very top.

Many companies, some large and some small, have installed data processing with high hopes that here was an innovation which would put an end to their problems and set them on the road to greater efficiency and profits. Today, several years later, they are still trying to make their computer control systems work. In the interim they have been plagued by expensive refinements, adjustments, and equipment failures. What has gone wrong? The executives of these companies are finding that very often they themselves are to blame for their troubles. Whether automated or not, the operation of a production line, factory, or company still remains a series of interdependent procedures. Just as the proverbial chain is no stronger than its weakest link, so it is with the complex business which has been linked together in an intricate information system. If just one element in it is weak, the addition of electronics will not help; the entire system will be weak or—worse yet—may fail completely.

Let us say it again: The ultimate goal of an effective management information system is to provide all levels of management with accurate, timely, and meaningful information concerning all developments in the business which affect them. The systems people, the data processing personnel, and those entering information into the system must know exactly which data to collect and which to tabulate, and it is up to management to specify its exact requirements.

More emphasis must be placed on communication between people to make the most of this revolutionary tool, the electronic computer, which modern technology has given us. It takes people, communicating effectively and performing their jobs efficiently, to utilize what the computer has to offer.

EDP Must Sell Itself

Each new development in management philosophy and techniques that comes along clamors for the company president's attention. He must then decide upon the action to be taken, and in the case of electronic data processing this has not always been easy. With the advent of the computer many chief executives automated data processing because their competitors were doing so, because it was the "coming thing."

That EDP has possessed all the characteristics of a fad is easy to understand. When one considers the fantastic speeds that are possible, the results that have been publicized so widely, and the many applications that have been suggested, one tends to overlook the fact that in numerous situations the value of the computer still remains to be proved. There is no doubt that the bright promise offered by electronics to business can and will be realized, but it is certain that a great deal of concentrated effort must go into making the new machines actually do their appointed work.

A Midwestern insurance firm installed EDP four years ago. A great effort apparently went into preparing the employees for the great day. Since that time a systems and procedures group has worked continuously to resolve the problems which have been created. Yet EDP has been unable to sell itself in this company. Management is still having trouble; the installation is not providing the anticipated results. It probably is not the fault of the equipment; nevertheless, in the eyes of these people this much-heralded electronic wonder is not performing as advertised.

This is only one of many examples which could be cited. The acceptance of the electronic computer has been extraordinary, if not unique; unlike some great innovations, it has assumed a very big role in just a few years. But it has by no means won the unqualified blessing of all who have sought to use it. In a recent study of more than 300 installations in 27 manufacturing companies it was found that 18 of the 27 firms weren't earning enough on the computers to cover their investment.*

The disillusionment and cynicism which all too often follow the hasty installation of an EDP system can, however, be avoided by a feasibility study. This preliminary step is in fact essential in view of the high cost of electronic data processing equipment, the long preparation period necessary to insure complete operational planning, and the difficulty of obtaining high-caliber personnel to run, maintain, and improve the installation. It must include a careful, thorough analysis of the following questions:

What is the objective of the EDP installation?
Where can and should it be used?
When should it be used?
Who will be involved?
How should it be used?
Why is it important?

If properly done, a feasibility study will quickly establish whether the company can efficiently use electronic data processing equipment.

And, with the growing trend toward profit planning and profitability accounting, EDP must be required to justify itself on the basis of real effectiveness. It must make a direct, measurable contribution to better planning and control. The systems/data processing manager must increasingly evaluate his operation in terms of overall company objectives, with the emphasis on profit. All of this will put a premium on administrative skill and broad-gauge planning ability.

Computers That Pay Their Way

EDP can sell itself if it produces such specific results as these:

- An accurate and timely comparison of sales volume by product, customer, area, salesman, or any other desired breakdown, indicating areas in need of attention.

* "The Boundless Age of the Computer," *Fortune*, March 1964, p. 108.

MAKING SYSTEMATION WORK

- Current data on returns by product, pinpointing defective or inferior items so that immediate corrective action may be taken.
- Dynamic inventory and material control data, permitting a 20 to 40 per cent reduction in inventory, a 35 per cent reduction in clerical personnel, immediate verification of lead times and customer delivery dates, and a 20 per cent increase in sales.
- Modernized wholesaling operations involving warehousing and materials handling, resulting in a 6.9 per cent greater volume of business and a reduction of 31 per cent in administrative costs.
- A 30 per cent return on the company's investment in the system, properly installed and integrated into the organization.

Almost without exception, the companies that have put computer-operation decisions in the hands of capable and well-qualified managers have experienced success. These managers have subjected themselves to rigorous discipline, constantly analyzing their businesses and looking for new ways to use the computer. They have also been willing to accept change, to revise their operating routines and their company organizations, if necessary, to exploit the computer. EDP has been able to sell itself to these tough-minded managers "on the go" because they early recognized its indispensability and are utilizing it as the valuable tool that it is. Their less enterprising colleagues may very well become the "has beens" of the business world.

Data processing is no different from any other phase of company operations. Once the feasibility study has arrived at anticipated costs, possible risks, and expected results, and once the project has received management's approval, careful planning must identify the steps required for implementation, together with manpower and time requirements. Then, after the work is under way, periodic reports of progress must point toward justifiable results.

As enthusiasm develops for the tremendous potential of electronics, it is easy to be carried away by the prospect of large dollar savings. These may very well be realized; but, on the other hand, the difficulties that may be encountered while converting an existing operation to a completely mechanized electronic system are often staggering. Before making the big decision to automate, management must therefore insist that the installation justify itself in terms of not only dollar savings but *increased speed, greater flexibility, much better operational control,* and *the ability to handle important new applications from time to time.* After installation, the flow of data and design of the system must be constantly re-evaluated in terms of performance. The use of appropriate industrial engineering tools can, within the framework of the productivity climate, yield impressive results.

The companies that are realizing the greatest benefit from their data processing installations find that it derives from savings in administrative and operating costs, improved manpower and machine utilization, fewer short runs and rush orders, better control of inventories, and more economical planning for marketing and sales effort. So that the computer may pay its own way, the tough-minded executive will take decisive action:

1. Personally concern himself with its installation and establishment as a valuable management resource. Ask probing questions instead of considering the operation as "privileged."
2. Staff the computer effort with highly trained, capable people who can visualize their contribution to the total organization and who want to be judged by it.
3. Clearly define performance requirements for the data processing function and its operating staff.
4. Establish realistic objectives; make sure that they are well understood and that they contribute directly to company and divisional objectives.
5. Continuously evaluate the profit contribution of the data processing installation and hold it accountable for total accomplishment.
6. Stress the need to strive constantly for a greater degree of performance excellence.

Measuring the Contribution

You can measure the contribution of your EDP installation by looking for—

1. The extent to which you are receiving the effective and enthusiastic support of your top executive.
2. The extent to which the top executive is receiving clear, concise management information and the degree to which established objectives have been attained.
3. The presence of a data processing chief who is able to communicate with all levels of management effectively and is himself of top management caliber.
4. Well-defined data processing objectives and policies which are thoroughly understood by all.
5. A data processing organization which can determine management information needs and can meet them through a simple but effective systems program.
6. Highly effective communication between the various functions of the business which depend upon data processing for the necessary flow of information.
7. The degree to which the installation is showing a net return on investment.

For, in the company where electronic data processing has been integrated in the proper manner, it—like all resources—must meet performance requirements established for it. If it is not justifying its existence, it must make way for some other, more profitable system.

Certain measures of efficiency can be built into the system's design. They must then be checked out from time to time to determine whether they are effectively measuring what they were intended to measure. Often, in those companies where the computer has failed to measure up to expectations, failure has not been inherent in the machine. Rather, it has been due to management's failure to avail itself of the full capabilities of the expensive equipment it has installed, to insist that the necessary provision for results measurement be incorporated in the program.

Two different types of altimeters were used in aircraft during World War II. The aneroid sensitive altimeter, which was the more common, operated by means of the effect that atmospheric pressure had upon its mechanism. However, inaccuracies could result from changes in pressure, which varies almost constantly; calibration tolerances, which might produce variances ranging from 15 feet at low altitudes up to 300 feet or more at very high altitudes; changes in temperature; and, to a certain degree, instrument "lag." The radio altimeter, on the other hand, was an extremely accurate instrument which gave what virtually amounted to an instantaneous reading of a transmitter which projected a radio wave directly to the ground and, as it rebounded, picked it up with a small receiver. The lapse of time was automatically converted to an altitude reading on the face of the instrument. There is no doubt which of the two devices made the greatest contribution to the pilot's confidence and peace of mind.

So it is with the computer as compared with older management tools. The executive today needs information virtually as it is created —not next month, next week, or even tomorrow, for by then it could very well be too late. The computer is giving it to him in just this way. With it he can confidently formalize the decision-making process and determine a logical course of action. And it is on this basis, in the last analysis, that the worth of EDP must be measured.

SUMMARY AND ACTION STEPS

When management takes a tough-minded approach toward systemation it can be made to work in a positive and dynamic way that will contribute effectively to the performance of the entire organization. Its value must be judged in terms of contribution toward company objectives—just like that of any other company resource.

How does management insure an effective electronic data processing system? Here is a suggested blueprint:

1. *Planning:*
    a. Establish and define clearly the specific objectives to be achieved by the EDP function.
        - Insure compatibility between these and overall corporate objectives.
        - Communicate the objectives carefully to all personnel and make certain they are clearly understood.
        - Assist and encourage personnel to identify their personal objectives with those of the department, division, and company.
    b. Determine the areas which must be considered.
        - Identify the divisions and departments which are directly involved. Make sure they are thoroughly aware of their responsibility and accountability.

MAKING SYSTEMATION WORK

- Determine the requirements for men, materials, money, time, and space.
- Define the management and operational techniques to be used: planning, organization, coordination, execution, control.
- Define the pattern of work flow: eliminate, combine, rearrange, simplify.
- Develop the procedures and schedules needed to accomplish each objective. Will the system perform quickly, efficiently, and accurately? Will its performance be measurable?
- Make specific provision for adjustments and follow-up when needed. Will processes be fast enough? What controls are to be provided for? What feedback mechanisms?

c. Determine effective patterns for control of operations. What standards are applicable? What department routings will be desirable? What machine assignments must be considered?

d. Develop a thorough understanding of the overall pattern and ascertain whether

- The operational details are all-inclusive. Are the data-handling steps clearly defined as they are interrelated? Procedurally?
- These details are consistent and compatible in time. Have the mechanics of flow been clearly outlined? Have the integration requirements been worked out?
- The operation as detailed will provide the maximum contribution to overall effectiveness.

e. Evaluate the anticipated contribution to the current needs of the organization.

- How closely will planned results approximate the objectives? Will the dollar savings be great enough to warrant the costs of converting to electronics and maintaining a computer center?
- Under what conditions would achievement of the objectives become more urgent? How would time and priority conditions then have to be altered?

2. *Organization:*

a. Develop a detailed organizational structure. Prepare a chart and evaluate reporting relationships and span of control.

b. Develop a detailed pattern for the timely provision of materials, facilities, funds, and personnel. (Here is an opportunity to use PERT, CPM, or some other effective system of programing.)

c. Visualize the overall procedural pattern. Will it insure a smooth operation? Evaluate it in terms of reducing the complex to the simple wherever possible.

DEVELOPING A TOUGH-MINDED CLIMATE

    d. Develop the new procedures which will be required. Present them in a way the worker understands.
    e. Provide means of compliance with prescribed procedures. Insure availability of copies for ready reference at all times.
    f. Establish provisions for integration of new operations by
- Adjusting the flow of supplies, availability of skills, and amount of manpower to meet required operating changes.
- Fitting specific operations into the overall operating schedule. Have the mechanics of flow charting shown clearly how integration is to be achieved?

    g. Determine whether the functional relationships between areas are reasonable and practicable. Will system requirements impose excessive or severe demands on personnel?
    h. Evaluate all elements in the organizational network to be sure they form a logical operational system. Can the system operation be simulated in advance to determine its reliability and its effect upon the organization?

3. *Coordination:*

    a. Determine which organizational elements are directly or indirectly involved in the execution of specific steps and the extent of such involvement. At what point do human judgment and interpretation enter the system? What are the control mechanisms which will regulate human responses?
    b. Provide means of insuring coordination of these elements through
- Proper liaison between EDP and other departments.
- Conferences and discussions between EDP personnel and general management.
- Formal and informal exchange of information.
- An understanding of common objectives and a constant, knowledgeable effort to achieve them.

    c. Insure that proper channels are cleared for the smooth flow of resources and that all persons concerned are thoroughly informed. Have the time requirements on output availability been described? Have peak load requirements been expressed? Have proper procedures been provided for?

4. *Execution:*

    a. Take positive and firm action to insure that
- Actual work gets under way and progress is maintained. Schedule the workload, determine the progress, evaluate accomplishment.
- The elements of the organization perform in accordance with the scheduled plan of action. Make certain of effective coordination, require thorough and timely feedback, provide for meaningful follow-up.

MAKING SYSTEMATION WORK

- Production resources—manpower, materials, and facilities—are integrated according to plan. See that integration requirements are clearly understood and adhered to.
- Working procedures and performance requirements have been clearly defined and are understood by personnel concerned. Stress the importance of referring to procedures frequently—and particularly when problems arise.
- Compliance is indicated by meeting the requirements of quality, quantity, and time schedules. Control workload, apply significant standards when applicable, carefully evaluate backlog and overtime requirements as they occur.
- Required changes in operation are made smoothly without disrupting production. Provide for thorough indoctrination of all personnel and for coordination of their efforts.

b. Conduct operations in accordance with the philosophy and policies of the organization.

c. Direct consistent efforts toward
- Greater employee productivity and high morale through good training, effective employee relations, and good working conditions. Close working relationships must be maintained, and sufficient information must be supplied to enable employees to meet commitments.
- Good publicity whenever appropriate. Strive to establish *esprit de corps*.
- Meticulous regard for employee safety. Insure it through knowledge of rules and equipment.

d. Continually explore possible improvements in operations.
- What takes the most time? Can the complex be made more simple?
- Is there misdirected effort? Assign definite work priorities.
- Are skills being used properly? Job classification is essential.
- Are workers performing too many unrelated tasks? Minimize activity.
- Are assignments spread too thin? Carefully assess manpower requirements.
- Is the workload distributed equitably? It must be properly planned, scheduled, and controlled.

5. *Control:*

a. Develop means for evaluating and measuring the progress of operations and use of resources, including
- A master installation schedule based upon a logical sequence of events.
- A reporting system which identifies problem areas requiring action.

DEVELOPING A TOUGH-MINDED CLIMATE

- A comparison of current forecasts against scheduled completion dates.

b. Determine the means of evaluating control information.
- Compare objective with actual performance.
- Analyze and explain variances.

c. Utilize planned corrective action by
- Removing all bottlenecks. Each system must be thoroughly tested.
- Replanning, re-organizing, and redirecting the operating elements. Use the integration concept to make the most of all data entering the system and avoid costly duplication.
- Evaluating results in terms of effective solution of the problem. Direct every effort toward achieving the best possible economic results from data processing facilities.

d. Determine the extent to which
- A clear understanding of the information required by all levels of management has been established.
- Information requirements are being translated into report form with emphasis on content and frequency.
- The relationships of report requirements are established throughout the organization.
- Integrated procedures are established to collect, process, and report management information.
- Installation schedules exist to provide optimum timing for all procedures.
- There is continual follow-up to assure that objectives are being met.

Do *you* have the self-discipline and thoroughness to use the efficient approach to systemation?

CHAPTER VII

Decision Making in the Space Age

ONLY THE TRULY TOUGH-MINDED EXECUTIVE WILL ENJOY OUR ENTRY into the Space Age. The luxury of second-guessing, procrastination, and poor management in general will be too costly for the efficient company of the future. Perhaps this return to a truly competitive climate for men and companies is what we as a nation need to regain our vigor, our hunger for excellence, and our individualism.

Hitler once said that we were soft, that our affluence had made us weak. What he thought is unimportant now—we were able to muster our strength and prove him wrong. Survival was an immediate need, a visible need, a commanding and demanding need that brought us to our feet fighting.

Today we face a more subtle problem. Our way of life is under attack just as seriously and aggressively as it was at Pearl Harbor on December 7, 1941—not from the "Red threat" that fills our news media daily, but from those both east and west of the Iron Curtain who seek to replace us as world leaders in productive capacity. War is something everyone can understand. It is more difficult to see that a loss of economic leadership will be just as costly as a loss on the battlefield. War is tangible, war is immediate; therefore, we are motivated to act accordingly. Economic destruction is slow, hidden temporarily by the fat of previous affluence; it stimulates little interest or action in its early phases.

It's Our Play

Because we have been and still are world leaders, we "feel" that "Yankee ingenuity" will always keep us so. True, we have the wealth, the natural resources, and the ability to out-produce all others today. However, we must become more tough-minded if we are to face the competition of tomorrow. West Germany, with its shortage of labor, has put the American computer to work. Its people have automated to a much higher degree than we and are moving forward rapidly in their ability to produce goods competitively. And they're not the only ones. Many sections of the world will soon be challenging our quality, our prices, and our flexibility to meet world needs.

It's only too clear that for our leadership to continue, our American eco-political climate must allow a healthy growth on the part of American business. But, urgent as this is, there is an even more immediate responsibility facing U.S. businessmen today. It is their job to take an analytical look at the tough-minded principles that will insure the American free enterprise system for future generations; to explore the requirements of management in an age when time, distance, and the purchasing power of the dollar are all being compressed.

The Decision-Making Problem

The day of the hard-nose who ran "his" company alone and knew how to face each decision squarely because he had faced them all before is not just fast departing—it's gone.

Decision making is the chief and most crucial function of management. Every day, however, in companies of all sizes, valuable time is wasted by the chief executive on decisions that could be made more quickly and more accurately by someone else if the company and each department in it had clearly stated, meaningful objectives to provide the necessary direction.

Of course, before a decision can be made, a problem or an opportunity must be present. Often management is unaware that either exists, that a decision is necessary. Many executives become bogged down with specific programed, deadlined tasks that multiply like rabbits and consume what might be highly productive hours for the company. Lack of direction (objectives), compounded by lack of delegation, is usually a good part of the answer.

It Sneaks Up on You

There are some exigencies facing management that demand prompt action and remedy, but most company problems show signs of their existence prior to becoming emergencies. Take the large

Midwestern financial institution that had to keep increasing its advertising expenditures to keep growing at the same pace as its competitors. These expenditures finally were twice those of any rival institution; resources and energies were being dissipated without even trying to discover the real problem. Had the signs been noted and correctly analyzed, management would have discovered that poor employee morale and antiquated equipment made it impossible to give the service demanded by the public. The ever-increasing advertising expenditures were necessary to bring in new customers to replace those who became dissatisfied and left.

Clear the Decks

To face tomorrow's pressures, it is imperative that the chief executive divest himself of trivia and keep watch over those indicators which are the key to his operation. Once he knows a problem exists, he is in a position to put all his forces to work digging for the cause or causes. After he has successfully isolated the problem, he will be in a position to scan the probable solutions.

Some of the problems the executive must face are sudden, unexpected, never before experienced. Innovations in the areas, say, of production methods or data processing may at any time confront the chief executive with the shocking realization that his resources are obsolete; that he cannot, with his present equipment, compete in the market. One of the leading automobile manufacturers, for example, has announced that through the use of the computer it will be able to cut the lead time on its new models from three years to one. This announcement has affected all other automobile manufacturers; because of it, they—like companies in other industries—will face many changes in the future. What these will be only time will tell; meanwhile, we must begin exploring their manifestations today.

Ready on the Right—Ready on the Left

There are certain things the managing officer can do to run a taut ship, to prepare for the Space Age with its expected environment of change.

DEVELOPING A TOUGH-MINDED CLIMATE

First of all, the direction of the company's efforts should be known to all who help steer its course. Objectives must be ambitious enough to be challenging, and they must be under constant review. Furthermore, it must always be remembered that objectives need men, money, materials, time, and space before they are attainable. Of these resources, men are the most important; therefore, in preparing for the Space Age, much attention must be given to manpower. Not only must we have the best men, but we must provide a climate in which they can do their best work. And not only must we hold them accountable for results, but we must reward them for their achievements along the way.

This is to say that the key decisions in any successful operation concern the effective use of resources, and especially important are the staffing decisions. Until you have the proper people in the right positions, you have done nothing. If the manning of the team is not right, the other resources will not be effectively utilized. At the same time, however, people—including managers—need facilities with which to work. We often see companies which seem to have everything but which disappear after a few years. The answer usually is that they had everything but manpower with the ability to manage. The officers did not know how to plan, organize, coordinate, execute, or control.

Wise managers are sometimes criticized by their colleagues for not immediately attacking the "heart" of a problem. They talk about attitude surveys, objectives, policies, housekeeping, testing, motivation, the right man for the job, accountability, morals, ethics, drives, when it is obvious that the problem is marketing. What they are doing is evaluating the human resources charged with responsibility for marketing. What others fail to see immediately, but may discover with guidance, is that business moves forward through the action of people: People are customers; people make the equipment used in business offices and plants; people move products from plant to consumer; and people make business operations successful or unsuccessful.

The success of the Space Age company will be dependent, then, on human—especially managerial—effort. It must trim down and retool to meet the demands of this new era with its increased competition. The pacesetters will be the businesses that are able to maximize the utilization of all their resources. And basic to successful maximization is the ability to make quick, accurate, and profitable decisions for the long and the short term.

Ready on the Firing Line

The Space Age manager must remove from his desk all decisions which can be better and more appropriately made by someone else.

1. He should have clear-cut objectives for his department heads that can be followed without constant supervision.
2. He should select men who have the ability and desire to meet commitments and hold them accountable for doing so.
3. He should set clearly defined limits of authority. Any problem falling within a department's authority should be handled by it in accordance with overall company and department objectives.
4. He should make sure his department heads know how to plan, how to organize, how to coordinate and execute, and how to control all their operations for maximum efficiency and profitability.
5. He should require from them, on a regular basis, clear and concise written reports of progress toward objectives.
6. He should have regular meetings with his subordinates to give them the benefit of not only his own thinking but that of other departments; also, to provide an informed sounding board which will help him in his decision making.

A subordinate who knows his assignment and knows he is to be held accountable for successfully carrying it out is in a position to keep a close look-out for indicators of trouble: a product which is not selling according to expectations, the costs of policing suppliers or distributors, and the like. He can spot these signs before they would normally become apparent to the chief executive, much less reach emergency proportions. And his proximity to the situation makes it simpler for him to isolate the cause of the problem and to take remedial action at once.

The manager, through the system of commitments and results

DEVELOPING A TOUGH-MINDED CLIMATE

measurement agreed to by his subordinates, has tight managerial control over his operation. He has built an awareness in his people of what is expected of them and how both their and the company's future depends on their ability to meet commitments. He has at his finger tips the information he needs about each area of his company. Finally, he has more time to give to making those decisions he cannot delegate.

Likewise the vice president or department manager can set up controls that will give him greater insight into his job.

1. He should regularly determine that his department is adhering closely to the company's objectives and the policies and assumptions which underlie them.
2. He should periodically make a complete reappraisal, clear-eyed and objective, of his total responsibility. This should be a prognosis as well as a diagnosis; it should not merely detect or correct difficulties but should also point to conditions, already above average, that can be improved.
3. He should train himself to be acutely conscious at all times that full control over his area of responsibility includes the most effective utilization of men, money, materials, time, and space.
4. He must institute procedures which will assure him that every activity of the department is being conducted in full awareness of its effect upon the total enterprise.

This manager should expect as much of his staff as is expected of him by his superior. As he watches the appropriate indicators in his area of responsibility, he will be evaluating the health of the operation and its progress toward stated goals. If he is the vice president of marketing, for example, he will systematically compare dollar or unit volume of sales against the department's objectives. Too great a deviation from commitment requires judgment and decision. The cause of the problem must be located, the relevant factual data compiled. This information can then be analyzed and a decision made; or, if action that exceeds the manager's authority is called for, the facts can be transmitted to his superior. In either event, much valuable time has been saved. Management has been made aware of a problem early and has the facts on which a decision can be made with a minimum of effort.

When a company's management team functions in this way, it is truly "unfair" competition for those men who are buried behind a mountain of operational details and unable to provide the leadership their firms need so badly.

Fire!

For years management books have stressed the importance of the personal objectives of the top man as the chief motivating force behind a company. This one is no exception in insisting that corporate objectives must give careful consideration to the private goals of this one man—an idea that may have some validity in those companies fortunate enough to have selected a tough-minded manager. What about the rest, though?

Our American colleges are considered by many to be ultra-conservative, almost archaic, in their administration. Since the end of World War II, however, college presidents have discovered that they must reach certain short-term objectives and make substantial progress toward long-term objectives or quit. Because of financial considerations, the clergy and professional educators of which college boards of trustees used to consist have more and more been replaced with representatives of business and industry. These men have seemed tough-minded; they have set objectives, introduced the concept of accountability, and rewarded or punished as the case demanded. But are they *really* tough-minded? As the Space Age and its climate make their own boards more interested, more active, more demanding, these corporate executives may be put to the test they have set the college presidents. Will they accept the challenge of the future and achieve success or, failing that, will they be tough-minded enough to resign for the good of their companies? We hope so.

The goals of the tough-minded executive are grounded in his philosophy of life, in fundamental truths, in sound moral and ethical principles, in a basic respect for human dignity, his own and others'. These provide the foundation on which each of his decisions is made. The inward guidance was there when he first accepted his responsibilities as an executive of the corporation, and it continues throughout his tenure of office; thus his personal objectives will be those that best serve the company's purpose. And they must emerge with increasing clarity, continuing to motivate his associates, as time goes by.

Just as there are specific indicators which are keys to the successful operation of a company department or function, the chief executive also has a key to successful administration. This is *profit*—which has always governed the corporate life span. Some companies begin life by making a high profit and then, for lack of long-range objectives and good leadership, die. Other companies grow, prosper, and live on successfully through prosperity, depression, innovation, and even changes in leadership; quite obviously they transcend the span of one chief. But profit is more important today than in the past 30 years and will be more important in the future. Why?

War, prosperity, affluence, and the lack of real competition have until fairly recent years minimized the need for real leadership. Profits were more or less measured by a positive percentage; few companies suffered fatal losses. The profit squeeze gradually became more serious, but markets still were not drying up.

In contrast, the chief executive of the future will face ever-increasing competition both from foreign and domestic companies and from new materials and techniques. He will have to make decisions that involve larger and larger amounts of money just to keep pace with innovation. Breakthroughs in automation, materials, transportation, communication, marketing and markets will force write-offs of equipment long before current depreciation and obsolescence allowances would have built up for their replacement. The company that cannot keep up will slowly but surely disappear. Objectives will have to be kept flexible; fat will have to be removed from all parts of the organization; any person or piece of machinery that cannot contribute to profitability will have to go. Operating costs will have to be controlled; lines of credit will have to be improved; new equity capital will be needed—in other words, all the factors in production must be known in depth so that decisions can be made quickly and accurately.

Future managers must realize once again that unless they own the company they, like the file clerks, are just employees. The only real difference between a file clerk and his president lies in responsibility, accountability, and salary. If either fails to do his job, he is of little value to the company. If profits fall off for any extended period of time, the chief executive may be replaced. This is not just a myth from a textbook on corporate finance, it is a cold, hard fact that must be faced.

A Man for Tomorrow

The executive of tomorrow will be quite different from his counterpart of today. He will in all probability be younger when he assumes command than the average new president of today. He may have an entirely different educational background; he will much more likely have a liberal arts degree than one in engineering, accounting, or business administration. If he worked in the plant, it was just a way of earning money to pay his college expenses. He probably played chess instead of poker in college. He will have a body as trim and as well trained as his mind, and he will know more about production, lead time, and the like than most presidents today who were raised in the factory. He will be able to tell in seconds where any job is in production and who is working on it. He will know current prices and markets for his and any other product or raw material—not only in this country but abroad. When he has to make a decision, he will be able to draw on hundreds of sources of information not currently available to the chief executive. If he wants instantaneous consultation with one or more of his officers, he will be able to get it without leaving his desk. The pressures of competition, however, and the need for quick action will restrict the proportion of available data which he can scrutinize carefully. He will be forced to make decisions on fractional information. His first decision, therefore, in solving any problem must be to restrict his research to key information.

We can only guess what tools will be available to the Space Age chief executive. Even today, however, we are seeing early applications of scientific developments in the more progressive companies: all forms of radio and telephone communication; closed-circuit television; EDP and IDP, satellite communication systems, jet travel, X-ray, atomic testing of materials, masers and lasers, high-frequency welding. Tomorrow's newspapers will keep adding to the list.

DEVELOPING A TOUGH-MINDED CLIMATE

With all this help, why will the Space Age executive have a more demanding existence than his present-day counterpart? Actually, he won't. His life, however, will be different. It will be geared to accountability not only for himself but for all. He will enjoy making decisions; he won't get ulcers from the process—in fact, as we have seen, he will spend his working hours making *major* decisions. Still, he cannot afford to be too busy with his daily job to understand that the world around him is changing at a rate faster than it ever has. The lead time from drawing board to finished innovation will not allow time for things to work themselves out.

In the final analysis, no matter how much science aids the Space Age executive, business will remain a human endeavor and success or failure will depend on the quality of the people who manage it. Automation may someday completely replace physical human effort, but human judgment—as embodied in the ability to make sound decisions and solve problems effectively—will remain a specific resource.

Problem solving does not in itself create opportunities for the company. Problem solving techniques, however, build mental agility and lay a procedural path for careful analysis of any given situation. To solve a problem, to evaluate an apparent opportunity, or to prepare alternate courses of action in anticipation of change, all the available resources of the company should be brought into play.

1. Assign the best people to make this particular study.
2. Consider what results can be expected and when the project is to be completed.
3. Evaluate the situation and locate all the known facts.
4. Collect all the additional information necessary to make the decision.
5. Present suggested courses of action and estimate the degree of risk connected with each course.
6. Compare these various courses of action with company objectives and resources.
7. Make the decision.
8. Put the necessary plans into operation.
9. Review, modify, or reverse action as needed.

The successful chief executive of the future will have the type of mind that can see three moves in advance. No gambler, he will be highly skilled in the art of problem solving; with a minimum of carefully selected information, he will make sound, progressive decisions. He will have accepted the challenge of carrying his company forward and, at the same time, satisfying its many publics.

SUMMARY AND ACTION STEPS

Today's actions, today's plans, are the foundation of tomorrow. Our colleges are preparing our Space Age executive; our society is building the stage on which he will have to perform. If our society continues as we know it, if a free choice continues to exist in the utilization of men, money, materials, time, and space, our Space Age executive must

1. Be aware of, and dedicated to the fulfillment of, the responsibilities of his position.
2. Want to be held accountable for his success in achieving the objectives of his company.
3. Select men of integrity and intellect to work with him in carrying his company forward, men who have the ability and desire to meet commitments and hold them accountable for doing so.
4. Respect his own and others' dignity.
5. Reward accomplishment; give leadership when needed; and punish or reprimand if necessary.
6. Provide clear-cut objectives for his department heads that can be followed without constant supervision.
7. Delegate authority to the lowest possible level of management capable of making decisions.
8. Remove from his desk all decision making not requiring his time and judgment, at the same time remembering that authority can be delegated but that ultimate responsibility remains.
9. Establish communications that not only transmit his requests to his subordinates but keep him fully informed as to the results achieved in all components of the organization.
10. Establish methods and techniques for studying problems of all types.
11. Know and understand the strengths and weaknesses of all the resources for which he is responsible (men, money, materials, time, and space).

DEVELOPING A TOUGH-MINDED CLIMATE

12. Plan for the future. Adapt strategy to various possible future contingencies. Make things happen; be a leader, not a follower, within his industry.

13. Be progressive but not a gambler.

14. Remember that human resources are his strongest and most valuable assets. Never make the mistake of believing that stored and mathematically treated data can replace human judgment based on knowledge.

15. Take the long view, not the short. Preserve a climate in which future executives will be able to insure American business's position of leadership for many generations to come.

CHAPTER VIII

Executive Motivation Through Incentive Compensation

MAXIMUM MOTIVATION WILL BE ACCOMPLISHED ONLY WHEN REwards are based on what an individual contributes to the goals of his employer. Hence the importance of executive compensation systems tied directly to performance requirements. In effect, expected results must be achieved before rewards are given and extraordinary rewards should be provided for extraordinary performance.

There have been many attempts to provide incentive bonuses for members of management, but more have failed than have succeeded.

The Well-Fed Executive

Some years ago, the president and principal stockholder of a firm manufacturing electronic components decided to share profits with his key executives. To gain a greater contribution from each of them, he assigned a certain percentage of net profits before taxes to each position.

Within a few years, since the economy was flourishing, his executives prospered and became wealthy. Yet none was really motivated to do a better job. Performance requirements had not been established for them which would stretch their abilities; also, individual rewards were based not on individual performance but on the success of the company as a whole. What additional effort resulted from the profit-sharing plan was no more than a greater concern for reviewing the financial records and monthly balance sheets to see what the semiannual bonus would be. The men became complacent. They accepted the fact that the company was in clover and accepted the credit for it. They joined country clubs, bought nice homes, drove big cars.

Then a temporary crimp developed in their area of the electronics industry. Not a single one of these executives felt he was responsible for the company's being in deep trouble, yet the good years hadn't been nearly so good as they thought they had. After-the-fact research indicated that although volume had grown during prosperity, percentage of market had steadily decreased—and was small enough that when the market receded the company was forced out of business.

We need not belittle profit sharing as an incentive, but participation in any plan should be related to individual performance. It is too easy for the well-fed executive to sit back and let George bring in the profits.

Up, Up—and Boom!

On the other hand, incentives tied *only* to individual performance can be equally disastrous.

A tired, aging chief executive, after hearing a number of lectures on management, decided that the easiest way to do his job would be to give almost complete autonomy to each of his immediate subordinates. This he did; and, among other developments, each major division—marketing, manufacturing, and finance—gradually installed its own incentive program. These plans were vastly different, but they had one common denominator: They all paid only on individual or individual unit performance. Individuals were motivated, but they were inspired to pursue their own personal interests and not the objectives of the company.

In the marketing division, "sales at any cost" became the policy. In spite of constant reminders by the controller, bad risks were given credit. Discounting was prevalent as salesmen's bonuses were paid on volume sold, nothing else. Quick delivery was promised, and manufacturing was harangued till the dates were met.

It was in the manufacturing division, however, that the real infection grew and finally burst. The managers of the smaller plants which supplied components to the larger ones were concerned only with individual success. Quality control slipped to get volume at minimum cost. Old equipment was constantly repaired, never replaced. The components shipped were just good enough to get by receiving inspection at the larger plants, which, because the trailers were being loaded quickly and poorly, had endless problems in unloading. The "buck" was passed whenever possible between plants and between departments within plants; everyone wanted to keep his skirts clean so as to get larger and larger bonus checks.

Meanwhile, administrative personnel became resentful and cynical. The company was being torn apart at the seams.

One July morning, the manager of the largest plant said, "To hell with it!" and walked off the job. Before the day was over, the chief executive had had a heart attack. He never returned to work, and a professional manager was brought in as president to salvage Company X. What was his first action? He abolished all incentive systems. This in itself, once the gloom wore off, helped tie individual units together.

A variation of this problem can be found in many companies where marketing and sometimes manufacturing personnel are paid incentives while others are not. Politics, buck passing, and overt resentment result from the inevitable jealousies.

The New Incentive Picture

Let's look at what happened to Company X when financial incentives were determined by a different method.

To begin with, the new chief executive called in his vice president of employee relations and directed him to design a system that would base financial incentives for officers and key employees on

- Total company profit.
- Total unit profit.
- Individual performance against standard.

While the vice president began work on the plan, the president and his executive staff established and documented corporate and divisional objectives. The vice president then was able to set up a system of incentives with the following goals:

1. To increase profits through more efficient management by offering an opportunity to key employees to earn compensation in addition to salary.
2. To base bonus compensation on the consolidated net income of the company and its subsidiaries in excess of a return on invested capital of a specified percentage, computed after all deductions except Federal income taxes and the incentive compensation payments under the plan.
3. To provide financial rewards in proportion to individual contributions and to stimulate maximum productivity on the part of all key personnel.

This new incentive plan for Company X spelled out the responsibility of the president and the vice president of employee relations for meeting with each vice president to discuss the *who, what, when, where, why,* and *how* of the system. This would insure a mutual understanding of the system's goals and the personal advantages it offered each member of the chief executive's staff. Then, after being suitably instructed in the plan, each superior was to meet with his subordinates and start them on a "get the house in order" step which required each manager to analyze his operation and take action to guarantee that the following principles of the productivity climate were being effectively implemented.

1. *Organization.* Each department must develop and maintain a clear-cut organization structure through which management could effectively direct and control the enterprise.
2. *Personnel.* Through personnel development or replacement all positions were to be filled by individuals fully qualified to meet the requirements of their jobs and of tough-minded management.
3. *Planning.* In consonance with corporate and divisional objectives, carefully framed departmental and individual objectives and plans would be established to provide a basis for authorization, a guide to achievement, and a measure of performance.

4. *Administration.* Guiding policies and procedures must be documented so as to enable all personnel to meet their responsibilities fully, effectively, and harmoniously. This would aid supervision, control the results of planning, and facilitate prompt, well-considered management decisions.
5. *Costs.* All costs, including manpower, were to be brought to an economic minimum and kept there, consistent with essential needs and profit goals.
6. *Employee relations.* All employees were to be assured of fair and equitable treatment and inspired to put forth their best efforts.

In Company X the "get the house in order" step was completed prior to moving on to the other steps in installing the new incentive system. (This is not necessary, so long as continuous effort is applied to getting it done quickly.) Three months later, each manager participating in the incentive plan was to have prepared his own listing of commitments based on the results for which he considered he was responsible—results targeted toward the achievement of established objectives. All commitments must be practical and attainable but tough enough to keep each man stretching. Each participant would then meet with his superior to get approval of his listing and insure a general meeting of minds.

The system provided forms on which each commitment or factor could be recorded. Performance on each would then be regularly posted. On a monthly basis each superior would review progress to date with the subordinate and agree with him on appropriate action. Provision would be made for extenuating conditions, beyond the control of the manager, which might affect his ability to meet his commitments.

Results would be measured annually, and the individual would participate in the bonus on the basis of the overall success of the company with respect to profit. Performance that exceeded established realistic standards called for maximum participation; performance that met but did not exceed standards, for partial participation. Performance which failed to meet commitments by a certain percentage resulted in counseling interviews with recommendations for overcoming areas of weakness, and performance which failed by an even wider margin to meet commitments brought such appropriate action as demotion, transfer, or dismissal.

The president of Company X and his staff were enthusiastic about the new incentive plan as presented by the vice president of employee relations. The "get your house in order" step was implemented, and within six months the system was in operation. It changed the situation at Company X considerably. Administrative personnel who had not been covered by previous incentive systems became members of the team, and the smaller plants were tied to the success of the larger plants through (1) overall company profit and (2) individual commitments affecting their service to the larger plants. The marketing division had commitments relating to profit, costs, and bad credit risks as well as sales volume; it concentrated on good profitable business and still exceeded its sales goals.

The new picture showed that individual executives were being motivated to achieve the company's objectives; they were no longer, as before, primarily concerned with personal interest. They were being held accountable for their own results as well as being rewarded for their contributions as team members. Company X survived and prospered.

Unified Whole

However, tying the executive incentive compensation system to individual as well as company performance is not enough. A good system requires much more; it requires that all parts of what is called the management process be done well. Actually, the installation of a topnotch executive compensation system forces a company to analyze its organization structure and its management skills. It virtually compels good management. For example:

1. *Planning:*
    a. Company objectives have to be formalized.
    b. Departmental objectives have to be developed.
    c. Timetables for accomplishment have to be set.
    d. Planning skills must be developed by each man.

2. *Organization:*
    a. Organizational structure must be evaluated and any overlapping functions eliminated.
    b. If necessary, the organizational structure must be redesigned with a view toward company objectives.
    c. Each executive has to re-evaluate his organization constantly as objectives and desired results change.
    d. Efficient subordinates must be developed.
3. *Coordination:*
    a. The *who, what, when, where, why,* and *how* of each position must be clearly understood and communicated.
    b. Each executive must keep his counterparts in other branches of the organization completely informed about pertinent matters and require that they do the same thing for him.
    c. Politicking is necessarily eliminated and cooperation achieved.
4. *Execution:*
    a. Operating policies and procedures must be established.
    b. Periodic meetings between superior and subordinate must be held to review progress toward objectives and explore methods of making greater progress.
    c. A total plan for execution must be set up with timetables attached.
5. *Control:* The system in itself is a system of control. It
    a. Reflects the nature and the needs of the operation.
    b. Provides for the measurement of every major function.
    c. Reports deviations from objectives quickly and simply.
    d. Is flexible.
    e. Shows where the organization is going as well as where it has been.

Thus a good executive compensation system based on performance requirements or standards will take management out of the need for constantly "putting out fires" and set it firmly on the road to long-range accomplishment. It can well be the backbone of the productivity-climate approach to sound management, providing, as it does, for both push and pull through (*a*) disciplinary action if commitments are not met or (*b*) rewards for exceeding commitments. The results are such that you not only are streamlining the total management process but are gearing management action toward results that contribute to profit. Payroll dollars can be considered an investment and the return on that investment measured. The artificial compensation criteria whereby people are rewarded for volume of activity rather than results are eliminated.

New doors are opening in the important areas of top management planning and control. An effective system of incentive compensation cannot help but play a vital role in the performance of tomorrow's new executive.

SUMMARY AND ACTION STEPS

A carefully conceived and skillfully installed system of executive compensation can, in itself, constitute a total, results-compelling management approach. Imaginatively tailored, it can help establish a productivity climate. It is a product of good planning; it contributes to sound organization, coordination, and execution; and it is a major and effective form of control.

In summary, the following steps make up the skeleton of such a tough-minded system:

1. Determine who will be responsible for the system.
    a. One individual must be given responsibility, accountability, and authority for orderly research and for the installation and administration of the entire system.
    b. A compensation review committee should be selected with the responsible individual as chairman.
2. Identify the objectives of the system.
    a. Determine the results desired from an overall executive motivation system.
    b. Determine company and departmental objectives as well as personal objectives for the key members of management.
3. Undertake the necessary research and analysis.
    a. Review the present organization structure; any existing position descriptions; present job evaluation system and ratings, if any; and present salary ranges.

b. Determine the results expected of each position by depth interviews with
   (1) Top management.
   (2) The incumbent.
   (3) His superior.
c. Determine how executives and managers are financially rewarded at present.
   (1) Salaries.
   (2) Bonuses.
   (3) Benefits.
      (a) Company-paid life insurance.
      (b) Company-paid hospitalization insurance.
      (c) Retirement plans.
      (d) Family assistance.
   (4) Stock options.
   (5) Deferred compensation.
   (6) Profit sharing.
   (7) Vacations.
   (8) Company automobile (or airplane) for personal use.
   (9) Paid physical examinations.
   (10) Other forms of compensation.
d. Research (but don't be unduly influenced by) current practices within
   (1) The industry.
   (2) The community.
e. Determine whether your current practices in compensation and motivation are consonant with the objectives of the company.

4. Organize to achieve corporate objectives.
   a. Evaluate your present organization structure and determine whether it is the best possible in light of your goals. Clarify or eliminate duplication or overlapping so that each individual can be held clearly accountable for results.
   b. Write results-oriented position descriptions.
      (1) Get participation and approval from the incumbent.
      (2) Get the approval of the incumbent's superior.
      (3) Get approval from top management if necessary.

5. Evaluate all positions for purposes of basic compensation.
   a. Evaluate each position with respect to its contribution to overall results.
   b. Establish a base compensation level for each position. This level will represent the dollar value of *minimum acceptable performance* toward the accomplishment of results requirements. (Point values may be used for later conversion to dollar values.)

DEVELOPING A TOUGH-MINDED CLIMATE

6. Develop a performance requirements program, using the results expected from each position as factors for which measurable yardsticks (percentages, ratios) can be established.
    a. Prepare a performance requirements (standards) sheet for each of several factors. For example:
       - Ratio of direct to indirect labor.
       - Scrap loss.
       - Turnover.
       - Average productivity per employee.
       - Average productivity per square foot of floor space.
       - Consumer complaints.
       - Lost time.
       - Vendor complaints.
       - Ratio of net profit to sales.
       - Ratio of selling expense to sales volume.
    b. Give each executive a set of these sheets or an appropriate master sheet.
    c. Concurrently with the development of this total system, counsel each executive on how to get his department in order, with emphasis on organization, administration, costs, personnel relations, operating improvements, and planning for the future.
    d. Have each manager review his operation and objectives thoroughly and then, with his superior, set commitments for each factor by month, quarter, or year as applicable.
    e. Work out extenuating circumstances in advance and agree upon them.
    f. See that each executive maintains a concise record of all commitments.
    g. At regularly scheduled intervals, have each subordinate furnish reports which will provide information on progress to date toward meeting commitments and any other data which may be desirable. A personal meeting between superior and subordinate should supplement this report.
7. Provide rewards for results accomplished. Two possible methods, in abbreviated form, are:
    a. Weigh the value in points of each performance commitment, conditioned by the degree to which the commitment was met. Was it just met, barely surpassed, or exceeded by far? Share of bonus available will be based on the ratio of the individual's base compensation to the total base compensation for all executives and managers.
    b. Establish a fund with a maximum bonus predetermined for each level of management. Exceptional performance on all commitments

will warrant this maximum bonus. For good to exceptional performance, payment will vary on a percentage basis determined by the quality of accomplishment on each factor.

Regardless of which method is used for determining payment, the consequences of not meeting one's commitments must be established. These will vary from counseling by one's superior to dismissal.

Rarely will any type of system work perfectly at the time of its installation. It requires constant follow-up and evaluation, plus modifications as necessary. The following rules must be adhered to for maximum effectiveness:

- The total bonus available must be based on the profitability of the company. This inspires coordination and cooperation.
- Each individual's participation in the bonus must be in proportion to his contribution to company objectives. This inspires him to meet and surpass his performance commitments.

CHAPTER IX

Candor, Courage, and Warmth

POINTING AT HIS ORGANIZATION CHART, THE COMPANY PRESIDENT asserted that while his four vice presidents were topnotch men in their jobs, "There isn't one of them who can take my job when I retire."

He explained further: The vice president of manufacturing had an excellent grasp of his specialty. Productivity was good, grievances were few, and programs of methods improvement and cost reduction were continually bearing fruit. The vice president and secretary/treasurer was a combination lawyer and CPA, described at times as virtually a genius. His grasp of legal problems and his financial planning were impeccable. The vice president of marketing had developed a fine sales organization which increased volume significantly each year and kept sales expense relatively even. He had organized a marketing research function that kept the company informed on conditions and trends and had resulted in substantial product changes. The vice president of research and development had several graduate degrees and had left the faculty of a major school to join the firm. The new products his division had developed accounted for 35 per cent of the total sales volume.

Why were these men not candidates for the presidency? "In spite of all my efforts," the president said, "none of them has developed a mix of mellowness and sageness to balance the urgency and dynamism of the younger executives."

Spoiled or Sparkling?

Real maturity of wisdom comes when an individual has learned to face himself, his times, his problems and their solutions honestly and still enjoy life. It requires that he be able to accept those things over which he has no control. Dr. Reinhold H. Niebuhr's famous quotation—which, in slightly different form, is also the Alcoholics Anonymous prayer—is pertinent here: "Give me the courage to change what can be changed, the serenity to accept that which can't, and the wisdom to know the difference."

This company president felt that it was his job to act as ballast for the top management team. A president needed to have the courage of his convictions—but the ability to face facts and modify his plans to accomplish objectives without quixotically tilting at windmills. Though his subordinates all were proficient in their present positions, all lacked the maturity of a chief executive.

Notice that the word this company head used to describe his type of management was "mellow." Sparkling wine is mellow; spoiled wine is not. "Mellow" means well ripened, not harsh and rough but mature and fully developed. "Mellow" management means drawing on years of training and experience to accomplish corporate objectives most effectively. It calls for courage, candor, sympathy, intuitiveness, compassion, and warmth.

A Keel of Candor

Another company, a manufacturer of aircraft components, was on the skids when its president died. He had gathered about him a group of seemingly weak subordinates, none of whom appeared ready for the presidency. The right man was found at the top of middle management in one of the nation's largest firms. He had a reputation as a results getter and a real "comer."

The new president had developed new plans to reverse old trends, but he would need a staff with guts, vigor, dedication, and vision. His predecessor had operated by subterfuge and manipulation, using his subordinates as whipping boys and scapegoats. Their courage, ambition, and imagination had dissipated under their superior's acidity, cynicism, and lack of direction. They had become obsequious yes men who did nothing to rock a ship that was already well off course. In contrast, the new chief laid a keel of candor. He emphasized his desire for a free and open exchange of information throughout the organization. He would, he reiterated, be candid with his people, tell them what was expected of them and how they were doing, and never use them unfairly.

It takes time to change a management climate, but gradually this company began to admire its new boss for his honesty, integrity, and drive. His subordinates began to emulate him, to become bigger men. Today the firm is rapidly becoming a leader in its industry. There are many elements in its success, but prominent among them is the new chief executive's insistence on candor.

It is basic to tough-minded management that we face up to every problem and situation, no matter how difficult, and talk it out. Candor as a way of business life insures that mistakes and misunderstandings will be recognized and corrected much earlier—so that people's energies can be applied to more fruitful pursuits. Candor is not to be confused with bluntness, frankness, or coarseness; it is a positive force that can be utilized for the good of both company and individual. It is dwelling on what a man can do—and should do —rather than on how badly he has done or may do. It should achieve some positive value, change something or someone for the better.

Candor can be most effective in a candid climate where people practice it consistently and accompany it with tact and graciousness.

Humility and Obsequiousness

Candor in a business operation sometimes finds a barrier in excess humility or servile, fawning obsequiousness. This type of behavior can only reduce the individual manager to a level of accomplishment far beneath his normal capabilities and, if prevalent within an organization, inhibit the interchange of information. This can be the case, unfortunately, even with true modesty and humility of spirit.

A capable production engineer, Bill Greenleigh, recently changed jobs. He somehow felt that outlining his very real capabilities to his new employers would be a form of bragging; it was only by accident that his co-workers learned about the many significant innovations he had brought about, over the years, in his former position. Actually, engineering management had hired him because of his accomplishments. However, after a few days of his deferential behavior, his bosses decided he must have been given credit that was not due him, so they were assigning him only commonplace projects.

Bill Greenleigh was a lion and not a cub, but because he was a lion without any roar, he was relegated indefinitely to ineffectual activities. He was responsible not just for inhibiting his own growth but for allowing his superiors to get only minimum results from his abilities. He had to learn that while modesty may be appropriate in some situations, in business it generally is not—that, in fact, there is such a thing as false modesty.

There is no reason for anyone in a company to be unnecessarily awed by his peers or even his superiors, to feel that others are on a much, much higher plane than he can aspire to. For one thing, the overly modest, deferential, easily awed person eventually tends to become obsequious, and obsequiousness is unpleasant. Besides, the obsequious man's motives are suspect: What does he hope to gain by his behavior?

As a cub reporter, the story is told, Walter Kiernan was assigned to interview William Howard Taft. His editor, seeing the young man was overawed, advised him to imagine that Mr. Taft was wearing red flannel underwear during the interview. He did this and found that his fear of Mr. Taft's prestige and position just melted away. Since then, Walter Kiernan has not been in awe of anyone.

If you have the problem of being overawed—and are in danger of becoming obsequious—mentally put your fears in red underwear and see what happens.

To Fill a Bigger Mold

At times, seeming modesty may be a sign that an individual wants to be left in a cozy situation where he will not have to extend himself and fail. This is common among children and young adults who are afraid of venturing into unfamiliar activities. A mature person, however, must realize that to fill a bigger mold he must have the courage to try new things.

Eleanor Roosevelt did an excellent job of explaining this need:

> The encouraging thing is that every time you meet a situation, though you may think at the time it is an impossibility and you go through the tortures of the damned, once you have met it and lived through it you find that forever after you are freer than you ever were before. If you can live through that you can live through anything. You gain strength, courage, and confidence by every experience in which you really stop to look fear in the face.

You are able to say to yourself, "I lived through this horror. I can take the next thing that comes along."

The danger lies in refusing to face the fear, in not daring to come to grips with it. If you fail anywhere along the line it will take away your confidence. You must make yourself succeed every time. You must do the thing you think you cannot do.[1]

This type of internal fiber is a necessity for the ambitious man. It is impossible to get anything accomplished without starting; but so many people, because they are afraid to fail, never start.

Not long ago an executive hired a university psychologist to test and interview a number of employees who were candidates for a managerial job. The psychologist recommended the man who he found had the greatest intelligence, the best personality, the best vocabulary and reading comprehension, and the most applicable work experience and training. The man was accordingly promoted. "Everything the psychologist told us about him is true," said the executive later. "He is intelligent and well adjusted. But he just doesn't get the job done. He has gradually allowed the number of people in his department to grow without any increase in volume, he won't commit himself on schedules, and he won't accept accountability. He is afraid to make changes even when they have proved themselves in other departments. We have invested a lot of time and money in him, but we are just going to have to let him go." The lesson here? Regardless of basic clay, if a man lacks courage and guts he is doomed to failure as a manager.

Some physicians claim the measure of a top surgeon is that "he cuts fast and deep and gets out quick." This is a good analogy for other walks of life. The surgeon who is unsure of himself can cut a little bit at a time and butcher his patient. The businessman can do the same thing to his organization.

To a certain extent an executive can learn to have confidence in himself, to be unafraid. "Courage," says Lyndall F. Urwick, "is in some degree a matter of facing dangers and learning that, if faced, they become less intimidating." But this takes time—and practice.

A successful insurance salesman felt he was ready to fill that bigger mold. He quickly found a position as a sales executive. However, he continued his concentrated job hunting and, before he had been

[1] *You Learn by Living,* Harper & Row, Publishers, Inc., New York, 1960.

fully tested in the one position, obtained another as vice president of agencies with a second firm. Here he had to make major decisions and direct a large sales organization. Instead, he vacillated, made excuses, and finally retreated to the preparation of sales promotion materials to keep himself busy. It became obvious that although he blamed other executives for not giving him enough information, he was continually in doubt about what direction to take. He had not developed the courage and the ability to fill the bigger mold and so returned to the personal selling at which he had been successful.

Roy Rollins, of the A. E. Staley Manufacturing Company, quotes a colleague of his as saying, "I may be wrong, but I'm never in doubt." A measure of this feeling will be found in most successful executives. This type of confidence, along with the courage to make major decisions and take the necessary action, keeps the wheels of industry moving forward.

Empathy, Insight, and Intuition

Empathy is defined as "projecting one's consciousness into another and so fully understanding the object of contemplation." More simply, it is getting out of your own shoes and putting yourself into the other man's, trying to see the situation as he would see it with his experiences, environment, attitudes, and education.

Edward Hodnett, in *The Art of Working with People*,[2] says:

> Through empathic projection you achieve insight into the minds and hearts of other people. Insight is a creative act of your mind and heart. It is an intellectual act because it requires your cool appraisal of problems as other people see them. It is an act of the heart because it demands your compassion for the human situation. It demands from you, therefore, both sensitivity of reaction and philosophical detachment.

This is difficult because we all have different backgrounds, but we need to be as understanding and objective as possible if we want to be effective in working with others.

First of all, we must know ourselves; the man or woman who is still trying to understand himself is not likely to understand someone

[2] Harper & Row, Publishers, Inc., New York, 1959.

else very well. Nor, just because we can identify with another in some way (for example, age, education, social position), can we assume that his desires and problems are similar to ours. Real empathy presupposes a familiarity with the many facets of life. We must continually broaden ourselves by reading; develop an appreciation of art, drama, and music; observe as we travel, virtually soaking in the living conditions, culture, and mores of those around us.

There is a retired executive who, like many American men, "lived, ate, and slept" business most of his life. After his retirement he continued to serve on his company's board of directors, contributing strictly a limited, facts-and-figures point of view. However, he remarried late in life, and his new wife exposed him to much broader vistas.

Now he is one of the more alert and alive members of the board. He demonstrates a deep understanding in many areas not directly related to the business; and, on top of this, he is getting much more enjoyment from life and has probably extended his span of years considerably.

One barrier to empathy is rigid thinking. Another, which similarly inhibits insight and intuition and goes far beyond just race, nationality, and religion, is prejudice. Too many businessmen have biases based on people's social position (or lack of position), politics, friends, and personal habits or on their geographic origin—even to the part of town in which they grew up. Rather, they would do well to remember that we measure people primarily by their deeds. Only in this way can we build a solid foundation for warm and profitable relationships.

Related to prejudice is jealousy, which blinds a person in his relations with others. A certain college professor, active in a number of cooperative efforts in which he must work with businessmen, has become so jealous of some of them, because of their income and prestige, that he no longer has any grasp of their problems or environment. He refuses to understand the business world because he feels the profit motive has become unfair to him and his academic colleagues. He has a low boiling point when he begins thinking about executive salaries, and this in itself is a wall against understanding. You can't understand as long as you're deeply disturbed or angry.

Practicing managers have stated that management is part science and theory but that a large share of it is intuition. They may be right. In any case, intuition requires empathy, insight, and compassion—and these you cannot have if rigid thinking, bias, prejudice, jealousy, or anger dictates the direction of your mind.

The Tap Roots of Warmth

A young businessman was undoubtedly intelligent, very alert, well educated, and informed on many subjects. Yet he lacked something. In meetings he showed little consideration for his colleagues, dominating them with his mental gymnastics. In the office he liked to clown, and, when he starred in his favorite arena, his barbed humor hurt and offended many co-workers. Moreover, he seemed bent on demonstrating his physical prowess. A weekend basketball game with other executives found him making most of the points while the older men, with less speed and stamina, got little chance to participate.

One of the group had to stay home for several days after being rammed into a tree by this young man in a touch football game. The executive vice president finally laid down the law: He had six months to grow up or, in spite of his abilities, he would no longer be employed by the firm.

"What in the world are you trying to prove?" asked the vice president. "What are you afraid of?" And at last the young man admitted he felt a compulsion to keep proving to others how capable he was both mentally and physically.

His superior asked: "Is charging so hard in a game that someone is injured the mark of a man? Is playing the cynic and the buffoon the mark of a man? Is displaying one's intelligence and verbal ability to the exclusion of others with good ideas the mark of a man? Is having a secretary cry because of one's so-called humor and lack of consideration the mark of a man?"

They agreed that this type of behavior was characteristic, not of a mature man, but of an adolescent. The vice president recommended that for the next six months the young man concentrate on being as effective as possible on his job and let his deeds speak for themselves. Along with this, he should try to reflect graciousness and warmth in his relations with his associates.

Surprisingly soon, this young man was able to show a sincere in-

CANDOR, COURAGE, AND WARMTH

terest in others; he became a much warmer and, consequently, a more effective individual. The point is that true warmth and graciousness cannot be developed as long as one is concerned primarily with one's own image.

American businessmen, more than any others in the world, are criticized for lacking graciousness. In Europe, for example, our executives are accused of having no time for the normal pleasantries of social interchange and, often, not being in the least concerned about the local country's customs and conventions. There is no doubt that American business has suffered economically from the Ugly American stereotype.

Remember, there is nothing tough-minded or masculine about being a bull in a china shop. A truly tough-minded individual is warm, gracious, and compassionate; he is sincerely interested in making life a little bit better for the people around him.

When you look at a tree, all you can see is above ground: trunk, branches, and leaves. But, if someone were to cut off the tap roots down below, the tree would wither and die. So it is with graciousness. If all you do is to practice the courtesies dictated by etiquette, without any real desire to do so, you are soon spotted as a phony. It is only when these courtesies are based on honest consideration for others that real warmth can result. It must come all the way from the tap roots.

SUMMARY AND ACTION STEPS

1. *To practice candor:*
   a. Dwell on what a man can do—and should do—rather than on how badly he has done or may do.
   b. Create the right climate. Sporadic or unplanned candor can be abortive and even cruel.
   c. Scrupulously avoid the temptation to develop whipping boys or scapegoats. Make sure others can speak to you candidly and openly.
   d. Recognize that candor requires real intestinal fortitude, must be thought through, and must always be accompanied by tact.
2. *To fill a bigger mold:*
   a. Determine the nature of the mold you want to move into next—in essence, where you want to go.
   b. Evaluate the requirements for this next move.

DEVELOPING A TOUGH-MINDED CLIMATE

    c. Evaluate your strengths and weaknesses in light of these bigger requirements.
    d. Delineate areas where you will have to develop further.
    e. Begin development immediately and continue working on it.
    f. Keep your sights on the bigger mold and let people know what you are doing.
    g. Re-evaluate your objectives occasionally to determine whether they are still realistic and whether you are still on course.
    h. Recognize your responsibility for investing your own personal time in working toward a bigger mold through reading, extension and correspondence courses, lectures (attending and giving), special home projects, visits to other companies while traveling, civic and other outside activities.

3. *To have courage:*
    a. Learn courage by living.
        (1) Recognize that you gain confidence and courage every time you meet head-on a situation that you were previously afraid of.
        (2) When faced with a situation about which you are apprehensive, come to grips with it. Do the things you cannot do.
        (3) Constantly try new things that you have not done before.
        (4) Forget the word "failure." Fear of it will prevent you from starting things that will never get done—unless you start.
    b. Remove fear.
        (1) Refuse to let your mistakes harness you. Be grateful that they show you what not to do in the future.
        (2) Realize that your feelings of inadequacy are imaginary. Regardless of who the other person is, there are some ways in which you are superior to him.
        (3) Take action *now*—there is no more favorable time. Besides, it will keep you busy, and there is no greater remedy for tension and fear than hard work.
        (4) Develop a mental image of yourself as a courageous person. Bolster this image with physical fitness—a key to courage.
        (5) Have confidence in yourself and in your fellow man.

4. *To have empathy:*
    a. Develop an understanding of yourself. Determine
        (1) What it is you want from life; your basic values, beliefs, and principles; your basic needs.
        (2) The extent of your integrity. Are you honest with yourself? With others?
        (3) What you have faith in; how stable you are mentally.
        (4) Whether you give of self or are looking out for what others can do for you.

CANDOR, COURAGE, AND WARMTH

  (5) Your prejudices and biases, if any.
  (6) Any tendencies toward jealousy. Is this one of your faults?
  (7) The people whose opinion you are most concerned about.
 b. Don't let common traits, background, or position lull you into assuming that other people's motivations, needs, and problems are similar to yours.
 c. Broaden yourself. The wider your interests, the better you can participate in and understand those of others.
 d. Avoid rigid beliefs and attitudes regarding people. Appraise your prejudices candidly. Don't be governed by your emotions.
 e. Don't let first impressions of other people sway you.
 f. On meeting people, when empathy is particularly important,
  (1) *Ask* questions—and more questions.
  (2) Be as objective and detached as possible.
  (3) Try sincerely to convey a sense of friendliness and understanding.
  (4) Where a problem is involved, determine the benefit and hardship which each possible solution would mean for the other person.
  (5) Where persuasion is involved, show the benefit, to him and others, of the recommended action.
  (6) Realize that the quality of your intuition as a businessman and a manager is in proportion to your ability to develop empathy and insight in your involvements with others.

5. *To reflect warmth and graciousness:*
 a. Be sincere. Remember that real warmth and graciousness can't be cultivated as long as you are concerned primarily with yourself.
 b. Give earned compliments freely. Accept earned compliments graciously.
 c. Don't blame anyone else for what you are *not*—but be grateful to those who have helped you become what you *are*.
 d. Be tolerant and considerate of the beliefs, habits, and attitudes of others.
 e. Try to prove yourself only through positive action. If you have been trying to impress people by belittling others, quit it!
 f. Learn to face yourself, your life, and your times honestly.
 g. Have "the courage to change what can be changed, the serenity to accept that which can't, and the wisdom to know the difference."
 h. Be compassionate.

CHAPTER X

Vitality, Security, and Dignity

SUBSTANTIAL, PLEASANT, SOLID-SOUNDING WORDS, THESE. WHAT DO they mean? Is there a need for vitality, security, and dignity in the lives of all of us? Why not just some people? Surprisingly enough, a few of us actually think in such terms—an unconscious rationalizing of our behavior toward other human beings.

Let's define, for our purposes, each of these dramatic words. *Vitality* might be said to be the contents of a personal storehouse of energy, vigor, ability, constructiveness, and latent potential. A crisp, crackling charge of personal electricity that can be unleashed and harnessed for positive results. Vitality can be physical, mental, or spiritual.

To know *security* is to feel physically, mentally, and spiritually well, to feel capable, to feel needed and wanted. An important part of security is the knowledge that you "belong" and that your achievements anchor you more firmly to your family, your friends, your company, and your country.

The person who has true *dignity* recognizes that every man and woman has some degree of basic dignity. This is part of his personal approach to other people, their problems, and his relationship to them. The truly dignified man respects and works consistently at helping others; his own storehouse of experience is always available in time of need. Often the man of wisdom and the man of dignity are one and the same.

We cannot presume to look at vitality, security, and dignity through rose-colored glasses, nor to see only the rosy picture that is more comfortable to the undisciplined personality who breeds and perpetuates mediocrity for his weak-kneed way of life. True, someone may say, "Why *not* look at the world through rose-colored glasses? That's just being a positive thinker." But positive thinking is much more than self-delusion—it is knowing and accepting the facts of a situation. It is knowing that something constructive can always be done and plunging ahead to accomplish constructive and positive results. Today, in this country of ours, we are living in a period of plenty. It is imperative that we almost literally strip away the rose-colored glasses from many of our people, including many of our executives. In increasing numbers, it seems, all of us—managers, office workers, laborers, farmers, miners—are guilty of wanting to do no more than is necessary to fill our bellies and enjoy our own lives.

How do we give people, in general and on an individual basis, the feeling that they have personal dignity, that they are secure? How do we build vitality into a sagging society? We had better be about our task soon, if we are not to abdicate world leadership to our enemies—but we are fully capable of meeting the challenge head-on and achieving our goals personally and as a nation.

The Search for Inner Space

Our socio-economic society is a cold cruel world to those who are unwilling to face reality. Instead of being willing to fight, to stretch, to grow, and to make a place for themselves, they seem to be in a two-way race: They must proceed far enough forward to make a living somehow, yet they retreat and regress emotionally under stress-producing conditions. Many people like this live an introverted life that is confined to themselves; they know no more about their environment, much less their true nature and their place in this world, than an unborn child. Before we Americans could set out to conquer outer space, we had to understand inner space—our own world—more fully. In the sciences, if not in other areas, we have attained this knowledge. Years of preliminary studies in many specialties preceded the glamorous activities which culminated on the launching pad and in the so-called race to the moon.

In the race of life, we businessmen and community leaders must know our own capabilities and strengths, just as, in preparing for an automobile race, the owner, the driver, and the mechanics all must be thoroughly familiar with their car—what it can do and how it will react to given conditions. The better they know their motor, their gear boxes, their carburetor, the better chance they have to win. What we are saying is this: We all must know our horsepower (brainpower), our gear box (capacity for self-expression), our tires (ability to meet human situations flexibly, responsively, and positively).

Every man and woman of us should have his own set of values and principles. What do we stand for? Often the response to such a question is amazingly slow in coming and difficult to extract. Asked, "What don't you like?" or, "What are you against?" the average person can reel off dislikes and complaints rapidly. It is a sad commentary that so many people today demonstrate purely negative attitudes. The words "don't," "can't," "won't," "isn't," "hasn't"—these can be insidious in destroying energy, initiative, and ambition in rising young executives when they are used all too frequently by old and not-so-old businessmen.

Moreover, provision must be built into our set of values for sharing ourselves with others. We need others; we need to be needed, to give to others. Man is a gregarious creature by nature; since the beginnings of time we have helped one another. This is all part of the grand pattern—it didn't just happen. Exploring the world around us, searching for the answers to its problems alone and with others, opens up an understanding of life and self that has astounded many.

Along with this new-found insight a man will experience a far greater feeling of personal security, a surprising upsurge of faith and confidence, a release of the natural vitality that formerly was chained and useless. Here is a man, then, who has explored inner space—who has found what he needed there and become a much bigger man. This kind of charged vitality in key executives can have a far greater impact on profit goals than any program or procedure. This is what it takes to make company programs yield full mileage—to achieve real results.

The Trim Silhouette

Have you ever watched a destroyer and an aircraft carrier moving in the same convoy or task force? How easily the destroyer moves back and forth in its zig-zag pattern, covering considerably more miles than the carrier with its additional bulk, girth, and weight.

Why the analogy? Simply because your vitality—your personal and managerial effectiveness—can be severely curtailed when your silhouette begins to show more than the normal padding. "Obesity" is not a word that suddenly describes you. It is a slow, silent gainer on the unwary and undisciplined mind and body. Look at such magnificent physical specimens as our Olympic champions. They train and care for their bodies; they know that physical discipline is tantamount to physical accomplishment. And physical discipline also can be converted into corporate fitness and trimness, which result in the low cost/high profit picture of many company histories. Whether head of a department or of a corporation, the man in a position of leadership must set the pace. If he is trim, tough-minded, and lean-thinking, he will develop key men of the same disposition and conditioning. With this team he has real corporate biceps that can be flexed constructively with truly spectacular results.

Just as people can be physically fat, so can they be mentally fat. We have too many junior and senior executives today with a roll of lard, real or figurative, around the middle. Does this lend itself to complex and demanding decision making? To inspiring leadership? Our world can and does kill men who are not in condition to weather its storms.

As a participant in the business arena, you know that the end results most sought after are company profit and personal dividends. You are much more likely to become or continue to be a hard-hitting, tough-minded, results-oriented businessman if you stay in good physical trim. Look at the ten most effective men you know. Do you still wonder why we place such heavy emphasis on physical tone?

The Anxious Vice President

Let's scrutinize the profile of the typical anxious vice president:

His assets:	*His liabilities:*
Physically sound.	Always looking for what's wrong.
Intelligent; well educated.	Afraid he'll be stabbed in the back.
Good looking.	Talks too much "confidentially" about others.
Personable, with years of sound related experience.	Can't give credit to others.
	Can't face up to reality.

Why should a man with intelligence, education, good looks, and a wealth of experience need to be unhappy, anxious, and insecure? What lies beneath the surface here?

VITALITY, SECURITY, AND DIGNITY

The development of a productivity climate, with personal and company goals in harmony, will of course help. This man needs to be provided not only with maximum profit motivation but with personal motivation. And you cannot motivate people—you can only create or develop an environment within which self-motivation takes place to bring about the desired end product. Moreover, this man is afraid. But he doesn't know where his fears spring from and therefore can't eliminate their source.

A major roadblock in the case of one such vice president was his poor relationship, real and imagined, with the company president. This relationship had not been defined precisely; certain authority and responsibility had been delegated to the VP, but other responsibility had been abdicated to him without authority. As a result, he had developed traits of inconsistency, vacillation, uncertainty, and insecurity. The damage was compounding itself in the actions of both men: They were building an atmosphere which lacked trust, faith, cooperation, and participation. They thought they were firm, fair men, but they were fluctuating from day to day, doing and saying only what the situation of the moment seemed to call for.

These men had to be encouraged—and to a great degree required—to sit down and talk to each other candidly; to learn to see each other as men, not only as two officers of a company. They had to practice using the tools of an effective, tough-minded executive:

Hard work	Decisiveness	Loyalty
Warmth	Fairness	Faith
Wisdom	Consistency	Empathy
Judgment	Guts	Giving of self

It can be a slow, painstaking process to change a man. It would be far easier, in fact, just to fire him. But how rewarding it is to see that man's life turn a corner and become a constructive force for positive results; to see him start living a fuller life; to see him become an example to others.

A vice president—or any manager, for that matter—who is insecure, anxious, and unhappy with himself and his achievements should seize the initiative. He must be his own catalyst. It is axiomatic that many a man in this position continues to delude himself

DEVELOPING A TOUGH-MINDED CLIMATE

into a false sense of security. Once he lowers his guard, however, you will often see that he is literally miserable over his job and his relationship with others. And a man who is capable of change but doesn't improve is worse off than the man who is incapable of change. His frustrations will reduce his confidence to zero.

The Exploited Boss

A few years ago a company president was dejected and hurt. To sympathizers he would recite all he had done for his employees.

"I pay over union scale," he would say. "I promote people when I can. I provide good working conditions and good working hours. I provide group insurance and steady employment. Even when a large contract was canceled, my machine operators scraped and painted machines, floors, and building, but they had a pay check every week. Why, I even advance people money." In other words, he had given his workers "everything"—and a thunderbolt had just hit him. The National Labor Relations Board had notified him of an impending union election. This disillusioned man felt his employees had turned against him; he felt exploited.

Is paternalism the answer? Had the president "looked after" these men and women too well? It is paradoxical that so many people who seem to have the "gimme" attitude don't want to acknowledge their gains as gifts; rather, most of them want to feel they have earned what they receive as fair and just compensation. The president therefore needed to make some immediate changes in both himself and the company's climate.

1. He stopped feeling sorry for himself and tried to look at matters objectively.
2. He informed the employees of his goals for the company and helped them understand the role they played in the achievement of those goals.
3. He sent several letters to the employees' homes, pointing out to them and their families the benefits they received from the company as rewards for their contribution.
4. He began to tell his employees and department heads the *why* of his directives and requests.

VITALITY, SECURITY, AND DIGNITY

5. He gave them full information which summarily killed the grapevine in the plant.
6. He learned to delegate authority and responsibility to subordinates and to hold them accountable for results.
7. Employees were given to understand that they were earning their compensation and benefits, that these were not gifts.
8. The president convinced the employees that he and they needed each other as members of the same company team.

Employees want understanding, warmth, consideration, and fairness; they don't want paternalism, benevolence, and other Santa Claus manifestations which seem to remind them that they are little children being given something for being good. When they receive the "little brother" treatment, they can rebel in several ways: The grapevine may become overactive, they may petition for a union election, grievances may increase, and annoying little cases of dissatisfaction break out like a rash. They want to be treated like individuals, like businessmen in their own way.

Many bosses say proudly, "I have an open-door policy. Anyone may come in and see me at any time." Is this really true? The door may be open, but will the employee and his problem be met with warmth, fairness, and understanding and given a full hearing? Apathy, disdain, and condescension can show through to a worker who is seeking help. To you, his problem is small; to him, it is a mountain of trouble. And, incidentally, the boss who maintains stoutly that he has an open-door policy should watch himself closely, or he will undercut the authority of the immediate supervisor who should be hearing the employee out.

A walk through the plant with a boss can provide much enlightenment about the climate existing in the company. Does he meet with warmth and enthusiasm? Are his greetings to the operators and the foremen and lead men genuine? Or does one worker say to another afterward, "The old man sure was friendly today. Wonder why?" In that case he clearly does not have a climate of productivity at work for him.

Paternal protectivism can have as bad an effect on a company as fear. Individualism can be stifled and initiative paralyzed. Naturally the boss will begin feeling that he is being "taken," that his people are not cooperating to their fullest.

DEVELOPING A TOUGH-MINDED CLIMATE

A business concern is not a philanthropy or a family. It is a profit-seeking organization of people, finances, equipment, real estate, and time. These assets must be harnessed in the most effective manner to produce a net profit. If no profit can be generated, the company cannot long endure; and every key person must know this. Sentimentality may have its place, and hardness may be desirable in certain metals. But, in the management of a business, the goal should be tough-mindedness of the highest order: warmth, flexibility, wisdom, and perseverance within a framework of performance commitment, performance measurement, and performance appraisal.

Levels of Productivity

Years ago a boy and his grandfather were cutting weeds. The grandfather said, "Let's stop and whet our scythes." The boy said, "No, I want to hurry and get done." If youth had listened to the wisdom of age, the boy would have known that sharp tools and skills will help you get more and better work accomplished—and sooner—than dull tools and skills. *People, like tools, must be honed and sharpened if they are going to function at their maximum potential.*

A good shop superintendent can become a superior shop superintendent if he will pursue a well-planned program of study aimed at a better understanding of people and their intricate interrelationships. A mediocre personnel director, for example, can thereby become an astute and highly capable vice president and contributing member of the management team. In addition, he should

1. Seek out associates and friends who are men of wisdom to provide him with personal insight and understanding.
2. Learn more about company operations as they concern other departments.
3. Look for problem areas and "hot spots" that will challenge and stretch him. Growth can take place only when personal goals are achieved.
4. Start thinking like a top-level executive in such terms as
    a. Long-range corporate planning.
    b. Company financial growth.
    c. Product innovation.
    d. Ratio of net profit to sales volume, as well as many others.
    e. Development of other people to their fullest potential.

VITALITY, SECURITY, AND DIGNITY

To sharpen his "people" tools, a man must have those often-mentioned personal, departmental, and company goals to shoot at. Ask a friend to go over to the wall and reach as high as he can. Then, after you have marked the spot, offer him some inducement to reach higher. You know the answer—he'll exceed his first effort. Goals, attitude, and motivation determine accomplishment—and pace—to a great extent.

Young Howard was a person of much ability and aggressive, positive attitudes. He had just been assigned to a new job as plant newspaper editor. His authority and responsibility had been defined; and, feeling he knew his objective, he set out with a full head of steam to achieve it. What happened? Howard, in the manner of many a newly created executive, proceeded down the road like a juggernaut. He simply had not been told of the results required of him in his new position, and he was running helter-skelter in a flurry of activity, looking busy, upsetting people, and costing the company more than he was contributing. Provided with a results-oriented job description, however, with full understanding of his accountability for those results, he was astute enough to reverse himself and make a valuable contribution to the company.

To encourage the highest practicable level of productivity and innovation from a subordinate, both you and he must have agreed on commitments for a specified period. Periodic review, progress reports, and personal counsel based on performance will serve to control and motivate the man's activities and results. With these you have the tools to do an organized, businesslike job. To insure achieving this high level of productivity yourself, you must make use of these same requirements and tools. Your organization must work hard, seek out and achieve their objectives if you are to achieve yours. They must understand the yardsticks by which their (say, a department's) and your (the company's) performance is measured and tie the two together. For example:

Company objectives:	*Production department objectives:*
20% increase in sales volume.	25% increase in production.
80% increase in net profit.	20% reduction in scrap and 50% reduction in returned goods; establishment of departmental news media and incentive systems.
20% reduction in turnover.	10% reduction in turnover.

DEVELOPING A TOUGH-MINDED CLIMATE

If neither you nor they know what you are looking for, how will you recognize it if you find it?

SUMMARY AND ACTION STEPS

In summary, to achieve the life of fulfillment which epitomizes the man with vitality, security, and dignity, we should recognize the constructive force of personal dedication and belief that carries a man forward. Dedication to principles and confidence in self—both of these are born of a well-grounded personal faith. Applied to the bread and butter of business —the profit column, the chief objective—this faith enables you to

1. Know and understand yourself better. You cannot understand others until you understand yourself.
2. Build your company in the image of complete integrity.
3. Have a happier personal life. Be a big person through hard work and giving constructively of self.
4. Help your employees to develop more fully. As they establish better work habits, attitudes, and values under your guidance, you too will continue to grow and so will be able to help them even more.
5. Resolve to be better respected by others. The tough-minded executive is more interested in being respected than being liked.
6. Improve your physical condition. Start the bloodstream surging again as it did years ago.

To achieve the full potential of the productivity climate, *whole men* are needed. In this admonition anyone who wants to achieve real success holds the magic key. But something must galvanize him into action. Let the suggestions under the following five headings be only the launching pad for a personal self-development program that will continue for years.

1. *Reading.* The list of helpful books on management is endless. Read carefully but retain a healthy dissatisfaction with both a particular book's content and your ability to apply it.
2. *Personal improvement* by
   a. Regular physical examinations and a physical fitness routine.
   b. Better family relationships.
   c. Positive personal and family objectives.
   d. Some real goals for stretching physically, mentally, morally, and spiritually.
3. *Better management practices*
   a. Selection procedures which stress tough-minded values.

b. Effective communication techniques. Be crisp, be warm, be organized, project complete sincerity.
   c. A personal commitment to developing all employees:
      (1) Try to bring out the best in everyone.
      (2) Set the pace for personal development, provide the example.
   d. Attitudes and terminology which focus constantly on *results*. Settle only for best efforts and results. Stress *excellence*.
   e. Empathy, warmth, and candor always.
   f. Time to *think*.
4. *Speaking*. Take advantage of opportunities to address local civic groups, trade and professional associations, or any group that can benefit from what you have to say. The tough-minded business entrepreneur of today has much to share with society.
5. *Giving more of yourself* to
   a. Your family.
   b. Your business associates.
   c. Charitable organizations.
   d. Your church.
   e. Industrial and professional associations.
   f. Boy Scouts and similar groups.

Take this list and add to it. These are only beginning steps. As you get under way in this program of self-improvement, you will develop your own momentum and it will carry you on to real heights of managerial and personal achievement.

CHAPTER XI

Integrity That Lives and Breathes

LUTHER HODGES, AS U.S. SECRETARY OF COMMERCE, ONCE WAS ASKED precisely when he planned to release an expected code of ethics for American business. According to Joseph W. McGuire, in *Business and Society*, Hodges replied, "It's hard to write a new Ten Commandments."[1]

Whether we call it ethics, honesty, or integrity, we are speaking of the same firm underpinning of a man's life in general. Whether we tie our thinking to business, to the nonbusiness enterprise, or to our life at home, this quality is absolutely essential. Dictionaries define integrity as an unimpaired condition, soundness; adherence to a code of moral, artistic, or other values; or moral soundness, honesty, uprightness. For the purposes of this chapter, however, let's treat integrity as a value in life, a precept for interrelationships between people, an acceptance of responsibility, and a commitment to one another.

A plaque at the entrance of Boys Town in Nebraska shows the picture, familiar to many of us, of a small boy carrying a still smaller boy asleep on his back. Asked if that isn't a pretty heavy load, the older boy replies, "He ain't heavy, Father—he's m' brother." To transpose the situation a bit, imagine someone asking about your obligations to your business today. Would your answer be: "I don't mind—it's my *responsibility*"?

On the premise that you know your responsibility for integrity in business, let's look at our socio-economic society closely and see what can be done about it.

Today—and Tomorrow

About the turn of the century someone declared it could only be by accident that the activities of a large number of individuals, all seeking their own private pleasures, should coincide in effecting the

[1] McGraw Hill Book Company, Inc., New York, 1963.

desirable end of the common happiness. The outcome would, more likely, be a competitive "war of all against all."

Are we laying our ethics and integrity aside in too many quarters today in the seemingly never-ending rush for greater pleasure, more spare time, and more money? Are businessmen possibly helping the country's integrity to slip backward into a morass of apathy and lethargy which destroys healthy and desirable relationships? Without the positive, powerful guidelines and governors that are imposed by personal integrity, could we find ourselves in an atmosphere of self-centered gluttony almost completely devoid of integrity and ethics?

The company president sat back in his chair, trying to appear both wise and composed. "If we don't terminate Henry," he said, "and if we don't include him in the executive development program, maybe he'll quit and save us the trouble of firing him. Besides, he's pretty well liked, and I don't want to antagonize his friends." There was absolutely no conception here of the lack of integrity, the lack of concern for a man's feelings and well-being, which these words implied. Henry's contribution to the company was so small that, in lieu of termination, the board finally agreed that his salary be cut in half, which would still leave him overpaid; there was not enough guts or integrity in the entire top management group to call Henry into the office, tell him he was out, and give him the reasons why. Owing to the emotional ramifications of more than 25 years' association, the president simply would not be that honest—even though, a year and a half later, he finally did fire Henry.

Men will speak of integrity, of honesty and fair practices, but too often they will not apply them personally. Integrity is not a living, breathing part of their lives. And, if today we fail to demonstrate a living code of integrity to our young people—our junior executives, our employees on their first jobs, our children—how can we legitimately complain about the prospects for ethics and integrity in our business society of tomorrow?

Managers Must Lead the Way!

In machine production work, each new contractor or job requires the machine operators to see that they are tooled up correctly before actual production begins. In business management today, should there be any less tooling up for the practice of integrity? Obviously not.

The president of a foundation, at a recent board meeting, asked that certain information be treated with the utmost confidence "for the good of the man concerned." Yet within two hours after the meeting adjourned this man had received the "confidential information." Some member of the board had forgotten all about integrity and his obligation to its principles. He just had never tooled up enough.

Integrity cannot be legislated, nor can it be given to a man with a hypodermic needle or in the form of a pill. Ignorance, while no excuse, is a factor to be considered. As one company spokesman has said, "It is not the crook in modern business that we fear, but the honest man who doesn't know what he is doing." Yet, for the modern businessman, the incidence rate chargeable to ignorance should be reduced to near nothing in terms of actions that are "right" or "wrong" according to a reasonable code.

The fact remains that integrity cannot be rationalized and diminished in importance. It is a matter of industrial conscience, of industrial morality. Who can lead the way better than our industrial leaders? In a *Harvard Business Review* survey, Raymond C. Baumhart[2] found that 94 per cent of the businessmen-respondents accepted the view that spiritual, ethical, moral, and social considerations should and do play a role of the utmost importance in profit making. As many as 99 per cent agreed that *sound ethics is always good business in the long run.* The problem, then, is one of living up to these beliefs.

When a company executive must make a tough management decision, when he knows he must face up to facts that deeply affect him and others, what should he do? How can he balance the many needs and values of a given situation to see that all are served well? How can he achieve his personal tooling for integrity? Find the effective, self-disciplined practitioner and you will very likely find a man who

- Meets commitments.
- Follows a realistic schedule.
- Is physically and mentally fit.

[2] "How Ethical Are Businessmen?" *Harvard Business Review*, July–August 1961

- Understands himself.
- Is a strong individualist.
- Operates by results, not activity, and measures others accordingly.
- Scrupulously insists on the truth.
- Continuously seeks new knowledge and growth.
- Conducts a periodic self-inventory and maximizes his strengths.
- Knows true creativity is impossible without planning, hard work, and follow-through.
- Develops pace and stamina.
- Can identify and eliminate trivia.
- Has happy domestic relations.
- Has a healthy balance of tension and tranquillity.
- Usually achieves empathy.
- Does not tolerate continued slipshod methods in others.
- Faces up to difficulties candidly.
- Gets to the heart of problems and talks them out.

The Contemporary "Con" Man

The confidence man is a skilled persuader who sells some unknowing or gullible citizen a story and extracts money from him. The citizen pays and is cheated. We all agree that this is not playing by the rules, not integrity in any sense. Yet we have books by the score on selling which advocate accentuating the positive and eliminating the negative—or at best diminishing the negative in size. They teach the double-barreled close, the various sales dynamites, the art of the gentle fib, and the skill of inferences. Selling built America, and it continues to be the prime mover in our free enterprise system. But should we condone the successful subterfuge as long as it suits company needs, or should we call it by its rightful name—dishonest selling or lack of integrity?

Is there any twilight zone of integrity? Must it always be a matter of black or white, honest or dishonest? Can there be gradations and degrees by which we govern our actions?

There is a company whose policy forbids the controller to initiate the sending of credit slips to customers who have overpaid. However, it glibly states that it will make a refund or give credit if requested.

This, the company feels, makes it honest. But isn't it a case of stretching a principle to the breaking point? By the last letter of the law, management's policy may still be honest, but it most certainly does not reflect any high degree of integrity on the part of management.

Integrity does not require that we be oblivious to selling skills or to accounting principles in an effort to be completely honest. Robert W. Woodruff, of the Coca-Cola Company, has commented that no act of salesmanship, in his opinion, is soundly successful unless something of the salesman goes with it. The man's *personal integrity,* his belief in himself and his product, must be an essential part of each sales agreement, if the company selling and the customer buying are mutually to benefit. This philosophy is easily stated, but it is more than mere window dressing—there are men who actually sell by it. If two salesmen from two different industries—one a firm believer in integrity, the other inured to every variety of sharp dealing—each made $25,000 a year, there would be no difference in their material reward. But imagine the difference in personal satisfaction and peace of mind.

Integrity Is Good Business

Deviations from integrity can manifest themselves in several ways. The individual executive may not realize it, but employees notice and condemn such actions as

- Asking his secretary to lie about his being in.
- Using company employees to paint his boat.
- Rummaging through subordinates' desks.
- Criticizing people destructively.
- Being overly concerned with status symbols.
- Indulging in moods.
- Philandering.
- Receiving kickbacks.
- Fixing prices.

This sort of man will most likely be suffering from "I" strain, thinking of himself to the exclusion of others.

An old expression used to have it that "a commitment made is a debt unpaid." Do we adhere to this workable principle enough today? Do we need a renaissance of integrity in American business? Have we gone forward or backward? Opinions will vary, but certainly we have the ability to move forward if we want to badly enough.

Several years ago an industrialist and financier could say, "The public be damned—I'm working for my stockholders." But IBM's Thomas J. Watson, Jr., says:

> If businessmen are sometimes thought to be self-centered, there is some truth in the belief. As in every profession, there are errants in business, men who put self-interest before everything else. Fortunately, however, they are few and their numbers are declining. The modern businessman looks upon business as a public institution, one which must be valued by the public if it is to endure. He respects public needs and he is aware of the responsibilities of business in the life of the nation. These are the things that give him his sense of values and make his career in business worthwhile.[3]

Variance from Standard

Benjamin Franklin once suggested to his parents that the family say Grace over the groceries once a week and ignore it at the table. This was a variance from standard that his father could not accept. Are there other variances, in business and elsewhere, that we can and must live with?

Adherence to the standard of integrity that should prevail throughout our business lives must be continuously honed on the grindstone of experience. It involves considerable circumspection and a constant weighing and assessing of our values and the accompanying restrictions and commitments. A willingness to compromise principles through a gutless, sheeplike attitude can only cost us needed profit in the long run. "No business can long exist without profits," says Charles H. Kendrick, Schlage Lock Company's chairman of the board. "Yet the practical businessman should think in long-range terms on this point. It does not help to make a penny today if one is to lose a dollar tomorrow, and *lack of ethical practice will surely bring this result.*"

[3] "New Opportunities in Business," in *Listen to Leaders in Business*, Albert Love and James Saxon Childers, editors, Holt, Rinehart & Winston, New York, 1962.

INTEGRITY THAT LIVES AND BREATHES

"Everyone's doing it" is not sufficient reason to go along with your competitors and rig prices or engage in some other dishonest practice. You may protest, "In our line we've always gotten together and decided our prices for the season. We have to do this to protect a legitimate margin." But somewhere along the years you've forgotten the principle of free enterprise that encourages striving for "the highest-quality product produced at minimum cost and sold in a competitive market at a legitimate price." When companies must fix prices to achieve a desired profit, they should retire from the battlefield of free competition. They are no longer serving society; therefore, their usefulness is at an end.

When sagging company profits indicate that something must be done, one or more of these steps must be taken:

1. Lower the quality of the product.
2. Increase the selling price.
3. Increase the productivity of shops and offices.
4. Reduce production costs through
    a. Improvement of internal manufacturing procedures.
    b. Reduction in noncontributing personnel.
    c. Use of new techniques and processes.
    d. Changing of worker performance and attitude.
    e. Development of supervisory and management employees.
    f. Willingness to learn from the experience of others.

This is the approach taken by a manager of integrity. He doesn't wait for someone to help him, he helps himself. He doesn't collaborate in price fixing, he has the intestinal fortitude to say, "I can't do that. It isn't honest."

There are no double standards—one for you and one for me. The same line of demarcation between right and wrong is mentally visible to all of us if we look for it. There is no personal tailoring of integrity to fit the exigencies of a given situation. We delude ourselves if we believe there is such a close tolerance between the acceptable and the nonacceptable in business that we can in all conscience proceed safely to develop the less desirable pattern of conduct.

Define in your own mind, and justify if you care to, the difference between these two men and their actions: your neighbor who beat the government out of $50 in taxes and bragged about it, and the man from across town who stole $50 from a safe in the U.S. Federal Building. Is there a difference? How much?

The acceptable standard of integrity in business that *you* know exists must be maintained. The line must be hewn to. With integrity, ethics, and dedication to principle, little or no variance from standard will pass inspection.

The Futility of Deception

The headlines sell themselves with their lurid and fascinating—yet disappointing—come-on: "Company *A* and Company *B* Indicted for Price Fixing." "Senator *X* Convicted on Income Tax Charge." In recent months and years we have been exposed to deception and lack of integrity in all segments of our society: price and bid rigging, share-of-market collusion, and misleading packaging in industry; quiz show scandals and disc jockey payola in entertainment; misuse of personal power, assistance in tax frauds, and minimal punishment for prominent figures in government.

The participants in these unscrupulous efforts, these hoaxes perpetrated on the public, may seem to escape lightly in many instances, but the personal loss in status and money takes its toll. Men are broken not only financially but physically, spiritually, mentally, and morally. Dishonesty is like battery acid—it's corrosive and disintegrating, working in an insidious way.

It could be that we as a society are at fault when, for example, we grade our schoolchildren on "ability to adjust." Are we not breeding easy conformity to easy standards? These children need to develop the ability to stand for the right instead of becoming only followers—sometimes not of the right but of the wrong. Society has a tendency to penalize the dissenter, even the leader, who steps off in a direction different from that of the pack. Being right may have its privileges, but it can be painful.

What price does a man *really* pay for deception and dishonesty? After World War II, Walter L. began a business in used equipment. He took advantage of any situation he could develop, and his success was phenomenal. He now has his millions, along with expensive automobiles, lovely homes, a family, all the tangible evidences of

STANDARDS OF INTEGRITY

For Guidance in Making Decisions in My Company and for Meeting Problems and Solving Them in My Business Life

I. I will live by the premise that to perpetuate my business and to be a good executive I must make the best-quality product practicable at minimum cost, market it competitively, and achieve the optimum legitimate profit in return.

II. I will recognize that my greatest resources in business are my employees, my associates, and my friends.

III. I will refuse to take advantage of a situation that will reflect adversely on the reputation of my company.

IV. I will refuse to take any advantage of a business opportunity if it may entail a violation of the morals, ethics, and laws of justice that I personally believe to be the foundations of society.

V. I will endeavor always to look for the positive, constructive, and developmental answers to problems concerning my employees and associates. I will try to demonstrate confidence in times of crisis.

VI. I will refuse to stretch honesty to the last letter of the law; my intention is more important than the act.

VII. I will practice—within the limits of wisdom—constructive candor, warm understanding, and helpful assistance to all who ask it.

VIII. I will confront my problems honestly and squarely, talking them out and solving them to the best of my knowledge and ability.

IX. I will recognize that both competition and cooperation built our country and that I must help to perpetuate these desirable attributes of our society for the future.

X. I will believe that the Ten Commandments are the supreme laws that should guide and inspire me.

financial well-being. Something, though, is missing. Walter L. has nervous tension and stomach trouble. His wife still lives with him, but Walter suspects she is staying only till their two children get through college. As for the children, they know their father only as their banker.

Is Walter paying for his deviation from integrity in his personal, family, and business life? It could well be that the great equalizing effect of life may have swung the pendulum of financial gain to the right in his case, but that the pendulum of real, lasting success has swung to the left.

SUMMARY AND ACTION STEPS

Frederick R. Kappel, chairman of the board for AT&T, puts it this way: "If you have any thought of taking part in a public service business, integrity and high character are the very first essentials, and there can be no misunderstanding about this." Kahlil Gibran, in *The Prophet*, says: "You give but little when you give of your possessions. It is when you give of yourself that you truly give." Tying together these two statements, Gibran's and Kappel's (the latter of which certainly applies to *all* businesses), we arrive at the concept of developing integrity in others through our own essential honesty. We sorely need emancipation from industrial and professional conformity. We need to achieve greater continuity of integrity in business. We need to promote the attitude that public acceptance or condonement does not right a wrong. We need to teach others, by the force of repeated example, how to operate by the rules. Only in this way can we change our ethical climate for the better.

It is easy to sit back and talk integrity. It is even easy to practice it—when it's convenient. But when it's not convenient, when it costs you money, to stand up for what you say you believe can be a realistic test.

How can the business executive take a forward step in building a climate of integrity in his own staff and company? This cannot be a one-shot treatment; it must have constant follow-through.

1. Determine precisely, in your own mind, what integrity is and how it should be applied to your company in such matters as companywide planning, man-to-man relationships, purchasing practices, quality of product, and marketing policies. Relate integrity to its effect on company profit and personal benefit.

2. Direct your key men to consider the cardinal points of integrity in the same thorough way.

3. Arrange for a series of executive sessions on today's problems in this area. These sessions will be much more than integrity-oriented, but one of the common threads can be the place of ethics and honesty in the generation of profit.
    a. Jointly work out a set of basic beliefs and principles for the company as a whole.
    b. Understand each other on a man-to-man basis, not only as department head to department head or subordinate to superior.
    c. Use constructive candor. Realize that none of you benefits unless you all say what you think.
    d. Concentrate on results, with heavy emphasis on *profit*.
    e. Discuss and understand the absolute necessity for deep and abiding loyalty to your company—loyalty which must be a two-way street.
    f. Stress the manager's responsibility for meeting commitments to other managers and to the employees.
    g. Understand the laws of communication and make them operative in your company.
4. Provide leadership by developing
    a. Company policies and procedures which reflect company integrity.
    b. A company creed or philosophy, documented and distributed to all of the company's publics.
    c. Company relationships with vendors, customers, government agencies, and others which show employees that the company practices what it advocates.
    d. Company attitudes toward employee participation in political, social, professional, and community activities—about which all employees are adequately informed.
5. Clarify for all employees the fact that integrity places a responsibility on everyone.
    a. Explain the management-union relationship in house organs or other media.
    b. Tell employees what the company's responsibilities toward them are, so that they know what to expect.
    c. Tell them what their responsibilities to the company are, so that they know what the company expects of them.
    d. Develop an understanding of the words "accountability for results." Make sure employees accept the fact that they will be held accountable for the desired results, know the methods by which their contributions will be measured, and understand the consequences of not achieving the goal to which they are committed. In the last analysis, accountability requires that a man do the job or get out of it.

DEVELOPING A TOUGH-MINDED CLIMATE

 e. Control as a manager should, knowing that the best controls are enlightened employees who practice integrity in depth.

This is tough-minded management in action. This is implementing the principle that only ethical performance counts in the long run. This is integrity that lives and breathes.

CHAPTER XII

Wisdom: The Stuff of Management

IN THE PAST TWO DECADES THERE HAS BEEN A TREMENDOUS INCREASE in the amount of time, effort, and money poured into the identification, recruitment, and development of management talent by American industry. That people are a business's most valuable resource, that the quality of management will determine its success or failure, and that its perpetuation demands a continuous supply of managerial talent—these have become accepted maxims hardly open to debate. And so, from business schools, training institutes, seminars, and job rotation programs *ad infinitum,* comes a steady stream of bright, polished, sophisticated "management timber." These young men are well schooled in the fundamentals and techniques of business—economics, finance, marketing, systems, planning, and of course human relations—and they are anxious to get on with their meteoric rise as captains of industry. And in fact these "comers" often do passably well in low-level staff and operating positions and win promotion quickly.

Then one day the smooth sophisticate finds himself in a management position. The rules are changed; he is faced with a situation demanding decisions but

- No time to make detailed studies.
- Problems of human motivation.
- A multitude of variables, some only vaguely perceived.
- Real accountability for results, for contribution to profit.

And the man falters. Talk and activity are no longer enough. He has no internal gyroscope to guide him, and sheer intelligence and knowledge are insufficient to meet the challenges that face him daily. He becomes tense and defensive, scurrying around in an attempt to get something going. He finds that he is almost entirely dependent upon his subordinates—that the only way to get things done is through them—but he also finds that neither threats nor cajoling or permissiveness will induce them to put forth more than a bare minimum of effort. In short, this bright young man lacks the stuff of management—wisdom.

Only People Get Things Done

It cannot be said too often that no matter how incisive the analysis, how thorough the planning, how lucid the memoranda and procedures, only people get things done. It is the job of a manager to manage people, not to administer through a plethora of reports, charts, memoranda, and the like.

Ed Jennings was a general accountant in a 40-man department of a medium-size public utility. He displayed a real flair for his work, and over a period of time had given top management sound, profitable recommendations developed from his analysis of financial and operating data. Ed was bright, ambitious, and persuasive and seemed the logical choice for the job of controller when it was vacated.

But the accounting department didn't operate very well after Ed took over. Needed management reports were issued late, and inaccuracies began to show up. The installation of an electronic data processing system had ground to a virtual standstill. Billing, accounts payable, and other administrative routines had fallen far behind. Ed was haggard and tense—quite a change from a few months before. A few probing questions opened the flood gates; and, as he poured out his frustrations and problems, a familiar pattern began to emerge:

- In an effort to get things done, he had rolled up his sleeves and dived into every accounting, systems, and miscellaneous problem brought to him in order to "get it done right."
- He had continued to do the financial analysis because he had no time to train the new man.
- Whenever one section in the department fell behind in the monthly closing schedule or on day-to-day routines, Ed would step in and personally help with the work.

WISDOM: THE STUFF OF MANAGEMENT

- In an effort to get the department's accuracy back up to par, he had taken on the task of personally reviewing all reports and supporting data before the reports were typed.

It was obvious that Ed was not managing the department; instead, he was doing the work—and running rough-shod over his subordinates in the process. He admitted to working more than 60 hours a week; yet the harder he worked, the worse things became. In short, he had abdicated his management responsibilities to become the chief clerk in the department. Why? Because he was highly intolerant of mistakes, by himself or others; believed firmly that clerical people are fundamentally lazy and will do as little as they can get by with; was convinced that people work only for a pay check; and felt that the only way to increase productivity in his department was through rigid procedures and well-defined quantity standards. As a result of these attitudes, the whole company was suffering.

Ed was demoted to his former position as a general accountant, much to his subsequent relief. Here his intelligence and initiative could be better used. He simply did not have the wisdom to manage others effectively. With experience, counsel, and a continuous self-development program, he may someday be ready for that big job, but not until he develops wisdom, the stuff of management.

There are a good many men like Ed around—men with brains, education, experience, and initiative who never quite cut the mustard as managers of other people, who never quite make the grade in the big jobs. But there are a few of the other kind too. These are the big men, the wise, tough-minded men who make companies grow and prosper. They take the same kind of people, machinery, plants, and methods that are available to their competitors and put them together in a climate of productivity to create a highly successful enterprise while others hesitate and fall behind. They can spot and nurture wisdom in other men, and they build on and with these men to make the impossible seem merely difficult and the difficult easy.

The development of people requires insight and understanding, both of self and of others. That elusive gift of wisdom is what separates the men from the boys when competition gets stiff or when technological or market changes threaten an industry's very existence.

DEVELOPING A TOUGH-MINDED CLIMATE

The Substance of Wisdom

Often the man of wisdom in business is pictured as a battle-scarred veteran of corporate wars who wears rumpled tweed suits and smokes a pipe, who smiles and nods knowingly as young executives scurry about him in a state of semipanic. This Spencer Tracy type has relatively minor responsibilities, but serves as father confessor and counselor to everyone from the president to the janitor. Hogwash! Business does not need father confessors and dispensers of sage advice. Business needs men of wisdom who can get things done—men who can develop other people and create the climate which will bring out the best in them. Business needs men who demonstrate the basic elements of wisdom: purpose, values, and concepts.

Before a man can be considered to possess wisdom, he must have worked out some *purpose* for his life. James Allen put it very succinctly: "Until thought is linked with purpose there is no intelligent accomplishment."* The wise man first of all recognizes a power greater than himself and has developed a personal faith which imparts real meaning and zest to his life. Second, he believes in what he is doing; he sees real value and opportunity for achievement in his life's work. Such a man draws no sharp lines between work and leisure, work and home, work and life. To work, to achieve, to build —this *is* life.

Part and parcel of wisdom is a set of solid, unshakable *values* and beliefs. Not opinions, nor ideas intellectually accepted, but rock-ribbed beliefs developed from introspective inquiry and examination, from keen observation, and most of all from the fiery crucible of experience. True beliefs are not only espoused but lived. They are as much a vital part of the wise man as his limbs and his heart. Among them:

- Knowing yourself is the first step to total effectiveness as your own man.
- People differ from one another, but all possess individual dignity.

* *As a Man Thinketh*, Fleming H. Revell Company, Westwood, N.J., 1964.

- True happiness comes only from giving of yourself to others.
- Integrity is a way of life with which there can be no compromise.
- Real zest for life and love of life flow only from work and accomplishment.

Concepts are the third essential element of wisdom in management. Well grounded in values, they translate thought into action and create the solid foundation upon which all management policies, practices, and techniques are built. They set the style and tone for the entire organization and create the *modus operandi* which molds the individuals in it into an operational whole which can achieve far more than the sum of its parts. Many of these concepts are already familiar to us:

- Management is the development of people, not the direction of things.
- Innovation and change are an essential, continuous part of business life and should be welcomed and fostered.
- Free enterprise must be lived and practiced in every aspect of a business, both inside and outside.
- Building on strengths unlocks the latent potential in people; their weaknesses will take care of themselves.
- Candor—honesty with warmth—is the essential lubricant in all effective human action.
- Tools and techniques exist for one purpose only—to help people get things done.
- People want to work and identify with objectives of the organization, and they want a hand in determining how they help to achieve those objectives.

This list will suggest the kind of pervasive and positive concepts which should provide the underpinning for all that managers say and do. They give living, breathing substance and backbone to the organization and unleash its power to fulfill the basic purposes of the enterprise and the individuals in it.

DEVELOPING A TOUGH-MINDED CLIMATE

The Development of Wisdom

The manager of plant engineering for a medium-size manufacturer had an excellent engineering background developed through formal education, wide experience, and continuous self-development. He also was highly intelligent, sometimes displaying real flashes of brilliance. But, for the most part, his work was disappointing and he achieved few tangible results.

This manager had a pronounced tendency to vacillate under pressure. He would state very positively the best way to handle a given problem in the shop, but he would nearly always reverse himself completely under probing questions about the *why* and the *how* of his proposed solution. Furthermore, although he could recite the principles of good supervision quite glibly, he always seemed to be botching up labor relations in the plant through apparent favoritism, poor communication, and indecisiveness. ("Put that machine here—no, over there! That's still not right; put it back here again.") Here, then, was a man who obviously lacked the wisdom to be an effective manager but who apparently had basic capabilities worth salvaging. To build some wisdom into him, to help him develop this elusive essential, his superiors had to

1. Help him to know himself. This entailed a sometimes excruciating but thorough and revealing inventory of personal goals, strengths, and weaknesses.
2. Help him to develop some basic beliefs, to work out at least a beginning set of positive values from within himself, not out of a book.
3. Work with him to develop some management concepts for dealing with others and motivating them effectively. This involved rolling up the sleeves and helping him to learn through trial and error in real-life situations.
4. Follow up continually to stretch the man's thinking.

Eventually the plant engineering manager's overall effectiveness soared far beyond his previous level; in fact, he was eventually named works manager. The point is that, if the basic clay is there in terms of ability and integrity, you can develop wisdom through continuous stretch and pull. Preaching is not enough. You develop the desired qualities in your people by working with them, listening to them, and showing them.

The Identification of Wisdom

One of the most important steps in achieving a productivity climate is to select the best people for key positions in the organization. And, since wisdom is the stuff of management, it follows that its identification and appraisal are essential to proper selection. The *how* here is simple in concept but difficult in practice—you must get to *know* your people.

To get to know someone is not so easy as it sounds. You can be acquainted with someone for years, maybe all your life, and still not know him. To appraise a man's wisdom, you must know him intimately—know his sense of purpose, his values and beliefs, his concepts. This isn't easy, but it can be done, and in an objective, systematic fashion. Significantly, the man who is wise is easier to know than the man who is not, for the man of wisdom has fewer fears, little tendency toward show or pretense, and a more realistic view of himself than the smaller man. It must be recognized, further, that the identification of wisdom in another person is subjective. There is no magic formula, battery of psychological tests, or rating form which will provide an objective, quantitative measure. There is no fit substitute for wisdom and judgment on your part in the identification and appraisal of another's wisdom. However, the following pattern can be used to good advantage:

- *Interview or discussion.* Ask many nondirect or open-end questions about the individual's goals, values, and beliefs; his concepts of management; and his strengths and weaknesses. Listen carefully and probe beyond superficialities by asking plenty of *why's*.
- *Testing.* Use psychological tests, professionally administered and evaluated, to measure strengths and weaknesses, attitudes and aptitudes. Correlate the test scores with results of discussion to determine how well the individual knows himself.
- *Observation.* Watch the individual in action. Observe how he

handles his subordinates, how he deals with others in the organization. Look at the results he achieves in terms of what is expected of him. Is his planning sound? How well does he develop his people? Does all his work reflect wisdom and judgment above and beyond mere technical competence? What do his peers and other associates think?

Hardness or Tough-Mindedness?

A good many people in this country, both in industry and in other sectors, have embraced the concepts of tough-mindedness as representing a sort of management "wave of the future." But there are others who obviously have taken the phrase without its substance and distorted it to mean something different. These are the people who equate tough-mindedness with "hardness" or "toughness" and who often justify their bull-of-the-woods brand of management as being not only appropriate but quite *avant garde*. This is sheer rationalization rooted in ignorance.

The tough-minded manager operates from strength; the hard or tough manager operates from weakness and achieves results of which the following symptoms are typical:

- Passive, compressed subordinates who turn out mediocre work but always look busy when the boss is around.
- Poor results—by any standards. Although people look busy, they seldom accomplish anything.
- High turnover—mostly among good men who want to grow and contribute. The poorer performers of course stay.
- High costs, stemming mainly from overstaffing.

What is it, in the last analysis, that distinguishes the tough-minded man from the hard one?

THE HARD MANAGER	THE TOUGH-MINDED MANAGER
1. He has many fears. For example, he is afraid that people will take advantage of him.	1. He knows himself and is happy with what he is, at the same time building a healthy dissatisfaction with the *status quo*.

WISDOM: THE STUFF OF MANAGEMENT

2. He is wrapped up in himself and his own interests.

3. He uses threats, bluster, "chewings out," and firings to keep people busy and in line.

4. He is critical of others' weaknesses and seldom acknowledges their strengths.

5. He lacks a real and abiding faith in himself or anyone else.

6. He hates to accept others' ideas and, if he does, represents them as his own.

7. His sole criterion for performance is usually "busyness"—activity but not results.

8. He has many doubts about his own character and abilities; so he tries to bring others down to his level through sarcasm and cynicism.

---

2. He lives the concept that management is the development of people and that it pays real dividends to both business and individual.

3. He knows that people will give their best if they are helped to develop a feeling of purpose and dignity.

4. He builds on his own and others' strengths and lets the weaknesses take care of themselves.

5. He lives integrity.

6. He welcomes and fosters innovation and change as a necessary and desirable part of progress. He welcomes others' ideas.

7. He believes that his people should be held accountable for results—not activity—and provides security, recognition, and opportunity on that basis.

8. He knows what he stands for as a man and continually strives to communicate his values and beliefs to every corner of the organization.

The differences between the tough-minded manager and the hard manager should be even more apparent if you will look at the results produced by each. The tough-minded manager will far outstrip his rival in building an organization of people who want to work, who want to see the company grow and prosper, and who direct their energies and wisdom toward the accomplishment of significant results for the enterprise.

SUMMARY AND ACTION STEPS

Wisdom is not a pie-in-the-sky philosophy which has no place in the modern business world. The stuff of management, it transcends mere competence and in fact is the quality which differentiates the excellent from the merely competent man. For the man of wisdom has the ability to

- Develop and focus his own abilities toward the building of others.
- Make decisions which are not only logically sound but appropriate, taking into full account the strengths and needs of others.

- Perceive and grasp the opportunities of today's world through a state of mind which looks for, welcomes, and nurtures continual innovation and change.
- Discern the emerging patterns of the future and plot his organization's strategy to shape and exploit those patterns.

Wisdom can be identified and fostered in an organization. There is no system, program, or method which will do the job; rather, an entire management way of life must be built upon solid, tough-minded concepts rooted in firm, positive values.

1. The top man must work out for himself his own basic beliefs and values and carefully define not only his purpose in life but that of the organization through
    a. Much disciplined thought and self-examination.
    b. Discussion with trusted friends, associates, and others.
    c. Wide reading and study of philosophy, religion, psychology, and the like.
2. The top man must reduce these values and beliefs to writing and communicate them throughout the organization. Anyone who cannot fully subscribe to the basic purpose of the organization should be asked to leave; otherwise, conflicts and cross-purposes will always exist.
3. Care should be taken to select only men of demonstrated wisdom for management positions. Wisdom can be judged by
    a. Evaluating results.
       - Has the man built and motivated people?
       - Has he achieved results through others?
       - Were the results ethically achieved? Does the man live integrity?
       - Has he made sound, appropriate decisions even where facts were sparse?
    b. Knowing the man.
       - What are his strengths and weaknesses? How realistic is he in his own self-appraisal?
       - What does he stand for as a man?
       - What are his basic goals in life?
       - Has he demonstrated the guts to stick up for his values?
       - Do his concepts of management reflect wisdom and tough-mindedness?
4. Continual effort should be made to foster wisdom in others, particularly managers at all levels in the organization, by
    a. Working with subordinates so that, by demonstration and by trial and error, they will gain valuable insights into concepts of effective management action.

b. Helping people to work out their own values and beliefs through discussion and counsel.
   c. Helping subordinates to know themselves better through discussion of their strengths and through objective, painstaking appraisal—supported, if feasible, by psychological testing.

The greatest strides that can be made toward fostering wisdom in an organization will come through the development of a productivity climate. This will offer vastly increased motivation and stretch, bring out the best in people, and provide the quality and quantity of accomplishment which will quickly move men from the level of technical competence to the higher plane of wisdom—the stuff of management.

CHAPTER XIII

How to Build on Strengths

THE ONLY PURPOSE OF ORGANIZATION IS TO MAKE ONE PLUS ONE equal three—or more. Two men must do more than twice the work of one man or there is no organization! A new concept? Startling discovery? Hardly. This fundamental truth has been recognized for decades. It is the source of methods improvement, of mass production and automation, of staff specialties of assorted shapes and sizes.

In fact, there is a growing feeling today that we are nearing the end of increased efficiency through organization. Many "sophisticated" professionals—personnel men, professors, psychologists, and consultants—are preaching that the true road to combined productive effort is through *dis*organization: job enlargement, decentralization, task forces, unstructured social interaction. Others believe that various permissive approaches are the answer; they advocate shared accountability, line-staff committees, junior boards, collective goal setting, and other so-called democratic processes. Some experts have completely given up trying to organize for greater human productivity and have turned to organizing machines instead of men. Yet all these solutions to the basic problem are superficial, piecemeal, patchwork makeshifts that fall pitifully short of the breakthrough necessary to realize the almost limitless and barely tapped potential of joint human effort. A complete shift of emphasis must take place.

Molding and manipulating people to achieve premeditated patterns of behavior and dropping them into preconceived slots on an organization chart may make you feel powerful and important, but it is about as effective as a square wheel in achieving excellence. Compressing a man to fit a job which has been carefully interrelated with other jobs (which are filled by compressing other men) may be neat and orderly, and will probably work moderately well if you get rid of the people who just won't stay compressed.

The issue is clear: Do you want an organization with no loose ends? A box for everyone and everyone in his box? An organization where exceptions to the rule (even in the form of exceptional men, who seldom follow the rules) are not allowed to exist or at best are barely tolerated? An organization which runs moderately well, is moderately safe and secure, makes a moderate profit, enjoys moderate growth, and provides you and your employees with a moderate degree of satisfaction and a moderate sense of achievement? If you prefer this approach, you need not feel guilty. Many do—and suffer no disgrace.

But you may want an organization which leads the parade; which sets the pace in profits, growth, products, methods, and concepts; which always seems able to come up with the breakthrough when it's needed; which keeps its competitors so busy catching up they don't have time for anything else. If so, if you want to reap the rewards which justice dictates must always fall to the victor, you must make a fundamental decision: to expand, not compress, men; to build on their strengths, not focus on their weaknesses. The weaving together of basically self-directed people, each doing what he can do best so as to achieve singleness of purpose and unity of direction, requires great artistry and effort.

If, finally, you decide to strive for excellence and seek exceptional performance, then you must back up your decision with demonstration, not just conversation, and begin building on strengths—starting with yourself. It is vital, in this context, that your basically self-directed men realize that the one best way to grow as individuals is to build others—constantly.

Know—and Accept—Thyself

"Know thyself." It's an easy prescription, but one that is hard to carry out. Since it was first laid down by Socrates in ancient times, men have sought better ways of appraising themselves objectively. But *there is no such thing as objective self-appraisal.* The very concept of objectivity presupposes that a large enough number of people agree on a certain point. When appraising yourself, you can accept the opinions of others in terms of the impression you are making, but only you can determine whether or not you like what you see. Everyone reads you differently, sees a different facet of you. Therefore, you have to abandon the idea of going out and taking a vote.

There is a good chance that you know yourself better than you think you do. It's a matter of sitting down and listing your strengths and weaknesses rather than any painful reflective process involving psychoanalytic symbolism. The main thing is to pull your thinking together and get it down in writing so that it doesn't keep sliding and slipping away from you. You begin defining yourself to yourself by taking a piece at a time.

First, you put down some of the more obvious things about yourself: for example, your age and other physical characteristics. Here you can throw in an evaluation of your total appearance and the impression you feel you make on people. Then you go on to describe your mental capacities, your ambitions, your energy level. You judge how persevering you are, how thoughtful and considerate. You state your physical stamina and well-being, the things you like and don't like, the times of the day you seem to work better than others, and why. It won't be long before you've developed a framework that will be a start at a self-description in terms of strengths, desires, and interests. Don't be concerned if some rationalization or bias creeps in; in any subjective analysis you are building largely on feelings and impressions.

The second step is to develop an ability to observe yourself in the various dynamic processes of life—at work, in the home, with friends. *A man is more what he does than what he thinks he is.* And, however strange it may seem, he often becomes what he says and does even though it may be contrary to his basic desires. It is important to decide whether you are actually yourself or whether you are trying to be something that you are not. To observe yourself in action, so to speak, you develop what might be called a "calculated schizophrenia." This is not as difficult as it seems. You merely have to set aside a small part of your thinking apparatus and pretend you are looking over your own shoulder as you experience life. You will be able to do this quite easily if you will make it a habit to keep a day-to-day diary—not necessarily a lengthy or soul-searching document but just an accounting of what you observed yourself doing during the day, why you did it, how well it was done, and what kind of results you achieved.

DEVELOPING A TOUGH-MINDED CLIMATE

Periodically you ought to go through your diary and sort out any recurring elements or patterns of behavior. Then you can go back to your initial description of yourself and see whether you are indeed acting the way you feel you are, whether you are being your own man or whether you are allowing pressures to make you behave in a way that is not natural and therefore will cause you frustration and bitterness.

The Theory of Crutches

Serious weaknesses and problems within an organization are not and cannot be identified or corrected because expedient and compensatory measures are informally effected to minimize the consequences of the weaknesses without eliminating the weaknesses.

In most companies, a strong, conscientious performer will tend to carry a poor one on his back, assuming the weaker man's responsibilities if it is necessary to get his own job done. Since his standards are always high, this situation is usually the rule rather than the exception; and, as long as the job does get done, the weak spots are neither revealed nor corrected. The situation persists primarily because of inadequate or poorly placed individuals over which the good performer has no control. Even when the weak people are on his staff, he often finds it easier to do their work for them than to face up to the unpleasant task of demoting or replacing them.

Here we come to the "theory of crutches," which recognizes that most people are inclined to avoid or work around problems rather than face them head on and solve them as they occur. This theory is at work in many companies, and it has a corollary: *No significant or lasting growth can be achieved in an organization until the crutches are eliminated.*

An insurance company had an extremely capable manager for its actuarial and underwriting functions—including responsibility for developing group health insurance rates for current clients who renewed their coverage each year. The historic method of developing these rates involved a 100 per cent manual accrual of claims paid to each individual in each group during the year. It also involved a similar recording of the premiums received from each group. The relationship between the premiums collected and the claims paid, when projected for the coming year, decided what the new premium would be.

Recently the company installed a large computer complex and developed a rather sophisticated data processing system designed to automate many internal paper operations. Among them was the critical but time-consuming manual accrual of claims paid and premiums collected.

As is customary, the new computer system and the old manual system were run parallel until the "bugs" were worked out of the new one. However, the vice president for actuarial and underwriting functions quickly detected some major flaws in the new system and attempted unsuccessfully to work them out with the manager of the electronic data processing operation. He therefore continued the old manual system on an informal basis after it was "officially" replaced. Thus the new computer system not only failed to improve service and reduce operating costs but also developed animosity between two key members of top management and shook people's confidence in the entire electronic data processing operation.

The problem was identified and solved by eliminating the crutches. The informal manual system was arbitrarily eliminated, and the vice president for actuarial and underwriting functions was relieved of responsibility for any consequences accruing from malfunctioning of the new system. (This was done on a dry-run basis to avoid possible long-term liability.) The flaws of the new system were of course immediately apparent, and it was modified accordingly.

This is by no means an isolated case. Similar situations exist in nearly every company. Often they continue for years and are corrected only by accident through the retirement or replacement of personnel. Always they inhibit the long-term health and growth of the organization, even though the crutches may seem an effective, expedient solution to an urgent problem.

Applying this theory to yourself, you can readily see that feeling and believing one way and acting another because of external pressures is using a crutch. It cramps personal growth and may completely block the development of wisdom. If you do not state your feeling or act on your beliefs, those feelings and beliefs will never be tried, modified, or matured. You will never be able to demonstrate their validity and durability to yourself, nor will you ever discover any built-in fallacies or erroneous assumptions in them. True wisdom and self-confidence are the outgrowth of a sound set of beliefs and principles which will stand the test of time and trial in many varied situations.

Most people so limit the scope of their experiences and associations with people that they are never able to develop or test broad principles or beliefs. They have a small closed circle of friends. They attend a certain church. They eat dinner in the same restaurant every evening. They work on the same job for 30 years. In short, they restrict the richness of their lives to such an extent that they never really can judge what kind of people they are. Adapting to their narrow world, they never know whether their principles are sound enough to prevail no matter what the external conditions or pressures.

You may actually have to drive yourself into new situations to try out your principles and, keeping the second part of your mind looking over your shoulder, evaluate the results. The ultimate test of their soundness lies in whether or not you have been able to achieve a high level of personal happiness and, in the process, contribute to rather than take from the happiness of those around you.

What Others Think

The third important step in learning about yourself is to solicit the opinions of people with whom you are in contact in various situations. Find out what your wife thinks of you, what your business associates think of you, what your fellow church members think of you. Select a few men and women and ask them for an honest evaluation.

This may be a little embarrassing, but it should not be impossible if you make it quite clear what you are after. Take special care to choose people who have had the opportunity of observing and working with you in different ways and under different conditions. Keep a written record of their evaluations, jotting down a few notes the first chance you have. And again, after you have done this with

HOW TO BUILD ON STRENGTHS

eight or ten people, go back and find any recurring elements. There should very definitely be a pattern in the way people perceive you, and you may be surprised that they don't see you in nearly the way you felt they would see you. This doesn't mean that you should quickly change your behavior so as to be all things to all people. The objective is for most of your associates to see you as you really are; if that is not adequate, if you still are not successful and happy, then you have to consider that possibly you should change the way you are.

It is not enough just to change the impressions of the people around you by changing the way you deal with them. You have to change your own thoughts, your own way of believing and performing. It is only practical to recognize, however, that individuals see you through *their* eyes; they judge you against *their* standards. Therefore, don't be alarmed if you are never successful in portraying the same image to all the people you meet. It's only the basic things you stand for and believe in that you want them to recognize in you —integrity, candor, warmth, wisdom.

As you learn the knack of calculated schizophrenia, you will begin to develop greater empathy. This doesn't mean knowing how you would feel if you were in another man's shoes; it means knowing how you would feel if you were actually that other man with his knowledge, fears, biases, and desires. Empathy will grow rapidly if you strive hard to sense how people feel about a situation in which they are involved, how they react to you and how they react to other people. And, with this greater empathy, with your new ability to read the impressions of your family, friends, and associates correctly, you will be better able to determine whether you are actually communicating what you want to communicate. You will truly begin to know yourself.

Inevitability of Mistakes

But an even more important part of knowing yourself is the willingness to accept yourself. Sometimes this is far more difficult. All of us have a tendency not to be happy with what we are, to set standards for ourselves that are far greater than any we would set for others; as a result, we may be plagued constantly by feelings of guilt and frustration.

Developing the ability to accept ourselves for what we are is the initial step toward changing ourselves into what we think we ought to be. We must not only accept ourselves but also accept the basic fact that we will always be making mistakes. We will never be so omnipotent that we can do everything right all the time or achieve the results we strive for. Unless we concede that we can fail and that failure does not mean total destruction of personality, we will never be able to achieve success and happiness. Nor will we ever be able to accept other people as they are and contribute to their success. Whenever we view ourselves as we are and then set out to define what we want to be, there will obviously be some gaps. The way to overcome these gaps is to select the one which we think is most important and to lay out a calculated plan for improving in this single area, recognizing that it may take time and that the important point is to make some progress each day.

Remember, we have to set our own standards. We have to arrive at our own conclusions and our own value system and then do our best to live accordingly. If the values and beliefs that we develop for ourselves do not fit in with our present environment—for example, the particular job we hold—then we must go find the kind of environment in which we can act in accordance with those values and beliefs. It is only when we have achieved the spiritual independence which is bound to result that we can proceed to build on the strengths of others.

Getting to Know People

Obviously, the place to start is a sound knowledge of others' strengths, but this is nothing you can acquire just by sitting back and reflecting upon this person or that. All you tend to do, in such cases, is to reflect on personalities, and the most natural thing is to concentrate on weaknesses and forget about strengths.

The only effective way to learn the strengths of your subordinates or colleagues is to work with them in a variety of situations where their mettle is tested, where you can see their reaction to pressure and stress, where you can see the quality of work they turn out and the quality of person they are. This means working with them not only in job situations but in social and other situations where they are called upon to contribute in quite a different type of way, as in the church, the Boy Scouts, the Community Chest drive, and so on. It is easy for a man to carry on an elaborate pretense, sometimes for many years, in connection with his job. However, it is virtually impossible for him to pretend to be something he is not in all aspects of his life.

In many cases, naturally, it is impractical to expect a top manager to become so totally involved with each of his subordinates and associates. He must often rely on the appraisals of others and extract the most out of each association. Psychological tests can help in getting to know others (as well as oneself), but a manager should not let himself be swayed too much by what they may reveal. These tests are based upon normal or average behavior, and the terms "average" and "normal" express a statistical, not a human, concept. No one is average or normal or typical in every facet of his personality; there is a great deal of unevenness about people, who generally are far more mature and competent in some areas than they are in others. A man may be a highly effective business supervisor, for example, but a weak husband and father and an obstructionist on the church vestry. He may speak well but write poorly. Or he may think well when he has plenty of time but come apart at the seams when he is under pressure.

As in getting to know yourself, it is important to put your observations in writing on a regular basis. Every time you work with someone in a specific situation, note down a brief description of what he did, how he approached his task, the results he obtained, and the strengths that made themselves evident. After you have done this over a period of weeks and months, you will see a profile of strengths developing. In most companies the opportunity to work with people in enough situations to evaluate their strengths is limited; sometimes it will have to be manufactured. You have to take a controller or sales manager or personnel director and try him out in other situations. This does not necessarily mean a hodge-podge of job rotation; it means bringing him in with you on a special project or problem whether it relates to his field or not. It may mean playing some golf with the man or going on a hunting trip with him. In any event, there is no short cut to knowing him. You have to expose yourself to him, work with him, make a conscious effort to arrive at a fair evaluation of his abilities.

Matching the Strengths with the Tasks

Then, as you build up similar profiles of all your subordinates and associates, you need to start thinking about how their strengths can best be used—how they can be focused and directed toward the realization of basic company or department goals. This takes a great deal of skill because you are dealing with a wide range of talents and strengths which you must match with the many tasks and functions for which you are responsible. In building a house it is not enough to know the clay and mortar you have to work with; you must have a plan or blueprint to guide you in their use. Similarly, in building on strengths you must know more than just the human material you have available; you must also know your objectives—what you are to build. Knowing your objectives, you will then be able to break these down into the small bite-size pieces that we call results requirements—single, discrete tasks that you can hold a single person accountable for performing.

For example, one of the objectives for your organization may well be the development of a new product. The first step necessary will probably be research to determine the market potential for the various products which you are considering. Another step may be the determination of criteria for selecting the product you will concentrate on: profit margin for first, second, and third years; return on investment; length of product life; or compatability with current equipment, facilities, and distribution channels. A third step may be building a prototype or making a test run of the new manufacturing process; a fourth, pilot marketing of a limited quantity of the product. In this way, you break down your objective till you have clearly defined all the basic steps you will have to take.

With your step-by-step list of tasks to be done, you review the list of strengths you have noted in studying your people and correlate the strengths with the tasks, regardless of lines of authority or position in the organization. This approach works equally well with special objectives like developing a new product or with such a general operating objective as meeting annual sales or production forecasts.

For a Dynamic Organization

Organizing by strengths takes a lot of self-control and self-discipline. It is all too easy to "type" people in the function for which they are responsible, without thinking how their strengths can be used elsewhere. In fact, such categorization contributes to a highly rigid organization structure and does more to stifle the potential of the people involved than it does to capitalize on their abilities.

Be careful to include your own strengths along with those of your staff. You too must be directly and deeply involved in the achievement of organizational objectives, use your own talents to accomplish specific tasks, not just sit back and oversee what is going on. This heavy involvement is necessary if you are consistently to review and reappraise the strengths of your people as they grow, to update your list of strengths, and—each time a new objective is set—to redetermine what tasks should be assigned to your key people according to their current level of development.

In this way you will develop a type of dynamic organization in your company that few have realized. You will constantly be establishing objectives, accomplishing objectives, assigning new tasks as people grow and develop new strengths. You will have eliminated the old crutches of seniority and promotion by personality, *rewarding people in direct relation to the results they accomplish.* They will be encouraged to develop new strengths and further exploit the strengths that they now have in the accomplishment of specific tasks. Each man will grow at his own pace, as rapidly or as slowly as his abilities, interests, and desires will allow. You will have ample opportunity to take advantage of the bright young men in your group, to stretch them so that they can grow much more rapidly than would ever be possible in a conventional organization. They will not find themselves blocked by organizational rigidity; they will experience the challenge that makes them want to perform for you in an exceptional way.

DEVELOPING A TOUGH-MINDED CLIMATE

However, building on strengths does require that you know your business and know it well. You cannot manage from your corner office or penthouse. You, like everyone else, will have tasks to complete. Not only will you plan and organize, but you will actually be an important factor in the execution of your plans.

Personal—to Company Presidents

Many company presidents exhibit the same type of mild but chronic dissatisfaction. They often ask, "Where do we go from here?" They feel they have things moving reasonably well, but they feel no sense of challenge or fulfillment. There are other presidents who say, "I've built this climate you talk about. I build on strengths; I challenge people—and they're working well, growing all the time. What do I do when they reach a level of excellence where I am no longer required? What will be *my* stimulation and challenge?"

The answer is quite simple: *This lack of personal challenge will never exist.* As you and your people grow, your company will grow at such a rate that new and challenging opportunities will always be there. You will always be searching out these opportunities and exploiting them to the fullest. You will be sharing in the excitement of accomplishment with your staff and business associates, relishing each success and spurred on by each failure.

Probably the greatest factor contributing to this vague sense of dissatisfaction on the part of company presidents is the fact that they no longer have anyone to share their success with. Their wives and families are not deeply enough involved to understand the trials and tribulations and excitement that went into getting the job done. Even their friends and casual acquaintances in the business world do not know the "people" problems, the crises, challenges, and rewards experienced in the social environment peculiar to the individual company. But these presidents can find full satisfaction working with their subordinates to the point where they savor with them the enjoyment that comes from being a real member of the team.

This kind of satisfaction never grows old, because as you reach one goal you immediately strike out toward another. It does not come entirely from achieving an objective; it comes also from the *process* of achieving that objective; from the association with competent people, the stimulation you receive from them, the leadership which you yourself provide. It is the source of the true joy of management—the sense of accomplishment that comes from building and guiding a successful commercial enterprise and at the same time knowing the ultimate in human endeavor—the building of men.

SUMMARY AND ACTION STEPS

The essential purpose of organization is to multiply individual productivity to obtain greater results through joint human effort. The basic assumption underlying all organizational concepts is that efficiency is gained through specialization, which can take the form of minute work processes or entail overall planning and decision making. The characteristic approach to dividing a project or function into specialized work segments is mechanical, sterile, and wasteful of human resources. To realize the huge untapped potential of human productivity, the division of work must be predicated upon the strengths of individuals even though it may not facilitate a neat and orderly organization structure.

Building on strengths requires knowledge, understanding, and acceptance of yourself and your associates. It also requires a creative and flexible approach to the assignment of tasks and functions in order to match the demands of the organization with the peculiar and changing strengths of its personnel. There is a tremendous gap between what people are doing and what they *can* do. It is impractical and idealistic to assume that we can jump this chasm with one great leap forward, but the gap can and must be bridged a plank at a time.

1. Identify and define your own strengths.
   - *a.* List what you know about yourself, beginning with such characteristics as age, physical traits, interests, and stamina.
   - *b.* Develop a calculated schizophrenia—the ability to observe yourself in action.
   - *c.* Expose yourself to new and different situations.
   - *d.* Keep a written diary documenting your day-to-day observations. Periodically review it for recurrent patterns of behavior.
   - *e.* Find out what other people think of you and put their opinions in writing.
   - *f.* List your successes and extract the major contributing factors. As you concentrate on these successes, any failures should become insignificant.

DEVELOPING A TOUGH-MINDED CLIMATE

2. Get to know your associates and staff as individuals.
    a. Develop empathy and work hard at applying it.
    b. Develop a close operational involvement with your subordinates. Give them as much of your wisdom and experience as you can, consistent with logical autonomy and accountability.
    c. Keep anecdotal records describing specific instances of your people's behavior and accomplishments.
    d. Utilize psychological test results and personal evaluations of others, but do not weight them unduly in comparison with actual performance.
    e. Make use of special projects or assignments to give your people the opportunity to display strengths not called for by their regular jobs.
    f. Prepare a written profile of the strengths of your people and regularly revise it as they develop and change.
3. Define in writing the performance requirements of the organization.
    a. Describe company objectives, both short- and long-range.
    b. Break each objective down into the discrete tasks necessary for its achievement.
    c. Break each task down into steps small enough that they can be assigned to a single person.
4. Match individual assignments with individual strengths.
    a. Change assignments as objectives change.
    b. Change assignments as people change.
    c. Assign specific tasks to yourself according to your own strengths, *not* according to your title or because of a stereotyped image of what a manager should do.
    d. Be flexible. Move quickly to change assignments when you are certain someone else can perform them better.
    e. Don't let weak performers cause you to overload strong performers. Either build up the weak links or replace them.
5. Above all, become *a part* of your organization—don't hold yourself *apart* from it. Management is more than "getting things done through people," it is getting things done *with* people. You must work with your staff, not hover over them, to perceive, balance, and build on their strengths.

CHAPTER XIV

Face Up to Company Politics!

DON WHITE, THE CONTROLLER OF A LARGE PRINTING COMPANY, WAS anxiously looking forward to the day when he would be executive vice president. He felt confident that he was the best man for the position, deserved it, and could do a much better job than was being done now. He also was concerned that his talents and contributions were not being recognized by the president or other members of the management team.

There were three obstacles standing in his way: The executive vice president would not be ready to retire for seven years, and both the sales manager and the production manager were definitely more qualified from the standpoint of experience and ability than he. The first obstacle he recognized; the last two he did not. Although he saw the other men as competitors, he could not admit their better qualifications even to himself.

Interestingly enough, White did not plan deliberately to sabotage either the executive vice president or his two younger rivals. He considered himself a man of integrity and high principles, and this certainly would be unethical. He did, however, almost subconsciously start looking at the three men for evidence of ineffectiveness, poor decision making, weak management methods, and personal idiosyncrasies to substantiate his own feeling of competence. His conscious motive, he would have said, was "deep concern for the company and its future welfare." To prove to himself that this was indeed his purpose, he became much friendlier and much more cooperative with each of the men.

White had ready access to the president since he was frequently required to develop special reports and provide needed financial analyses. Occasionally, too, he saw the president socially or played golf with him. He used these occasions to indulge in informal discussions about the company and, of course, its people. Wasn't it his duty to keep the president informed of what was going on, to evaluate situations and people objectively and unobtrusively?

White was quite voluble in his praise of his three rivals. A typical remark about the executive vice president might be: "You probably noticed I agreed with Charlie in staff meeting today. I think he has the glimmering of a good idea; and, frankly, I think his confidence needs bolstering. But I honestly think he's out in left field as far as timing is concerned. Does it seem to you that Charlie's been slipping lately?" Or: "Charlie sure has been working hard. Do you think the strain is beginning to be too much for him?" And additional seeds might be planted at another time in a comment about the tremendous growth the company across town had achieved since it installed an early retirement program and got some young blood into the organization.

It wasn't many months before the president started thinking of Charlie as a possible early retiree instead of an executive vice president. White "forgot" this was his idea when it was mentioned confidentially by the president; he offered to assume some of Charlie's responsibilities along with his own so that Charlie could stay on. But within a year the executive vice president was slated for retirement at 60. Obstacle No. 1 had been overcome by Don White —and he would be the last to admit he had anything to do with it. "It was just one of those things that happen in business—and have to happen, no matter how unpleasant, for the good of the company."

Now the only obstacles left in White's way were the sales manager and the production manager. Actually he had carefully removed both of them from the running, in the eyes of the president, while retiring Charlie. He thought up some additional techniques, however. In the case of Jack Larkin, the sales manager, reports showing unfavorable sales trends found their way to the president with the note: "Here are the figures on customer purchases I developed for Jack. I haven't analyzed them yet, but I thought you would be interested." The president *was* interested to see that sales to one of the firm's best customers were off 50 per cent. White steadfastly defended the sales manager with every weak excuse he could think of.

As for the production manager, Bob Johnson, his request for a new press had been turned down and the president, concerned about his reaction, asked White how he took the decision. White's answer

FACE UP TO COMPANY POLITICS!

again proved his loyalty to his fellow manager: "Look, I like Bob. I wish you wouldn't ask me that question." When pressed to amplify, he said reluctantly, "Let's just say he was a little vindictive, didn't use the best judgment, and let it go at that." The implications were considerably greater than the facts warranted.

When it came time for the executive vice president to retire, few were surprised to hear that Don White would succeed him because of his loyalty, dedication, dependability, and hard work. *This is company politics!* Such situations might be unbelievable if they weren't happening in hundreds of companies across the continent right now.

The most insidious result is the waste in human resources. Look at some of the losses incurred by Don White's company:

1. A good share of the controller's time and effort was directed toward personal gain instead of company objectives.
2. The effectiveness of three men was reduced, both by the president's diminished confidence in them and by their concern over their decreasing status.
3. Because a less capable man rose to a position of higher authority, the company risked much of its potential for growth and profit.
4. The contribution of a capable, experienced man was terminated abruptly by forced retirement.
5. Because morale and individual incentive suffered throughout the organization, overall productivity slumped.

A Matter of Climate

How does a situation like this get started? How can it continue to fester and weave a web of destruction within a company? There is only one answer—because it was *allowed* to exist and there was a climate present that encouraged its growth. The fault of this president lay not so much in the fact that he was taken in by a clever operator but, rather, in his lack of a positive way to evaluate the contributions of his key people. He was open to hints and innuendoes because his only measure of performance was subjective.

Probably there is no work situation in which politics cannot exist.

DEVELOPING A TOUGH-MINDED CLIMATE

It is possible, however, to create a climate in which it is difficult for politics to exist and, even more important, to create a climate in which there is no need for politics. This can be done by

1. Squelching any activity that smacks of politics the minute it starts.
2. Letting everyone know he will be judged solely on the basis of results.
3. Making candor the rule.
4. Stressing integrity and honesty.
5. Understanding the causes and motives underlying political activity.
6. Establishing methods for measuring results objectively.

An individual resorts to politics basically out of fear. This is always the hidden motive, but there are many surface ones linked to human needs for status, approval, power, authority, money, prestige, privilege, and responsibility. Politicians can operate effectively, however, only in situations where the top man ignores or condones the practice. Unfortunately he sometimes encourages the politicians in his organization by participating in company politics himself.

The president of a small electrical equipment manufacturing company felt quite insecure. Although he owned a controlling interest in the company, he desperately needed the approval of the people around him. He found the president's job lonely—he needed someone to talk to. As a result, he often took individual members of his staff into his confidence. Basically this was fine, since it brought his people closer to him, but he couldn't resist the temptation to discuss men's weaknesses with their peers and subordinates. To him this was not nearly so unpleasant as criticizing them directly, and at the same time it let his people know he knew what was going on. In addition, this president had a tendency to hedge any major decisions so that he would have an excuse if they turned out to be poor ones. For instance, his sales manager developed a campaign for the dealer organization, an approach that had never been tried in the company and would require the cooperation and united effort of the entire staff. The president agreed enthusiastically that the program should be undertaken. A few days later, however, he was overheard remarking to another staff manager, "I don't know why I let Joe talk me into that campaign; I don't think it's going to work." He was right. From that moment on, staff effort and enthusiasm diminished to the point where only mediocre results could be expected. The final outcome was a loss of respect for the president and the development of a feeling of distrust. The staff became more concerned with what the president was going to say behind their backs than in their contribution to company profits. Their strategy and planning revolved around feeding the president's ego rather than meeting commitments.

The Crisp Crackdown

The surest and easiest way for a manager to put a quick stop to any political situation is to apply three principles: directness, candor, and honesty. When a manager sees tell-tale evidence in his organization, he should evaluate it to determine who are involved and what their motives may be. Armed with as much information as practical, he should call in these individuals, inform them of what he suspects is happening, state categorically that it will not be tolerated, and firmly review the manner in which he expects his subordinates to conduct themselves.

Here is an example of the tough-minded approach needed: Harold Bliss was the president of a life insurance company, a very successful one. Rapid growth had created the usual problems; and, in addition, the decision had been made to build a new home office building. For six months, Bliss's attention had necessarily been diverted from the day-to-day operations of the business; however, he was beginning to have an uneasy feeling that all was not well, that his staff was not functioning as smoothly and effectively as it had been.

In staff meetings recently there had not been the usual free flow of ideas and opinions; people were reticent, they chose their words carefully, and they glanced meaningfully at one another. Three of the group tended to agree with each other more than usual and to defend each other's points. During individual talks there had been innuendoes that he ignored at the time—such as the agency director's remark when questioned about the month's sales goal: "We could make it if we'd get any cooperation from underwriting." Two of the staff members had seemed a little oversolicitous, a little too agreeable, and he'd noticed a trace of false heartiness and a definite undercurrent of intrigue.

Bliss called in a vice president whose judgment and integrity he respected. "Jim," he said bluntly, "I don't know what's going on in our management group, but something is and it isn't good. What's up?" He found out! During his absence from staff meetings jockeying for position had caused jealousies and resentment, a breakdown in communications, and some heel dragging when cooperation was required. There had been speculation about who was going to be located where in the new executive offices. All in all, the reasons behind the unrest were petty, but it was beginning to permeate entire departments.

The next day the president called in the management group, told them what he knew, and concluded with the following statement: "I do not believe there is a place for political activity in this company at any time. Not only does this apply within the management group, but it is your responsibility to be sure no political situations exist in your departments. I want to emphasize again that every person in this organization is judged by results and results alone. If people are interested in promotions, bonuses, salary increases, increased responsibility, or any other benefits, they can earn them on the basis of contribution to company or department objectives."

Compliance with a few basic principles should insure a working climate in which maximum productivity is possible with a minimum of political activity and the attendant unpleasantness:

1. If you have something to say about another person, don't say it to anyone else unless you already have said it personally—or expect to say it—to the individual involved. If the situation is of such a nature that the person cannot be told about it, his superior should be informed directly and candidly.
2. Don't hint or plant sly innuendoes. If you have something to say, say it.
3. Make certain that everyone knows exactly what is expected of him to the extent that he can judge himself how well he is doing and therefore be certain where he stands in the eyes of his superiors.

It is not easy to detect the beginning of political activity within a company or department. The president or manager is generally the

FACE UP TO COMPANY POLITICS!

last to know unless he is constantly alert. Once his suspicions are aroused, facts and positive action are necessary to meet the situation firmly and directly.

Stacking the Deck Positively

Men engage in company politics because they believe they can best achieve what they want in a devious, indirect, or underhanded way. Where they know that this type of activity will gain them nothing, few will engage in it. The one determining factor, then, is the leader of the group. If a president, manager, or supervisor rewards a subordinate in any way for engaging in political action, he merely encourages increased action on the part of that individual and similar action by others. The leader who reacts negatively to politicking, who rewards people solely on the basis of results, has no problem keeping such activity to a minimum.

If the elimination of politicking is so simple, why don't more managers do away with it? They close their eyes to it, they don't recognize it for what it is, or they don't know what to do about it. Possibly they have become inured to it and feel it is inevitable. Or they simply are not able to measure results and so cannot make good on a promise to judge their subordinates purely on the basis of individual contribution. They are confused; they don't know when people are doing a good job, working to their full capacity, and when they aren't.

Take sales, which has always appeared to be one function in which results can be easily measured. For example, a manager has five men with annual sales as follows: Salesman A, $152,000; Salesman B, $175,000; Salesman C, $167,000; Salesman D, $203,000; and Salesman E, $225,000. It should be obvious that Salesman E is doing the best job, but is he really? His territory has more people, more dealers, and our product is more widely accepted there. Is he working at his full potential? Let's look at the share of market obtained in each territory: A, 16 per cent; B, 14 per cent; C, 12 per cent; D, 19 per cent; and E, 15 per cent. According to this standard Salesman D stands head and shoulders above the rest. Can we assume that he is making the maximum contribution? We could, but we shouldn't. Instead, let's look at the gross profit contribution from each territory: A, $45,600 (30 per cent of sales); B, $49,000 (28 per cent); C,

$40,080 (24 per cent); *D*, $44,660 (22 per cent); and *E*, $56,250 (25 per cent). In this case Salesman *A* is certainly doing the best job of keeping his expenses low and maintaining price, but Salesman *E* has contributed the most profit.

In other words, the sales manager who uses these yardsticks knows a man's contribution only in relation to that of others, not in relation to the potential of the man, his stage of development, or the possibilities of his position. To measure contribution effectively, he might set up such results requirements as these: Annual sales: Product *M*, $75,000; Product *N*, $95,000; Product *O*, $60,000. Share of market: 18 per cent; sales expense, 9.5 per cent or less; gross profit, $62,100 (27 per cent); new dealers, 6 (more than $5,000). Then he would have a basis for measuring performance at the end of the year and controlling it throughout.

Specific results requirements of this type, incorporated into individual position descriptions along with strict accountability requirements, should enable every man to know the *what, where, when, who,* and *why* of his job, and to know beyond any reasonable doubt just how he is measuring up to it. With this knowledge he will recognize that the road to advancement lies in superior performance; he is not likely to be seduced into the byways of company politics.

Masters of Manipulation

There are few of us, to be sure, who have not at one time or another engaged in political activity—have not tried to influence the behavior of another person or persons through devious means. Our maneuverings are constantly apparent in the family, in the neighborhood, in the church, in clubs and schools. It is quite natural that such activity should carry over to the office or plant. It is also quite natural that it should be even more prevalent there. After all, isn't the prize a big one?

Inevitably, business organizations have developed some shrewd manipulators, skilled in the art of twisting people and situations to suit their own ends. There is no particular type of person who becomes involved in company politics—anyone can play, from the president to the office boy, from the bullying extrovert to the frightened introvert—and there are probably as many techniques as there are practitioners. Some of the common experts are quickly described.

1. *The yes man.* He is always agreeable to any suggestion or proposal because he wants to be liked. Basically he is insecure in his position and lacks the courage to disagree, particularly with his superior. His presence in an organization usually indicates a weak manager who needs support for his decision making and direction.

2. *The fence sitter.* This is a yes man with a different motivation. He can make a decision and stick by it, and he can disagree when necessary. However, his primary concern is being on the "right side," so he doesn't make a decision until he sees how the wind is blowing. In meetings, he watches the reaction of his superior to a proposal and, when he feels he knows how the boss is leaning, jumps in decisively. Even more insidious than the ordinary yes man, he is much harder to detect; and his contribution, since it is not based on fact or judgment and his motives are solely personal, is practically worthless.

3. *The responsibility reaper.* This man collects responsibilities the way some people collect stamps. He builds his personal security by attempting to make himself indispensable. He is selfish about delegating any but the most routine matters, and he is a source of much information because he guards anything in his head or his personal files zealously. He takes pride in the fact that he hasn't had a vacation in ten years; the department just can't run without him. While it it true that he might be missed temporarily, he does great harm by impeding progress—simply because he fails to utilize or develop the talents of his people.

4. *The climber.* He is heavy on ambition and sometimes, but not always, light on talent. He has a firmly established goal which he is going to achieve regardless of the cost—to others. If he has ability, he either doesn't recognize it or doesn't trust his superiors to recognize it. He believes that rewards are based upon whom you know rather than what you know. He courts favor with superiors, is resentful of his peers, and uses his subordinates. He is unable to look at any situation objectively since his personal motives are always foremost in his mind.

5. *The empire builder.* Here is a man who collects people. In companies that base compensation on old-fashioned methods, this pays off handsomely in salary increases; in others, it adds to the man's feeling of importance and his apparent prestige and security. The

empire builder is a master at making any job difficult, is dedicated to multiplying work, and tends to build an organization whose primary objective is keeping busy.

6. *The information center.* This man has to be in the center of everything. Anyone wanting an answer to a question always checks with him; if he doesn't have all the facts, he can be counted on to invent a few—which is why he is often the source of the many rumors floating around the organization. He usually specializes in analyzing the boss, interpreting his moods, translating his directives, and freely offering advice to others on when and how to approach him.

7. *The shirttail clinger.* Found only in large organizations, the shirttail clinger attaches himself to his immediate superior and moves up through the ranks with him. Because his future is dependent upon the boss's, much of his political effort is designed to promote the big man.

8. *The politicking superior.* He loves the political situation; he enjoys the fawning, the favors, and takes advantage of his position whenever possible in business or socially. He often has a wife who enjoys playing the same role with the wives of his subordinates. He expects his people to emulate his dress and his habits (if he drinks martinis, everyone drinks martinis; if he works late, his subordinates work late). He treats people like pawns, playing one against the other and purposely creating unpleasant situations. He manages by fear. Unable to trust or be trusted, he receives little respect from his people.

9. *The retaliator.* In return for a real or imagined hurt, the retaliator strikes back viciously to even the score. He uses his strengths negatively to harm the individual involved and, in doing so, many times harms the whole organization.

SUMMARY AND ACTION STEPS

There is a fitting sequel to Don White's case. Soon after he became executive vice president, he started cultivating several of the board members, developing a warm relationship with two of them. He assumed responsibility for keeping these men fully informed of all pertinent happenings within the company, and occasionally he favored them with "objective" evaluations of the president—along with much praise. He

FACE UP TO COMPANY POLITICS!

found it necessary to defend the president quite often, for the company wasn't doing too well—the sales manager had left and the production manager had lost his old enthusiasm. Don's loyalty earned him the president's job in just two years. There he lasted 18 months. He found himself in a position where the only thing that counted was results. The one thing he couldn't influence or manipulate with glib innuendoes was the profit and loss statement.

The interaction of people within the organization—individuals with varying motives, distinct personality differences, divergent objectives, and their private fears, ambitions, doubts, and feelings of inadequacy—is the basis for politics. The function of the organization itself requires people constantly to work together, to react to each other, to change the behavior of each other while at the same time carrying on their assigned duties. Each man is *forced* to influence his superiors, his peers, and his subordinates. It is this that creates the opportunity and the motivation for political activity.

There are few, if any, organizations in which politicking does not exist. There are even those who claim that it is necessary. However, a particular type of environment is needed to nurture its growth, and a tough-minded company simply does not provide the right climate.

Creating the tough-minded type of climate, in which political activity is held to a minimum, requires personal leadership of the highest order. For success the manager must

1. Recognize that politicking will exist in any organization or group but that its extent is directly related to the boss's attitude and that it can be controlled by him.
2. Demonstrate that political activity will not result in benefit to any individual by reacting negatively to political overtures and basing all rewards upon individual contribution to company objectives.
3. Identify political situations quickly and deal with them firmly and openly.
4. Know when people are making an optimum contribution to the company and when they are not.
5. Have the courage to bring unpleasant personal situations into the open. Be intolerant of hints or innuendoes; require people to say what they think in a candid, straightforward way.
6. Create the necessary tools and administrative procedures within the organization to insure that people
    a. Know what is expected of them in terms of specific results requirements.
    b. Know where they stand—when they are doing a good job and when they are not.
    c. Know why they are working in terms of clearly understood objectives and individual contributions to them.

DEVELOPING A TOUGH-MINDED CLIMATE

    d. See beyond themselves; are as concerned about the company and its welfare as with their own well-being.

The connotation of internal politics is almost always negative—it saps the vitality of a company, creating a climate in which the full productivity and potential of its people cannot be realized. The truly productive individual will not become a part of such a climate or remain with such an organization; he knows it will drain him of enthusiasm, dedication, ambition, loyalty, and self-satisfaction. The capable individual wants and needs to be judged on his worth. The capable manager wants and needs men like him.

CHAPTER XV

Personal Organization for Tough-Minded Results

THE FACT THAT YOU ARE READING THIS BOOK IS SIGNIFICANT. IT INDI- cates that you have an inner spark which sets you apart. You are a member of that select group who actively seek personal improvement. Your inner spark may be flaring brightly, or it may only be smoldering. Perhaps you are searching for answers to problems of self, professional advancement, and your personal future. In any event, understanding *and practicing* tough-mindedness offers you rich rewards.

Tough-mindedness is not a package deal replete with glowing promises of instant success. It is, however, pervasive and its influence on all phases of living is inevitable. It is a way of life which can yield positive values in self-fulfillment when properly understood and practiced.

"Tough" in this context means flexible, not brittle; malleable but strong and tenacious. Cast iron is tough, but it is also brittle. Rawhide is tough and flexible and brings to mind things lean, strong, and durable. These qualities of toughness have no relationship to the bully, the rowdy, the tough guy of fact and fiction. We want no part of him.

As Senator and as Vice President of the United States, Harry S. Truman was, in the opinion of many, a creditable performer but not in the same league with Franklin D. Roosevelt. Yet, when circumstances placed him in the most responsible position in the world, he was equal to the results requirements of the job. He proved to be tough-minded. Did he rise to the occasion, or was his apparent tough-mindedness present all the time?

DEVELOPING A TOUGH-MINDED CLIMATE

What Is New About Tough-Mindedness?

Certainly the old statement that "there is nothing new under the sun" applies here. But mayn't there be something new about tough-mindedness? Plenty, of course—not newness in the sense of fundamental and accepted truths but newness in terms of application to you as a whole man. In your life you play all sorts of parts: husband, father, worker, provider, friend, neighbor, citizen, and many others. Hence, to concentrate only on your "provider" role, regardless of your success in it, is to build the lopsided man.

To illustrate: John H. is in comfortable circumstances. He is an officer of a successful company, his children are grown and married, and his financial future is secure. Yet, despite all the traditional trappings of success and security, by his own admission he is not a happy man. Indications are that he is a victim of the "work syndrome." Years without number have found him at his desk long before and long after regular working hours. Often he has been so exhausted that he went to bed immediately after dinner. Here, in short, is a lopsided man caught in an unhappy situation of his own making.

Zest, eager anticipation, a sense of accomplishment, a feeling of well-being—these are only a few of life's pleasures a man like this can allow to slip away.

Cult? Fad? Doctrine?

Each of us has been exposed to a fantastic array of cults, fads, and doctrines. Name the condition or the situation—someone has an answer to it if only a potent brew of noxious-smelling herbs or a bit of copper worn around the ankle. This is not to make light of man's eternal search for solutions to his problems. But it must be confessed that the pat answer, the magic formula, the overnight results are largely the figments of wishful thinking.

What we are all seeking, in one way or another, is the fulfillment of our dreams, hopes, and ambitions. Now, what you want and what I want are probably two entirely different things; however that may be, if we are honest we will readily admit that we have fallen far short of our original hopes—at least in some respects. It is a rare man who can look himself in the eye and make himself believe that he measures up to his best in all phases of living.

Meet Thomas L. This is the man who took you to lunch—come to think of it, he sold you an order. It was a pleasure to do business with him. Yet this was also the man who in a counseling session confessed to a host of personal problems. Far from being the suave personification of the successful salesman, he was plagued by self-doubts and fears—climaxed by his failure to be named sales manager. Fortunately, he was able to stop and look at himself a bit, to recognize his own strengths and weaknesses and build on the strengths. No, he did not become sales manager. He did, however, learn to live with himself, and he has made a happier and more successful career.

By the time you have read and digested this book—it cannot be absorbed in one gulp—you may well conclude that it espouses a doctrine. This is not important. What *is* important is that here is a practical, down-to-earth, meat-and-potatoes set of principles which is applicable to you personally regardless of your present management status.

What It Takes

Like anything of real and lasting value, tough-mindedness has a price tag. It requires soul searching to the end that you may know and face up to the real you. It takes perseverance, courage, and determination—in short, guts.

Tough-mindedness takes planning; and, since the road to hell is reputedly paved with good intentions, this planning must be based on fact and on cold calculation if you are to achieve the specific results you want. Again, this may not be completely pleasant. It does require thought and work.

It also takes patience, determination, and continuing evaluation to follow your plan. Not that you must abandon all your comfortable habits and patterns. You are simply going to capitalize and build on your strengths, recognizing and improving those areas vital to your progress toward your goals.

Above all, tough-mindedness takes continuity. Your personal program cannot be an on again, off again operation. Results will be in direct proportion to your continued application and practice. It is far better to move slowly and consistently rather than to explode into periods of frenzied action alternated with lapses into nothingness.

What There Is in It for *Me*

"Profit" as a word immediately brings dollars to mind. Dollars are important, but is it not reasonable, also, to consider other types of personal gain as personal profit?

First let's face up to the fact that personal gain is a basic motivating force; no one questions the urge to earn dollars. But consider for a moment the members of your school board, the church workers you know, the volunteers for charitable drives. Their motivation certainly is not economic. And what of the high-salaried man who sets aside personal affairs and runs for public office? Again, his motivation can't be dollars; it has to be an inner need of some kind, a personal kind of gain or profit.

Psychological research has sent probing fingers into all aspects of human behavior. These findings to date have been significant, but you and I often view much of the resulting theory with some uneasiness. However, one set of guideposts we can all accept both intellectually and emotionally is the four basic human needs for recognition, security, sense of belonging, and opportunity. Note how each of these encompasses all phases of personal profit when profit is considered as economic, social, political, and spiritual. This is an idea we can get our teeth into and hang on to.

What does tough-mindedness hold for me? Most simply, personal profit.

How Do I Start?

There is only one place to start your tough-mindedness program, and that is with a carefully conceived plan. No plan—no results.

Remember those old-time movies which pop up from time to time on TV? The house catches fire. The characters dash about, grab opposite ends of ladders, charge in and out to rescue birdcages and other useless impedimenta. Pandemonium. Confusion piled on more confusion—all for lack of a planned approach.

To develop your personal plan, we must first consider you as a manager. We must examine your company and your relationship to it. Later we will equate your personal goals with the goals of your company. A divorce of the two is no more compatible than an attempt to operate at peak efficiency on a daily diet of carbohydrates with no proteins or vitamins.

The company's goals. Expressed or not expressed, your first job is to determine as exactly as possible the goals of your company and its plans for reaching those goals. You may be fortunate enough to work for a concern that has a sound planning procedure, both short- and long-range. If so, you must review these plans thoroughly. Unfortunately, however, most firms do not have a comprehensive, documented plan for accomplishing specific objectives. If this is the case, here is your first challenge.

If you are the chief executive, there will be no hierarchy problems. If you are in a lesser position, work your way skillfully through channels to the top of the ladder with a carefully prepared set of questions. This will challenge your ability as a communicator and as a salesman. Remember that so far as your company is concerned, your immediate goal is to become a better manager.

Pick an arbitrary time period, not less than two years and not more than five, as a base for your questions. Where does the company want to be five years hence in the following categories?

1. Innovation: new products, new services, new methods, new uses for present products or services.
2. Market standing: share of market, penetration, new markets.
3. Manager performance and development; manager requirements to accomplish goals.
4. Worker performance and attitude; worker performance to accomplish goals.
5. Physical, human, and financial resources: new plants and equipment, people, and money required.
6. Productivity: results required from each segment of the business from top to bottom.
7. Public responsibility; requirements as a member of the community and as a participating citizen.
8. Profitability: return on investment, reserves, debt retirement.

DEVELOPING A TOUGH-MINDED CLIMATE

These, of course, are *what* steps, but they are the base of the pyramid for your personal *how* steps.

Personal goals. Again let's prepare a checklist to help determine your personal goals.

1. As a member of management:
    a. Eventual position I desire to attain.
    b. Size of company and type of product or service I prefer.
    c. Geographical location I consider most favorable.
    d. Schedule or timetable that will be required.
2. As a provider and family man:
    a. Standard of living I aspire to.
    b. Income I will need.
    c. Family relationships I desire.
    d. Health standards I will adhere to.
    e. Insurance I will need.
    f. Participation in church affairs I consider proper.
    g. Social activities I want or my family needs.
3. As a citizen:
    a. Civic responsibilties I want to assume.
    b. Political activities I want to assume.
    c. Civic and service clubs in which I will participate.

Most certainly this checklist should be expanded to meet your particular needs. At this point it is a "thinking" list only.

Personal goals related to company goals. Although we must recognize economic gain as a normal and desirable goal, balance is essential. It is the key to the whole man. Our next step, then, is to strike a balance as we equate personal and company goals.

Take a full sheet for each of the goals established by your company. Now, with your personal goals checklist in front of you, examine each company goal and your responsibility toward it in the light of *all* your personal goals. To the best of your ability put down

- What you want or need to do toward achieving that goal.
- What methods you will use.

- What additional training will be required.
- What your end objective is in terms of your personal goals.
- What your general timetable should be.

In simplified form one of your sheets might look something like this:

1. Innovation [company objective]
    a. A market-tested new line of plastic kitchenware complementing our present metal line to
        (1) Provide an opening wedge into the plastic market by January 1, 1967.
        (2) Increase our present share of market 20 per cent overall by January 1, 1969.
        (3) Provide continuing employment for present workforce.
        (4) Provide a gross profit of
            (a) 2 per cent by July 1967.
            (b) 3 per cent by January 1968.
            (c) 5 per cent by July 1979.
            (d) 8 per cent by January 1970.

And so on. This example, of course, shows only a brief *what* part of the company's objectives. Properly completed, your sheets will cover all phases of *who, what, why, when, where,* and *how.*

As our next step we must assume a specific position for you in the organization—say, manager of the kitchenwares sales department. Now let's relate your personal goals to the company's goals. This requires a second series of sheets.

PERSONAL GOAL	RELATIONSHIP TO COMPANY GOAL
1. As a member of management:	
a. Eventual position I desire to attain.	Next logical step or goal is division manager of consolidated kitchenware division.
b. Size of company and type product or service I prefer.	No change at this time.
c. Geographical location I consider most favorable.	No change at this time.
d. Schedule or timetable that will be required.	Present responsibility will be increased to cover plastics at start. Additional sales and new products will be required to create demand for division status. Start additional

PERSONAL GOAL	RELATIONSHIP TO COMPANY GOAL
	market research on new products immediately after approval of current project. Target date for approval of additional products to manufacture: July 1967.
2. As a provider and family man:	
a. Standard of living I aspire to.	No change.
b. Income I will need.	$5,000 increase on basis of above.
c. Family relationships I desire.	Schedule self-improvement so that time is not taken away from family.
d. Health standards I will adhere to.	Eight hours' sleep; daily exercise; annual physical checkup.
e. Insurance I will need.	No change at this time. Review each year (possibly start college education policy).
f. Participation in church affairs I consider proper.	No change.
g. Social activities I want or my family needs.	No change.
3. As a citizen:	
a. Civic responsibilities I want to assume.	No change. Maintain present memberships and obligations.
b. Political activities I want to assume.	
c. Civil and service clubs in which I will participate.	

Thus, at this point, we have arrived at basic personal goals, each with a definite relationship to our first company goal. The same process should be followed, in turn, for the other company goals. This is the foundation upon which we will build the specific steps required to achieve the sum total of your objectives.

Personal assets and liabilities. Next we must examine what we have to work with. This is necessary in order to capitalize on your present strengths and develop the new ones you will need.

To know yourself is a formidable task and challenge. In a piecemeal sort of way we all ask ourselves occasionally what we stand for, what we believe in, and why we have not achieved the measure of success we feel we are capable of. But there is a certain magic in an orderly method of writing down the answers to these questions. The cold written word stares back at us; it won't slide off into thoughts

PERSONAL ORGANIZATION FOR TOUGH-MINDED RESULTS

of yesterday's ball game. It is concrete and solid, lending itself to further study and positive action.

Certainly, to assure a reasonably objective analysis, you should use all the resources at your command. The real you may be considerably different from your mental picture. First of all, there is the possibility of complete testing, by your company psychologist or a qualified consultant. In addition, your superior can help—provided you have established the right rapport with him. So can carefully selected peers; your pastor or doctor, if either knows you well enough to qualify; and your wife, if you have a sense of humor and can take her criticism. Finally, you can answer your own questions on the basis of results achieved. Beware, though, of the "I was right but..." rationalization and all its relatives.

Now for the analysis—the most fascinating you will ever make. Its subject is you. Don't be afraid to let yourself go and make copious notes—you can boil them down to essentials later. (Note that in the following checklist we follow the basic steps shown under "Personal Goals.")

	ASSETS		LIABILITIES
1. As a member of management:			
a. Education	B.A. in Business Administration.		Need further education in marketing.
b. Experience	Ten years' varied managerial experience.		Short in broad, general management experience.
c. Ability to manage	*Excellent*	*Good*	*Fair*
(1) Communication	———	———	———
(2) Empathy	———	———	———
(3) People development	———	———	———
(4) Integrity	———	———	———
(5) Acceptance of change	———	———	———
(6) Intellectual curiosity	———	———	———
(7) Relationships with			
(a) Fellow managers	———	———	———
(b) Other workers	———	———	———
d. Significant results accomplished			
e. Unsatisfactory results			

And so on. Then, adding still another sheet to the profile you are preparing, you set up two headings: on the left, "Uses of Capital"; to the right, "Reduction of Liabilities." The first side of the page should be used to summarize the best application of assets to the specific reduction of liabilities. On the second you list in detail the exact steps you propose to follow and your schedule or timetable.

Our approach to tough-mindedness, it should be clear by now, is a purely personal one. We have indulged in no flag waving, concentrating on "what is there in it for me." Yet it is fundamental that the tough-minded manager (or man) gives more of himself than he receives. It is no anomaly that by being selfish he moves more and more to selflessness.

Where Do I Stand Now?

Next comes the *do* step. Your plan is of your own making. It is based on your best judgment and best thinking, designed to accomplish specific objectives according to your own timetable.

A properly conceived plan is the best-known method for achieving an objective; but carrying it out, like most things, requires practice and experience. Moreover, a good plan is not rigid; because circumstances may alter its validity, common sense demands it be flexible. Consequently, periodic review and evaluation are necessary. For this purpose, add a sheet to your profile analysis. From left to right you will then have at a glance your assets, your liabilities and their reduction, and your follow-up or score. By all means keep a full record of your progress. It will be your constant guide.

How to find the time? This is indeed a question; each of us has a multitude of projects shelved for "when I have time." It is obvious, however, that unless we bring pressure to bear on ourselves, we never will find the time. We cannot make or create additional hours in the day, so something has to give—and it will if we plan properly.

Let's admit that few of us use our 16 waking hours to the maximum. To put it in less than erudite terms, we "goof off." Of course goofing off can be constructive; if it isn't, we can make it so by turning part of our unproductive time into productive time. For example:

> *Lunch hour:* Use half for reading three days per week. (Total: one and a half hours per week.)

Delegation: Keep a chart. Determine what chores can be delegated to your subordinates. Use the time saved for company projects related to your personal goals.

Evenings: Substitute one hour of study two times per week for TV. (Total: two hours per week.)

Weekends: Schedule a minimum of two hours of work toward your objectives.

Each man must tailor his schedule to his own situation. The examples shown are quite flexible and allow time for family and outside activities. Yet, in 50 weeks (allowing two for vacation), you will have moved toward your objectives to the equivalent of a solid 30-plus eight-hour days. If you are an eager beaver, you can do materially better and still maintain an excellent balance of all your activities.

Better utilization of time has been a subject of concern for ages. Yet, in the final analysis, many of the suggested remedies leave something to be desired in practice. Here, again, the most satisfactory method is to have a definite plan and follow it. A little browsing in your library will supply all the ammunition you can use. Here are a few additional possibilities:

- Get to work 15 minutes early each morning. Use this uninterrupted time to plan and organize your day.
- Ponder the "first things first" method reputedly used by the legendary Charles Schwab. He is said to have listed the six most important things to be accomplished each day, then taking them in that order.
- Discourage "chatterers"—in person or on the telephone.
- Listen more carefully; get the message right the first time.
- Learn to say no when you have to. You can't be all things to all people all the time.
- Handle your time the way you do (or should) handle your money.

SUMMARY AND ACTION STEPS

Many of the ingredients necessary for the successful pursuit of your goals you already possess. As a man and as a member of management, you have used them in your progress to your present position. These are strengths. Capitalize on them. Basic, perhaps, are the following: belief in self, drive, perseverance, and above all enthusiasm.

Systematically, according to the program suggested here,

1. Examine tough-mindedness as a way of life for the whole man.
2. Examine your company's goals—what your company wants.
3. Examine your personal goals—what *you* want.
4. Equate your personal goals with the company's goals; make the one a means to the other.
5. Determine what it will take to achieve these goals; set up a plan of accomplishment for yourself.

Be *un*satisfied but not *dis*satisfied. Push hard toward success. Don't let anything sidetrack you or stand in your way.

CHAPTER XVI

Counsel, Don't Advise

THE TRULY BROAD-GAUGE MANAGER, THE MAN WITH REAL DEPTH, THE true leader can readily be identified by the percentage of time he devotes to counseling rather than advising those with whom he works. The more time he spends in this way, the more likely it is that he has a realistic grasp of the primary requirements of the management job. Anyone can give advice, but it takes a man with depth of character developed over a period of years to counsel others patiently so that they understand not only what is expected of them but *why* it is expected. Advice may or may not be acted upon; but counsel, properly given, makes the *why* of an action so crystal-clear that the action itself may be anticlimatic.

The Tools of Counseling

The prime tool for counseling is perhaps the most complex, but without it all other tools are ineffective. This is self-knowledge. Without knowledge of ourselves, the counsel we give will ring hollow, and the recipients will spot us as phonies. The effective counselor and builder of men first of all knows himself and has developed an unshakable confidence in what he can do. He approaches the challenges of life without all the answers but confident that somehow the answers will reveal themselves at the appropriate times. He is by no means self-centered and introspective, but is able to escape himself and view life through other people's eyes. In short, he is objective but friendly, businesslike but compassionate, well equipped to use the other tools of counseling.

His second most important tool is a well-developed knowledge of people, a keen insight into their needs and motivations. As Clarence B. Randall, retired board chairman for Inland Steel, once stated, to be worthy of management responsibility today a man must have an awareness of human problems, a sensitivity toward the hopes and aspirations of those he supervises, and a capacity for analysis of the emotional forces that motivate their conduct. Otherwise the projects entrusted to him will not get ahead no matter how often wages are raised.

Insight into other people is achieved to the highest degree when developed in a practical way through conversation, the exchange of thoughts and ideas on a broad variety of topics. This is a two-way street—a man must be willing to share if he is to gain insight into others' feelings, and the man who knows himself and likes what he sees has no fear of sharing. A word of caution, however: Don't limit your conversations to a select group; instead, reach out and share with people from all types of backgrounds and interests. Be alert for opportunities to talk with everyone you meet, including neighbors, fellow commuters and churchgoers, barbers, the garbageman. The overall goal is continuous improvement in your ability to use *empathy*, the art of being able to place yourself in someone else's shoes.

The effective manager/counselor has an almost overpowering drive to help others help themselves—a drive which cannot be contrived but must be sincere. He fully accepts the statement that "you can never do more for others than you will receive in return." This is not purely altruistic; it is businesslike and practical. The manager wants to help others because he himself expects help when he needs it—not from the same people but from people in general. Above all, he avoids any tendency to manipulate others; instead, he helps them use their capacities to come to logical decisions.

People have a wide variety of interests. The manager bent on becoming an effective and tough-minded counselor must therefore have a broad storehouse of interests and knowledge that he can call upon in establishing rapport. Moreover, he must keep this background information current by a vigorous personal reading program. The average manager simply does not read enough in the field of management, let alone in the many others available to him. Insufficient time? Nonsense—for the man on the go, time expands to meet the need for it.

Another vital tool is a climate conducive to communication. The burden of building this climate is on the manager; he is the one who initially wants to get something done, not his staff. Moreover, it cannot be brought about overnight, yet it can be wrecked within a few minutes. The staff will place the manager on a pedestal until he does or says something which destroys all confidence in him. Like it or not, everything he does or doesn't do, says or doesn't say, whether at work or away from the office, influences his people's opinions. A single action that is not consistent with what has been previously communicated can seriously damage rapport.

The manager/counselor must recognize the value of listening. Silence is often more important than any number of words. However, there is no denying the importance of being able to express oneself simply. This is an art, and its secret is the knack of reducing the complex to the simple. Some key guides:

- Break down what you have to say into bite-size pieces.
- Use nickel words rather than the two-bit variety if they will make communication easier—as they generally will.
- Keep the other person's vocabulary in mind. Provide stretch, but don't talk down or overshoot his capacity to understand.
- Cut to the heart of what you have to say. Don't skirt the issue.
- When in doubt, use the trial-balloon technique: Phrase a statement several ways and examine each wording with the other person for a more precise understanding.
- Don't assume you have communicated: Contrive some sort of feedback on whatever was agreed to and why.

If action taken as a result of counseling is not as agreed, it is likely that one of the parties did not receive sufficient *why* or the facts have since changed.

Counseling sessions are intended to provide answers to challenges and problems and so generate profitable results. The "compleat" manager takes pride in the answers arrived at, not in the fact that his personal answer may have been better than that of the man counseled. He is more interested in the results than in the process that was used to get them. He has developed the true "we" spirit.

Expand the Whole Man

To judge by the tremendous growth experienced by men who suddenly are motivated to produce, it is a fair assumption that people rarely use more than 50 per cent of their capabilities. Hence the enormous possibilities in releasing unexpected potential through counseling.

The president of a medium-size specialty manufacturing firm doubled his personal sales within one month after a counseling session had confirmed his opinion that he was a better salesman than manager—during the off season for the industry. Even more remarkable was the fact that through enforced delegation to others he soon gained confidence and unleashed his latent abilities as a manager.

Much too often counseling falls short because the counselor restricts himself to what he considers work-connected developmental needs, whereas the counselee is acutely aware that the man on the job is only a part of the whole man. This whole man receives stimuli for development from many external sources, not just from the job. To expand, he must not only understand why change is necessary but see how the change will affect other aspects of his life.

The manager who has a deep desire to free the untapped potential of his staff needs to view its individual members in the round if he is to give them sound guidance. This means he must be aware of the whole man, but it does not mean that he should necessarily provide counsel on all that man's problems. He must recognize that his counsel will affect the man on and off the job and have faith that the principles he helps the man to formulate will be of value in other aspects of his life.

The counseling relationship must be built up over a period of time and should be based upon mutual confidence and a solid conviction that the company's goals, with emphasis on profit, are worth striving hard for.

A Blend of Objectives

The mature manager/counselor will rise to the challenge of assisting his subordinates to blend their personal objectives with those of the company. Each individual in turn should accept the responsibility for identifying with the organization sufficiently. Only in this way can he realize his fullest potential, for himself and for the company.

Should such a blending be manifestly impossible, it is to both parties' best interests if they agree to break off relations. The managerial or supervisory employee who recognizes that he is hopelessly out of step should have the guts to leave. His superior, once he has exhausted the logical avenues for the necessary blending of objectives, is responsible to the employee as well as the company for taking decisive action to remove the employee from the payroll.

Blending the objectives of individuals with those of the group will bring about the only reason for organized effort: *the achievement of results in excess of the sum total of the results that the individual members of the group could achieve as individuals.*

Principles Build Practices

The manager's counseling role should not be construed as that of an "answer man." Cranking out a solution each time a problem comes up doesn't build people; in fact, it weakens them for the challenges that arise when no one is around to help. The manager's proper role is to promote understanding of the basic principles of the problem-solving process that will lead to the answer.

The manager who helps his staff in this way is far ahead of the one who automatically provides answers to current problems. The first has a staff capable of solving future problems and can manage "by exception." The second has weak-kneed learners who will soon sap his energy.

Much has been written about those Americans who were brainwashed during the Korean War, who betrayed their countrymen and defected to communism. Lacking a thorough understanding of the principles underlying our free enterprise system, these men had never tested their beliefs and so had failed to develop firm convictions. Thus they were susceptible to brainwashing. A manager can expect the same kind of negative results from a staff that has not been provided with tough-minded principles which they can integrate into their work through practice.

The "Go-Giver"

Most managers have achieved what they have through the help of others; they have already received more than they can expect to give others in a lifetime. Knowing this should provide the incentive

DEVELOPING A TOUGH-MINDED CLIMATE

for giving of themselves insofar as they are able. The "go-giver" as a manager achieves not for himself but for all those with whom he is associated.

Complete altruism is not his objective; this would be naïve. He recognizes that through giving he will receive back, not necessarily material rewards, but rather the continuously reinforcing feeling of having shared his own strengths in the attempt to build those of others. The fact that he can never be absolutely positive of success does not discourage him; in spite of it he has vowed to do the very best that he is capable of doing.

The manager who is most likely to succeed at helping others knows that maximum success is achieved only when the person to whom he is giving has recognized the need and asked for help. Otherwise, advice that may or may not be appreciated is all that has been given—and it may or may not be taken. However, he has developed the maturity and patience to recognize that at times he must stand by while people he would like to help fail simply because they haven't seen the need and asked for counsel. He knows that because of the failure he may be in a better position to help. At the other end of the scale the same manager recognizes that as he provides counsel to employees, it is likely that some will soon outgrow their present positions and, in some cases, be promoted to higher positions than his own, either inside or outside the company. This type of manager draws deep satisfaction from his staff's personal growth; he never holds people back because he has confidence that others will take their place and be guided to success.

At least one company, in the electronics field, has followed the practice of never standing in the way of men who wish to leave the organization; in fact, it has always wished such men luck; managers have been encouraged to help them in whatever way is practical. At the same time, this company has built a reputation for never turning a cold shoulder on a man who wants to be re-employed simply because he once quit the firm.

One manufacturing manager explained the company's policy in the following manner: "We figure that if a man is intrigued by what he thinks is a broader-gauge job, he'll never be completely satisfied until he makes the attempt and he won't be able to use his full capabilities in his work with us. We are better off if we find someone who is similarly challenged by the position we have to offer." Then he added quickly, "Besides, the fellow may learn something and come back to us a better man than when he left." Experience indicates that those who do return are more mature and can be counted on heavily to become longer-service employees. And the sales manager points out that many ex-employees of this company are major purchasers of its products.

Needless to say, management has received value many times over for *giving* in a situation where other companies have *taken* by holding people back.

Counseling's Emotional Context

It has long been recognized that learning is most likely to take place when the person who is learning becomes emotionally involved in the process. Thus the counselor strives to bring about emotional involvement on the part of the counselee. Although fear can be a partner to learning, pleasure is much more desirable since it is conducive to *positive* learning; and enthusiasm, as a combination of emotions, is still better. And remember—learning does not take place unless behavior actually changes. Thus, if attitudes are to be fused like pieces of metal, heat must frequently be generated and applied.

The manager/counselor's first step often is to develop the type of relationship in which the learner feels free to show his emotions. Inhibition prevents a man from experiencing the excitement that accompanies new insights and intellectual breakthroughs. During counseling, the manager should be alert to detect signs that indicate when emotions are near the surface and whether they are signs of cooperation or resistance. Restless and fidgety movements may be the first indications that communication is occurring.

The counselor frequently will not know for certain whether the person whom he is counseling plans to act on what he says; the counselee may merely listen without comment. The counselor is quite likely, however, to know when the other person is not receptive to help. He may, in fact, learn this in trying circumstances; his man may emphatically not be buying and may point out that he has no business interfering. By previously establishing the need for counsel, getting permission to provide it, and developing confidence on the part of the person he is counseling, the counselor can justify the arousing of emotion by simply explaining that this is a part of the process of reaching an understanding.

Perceptive observation of the emotional changes in the counselee during the session often will reveal when a point has been communicated and when there has been a breakthrough in thinking. Often the counselor will not know why this occurred—in fact, he may never know. Nonetheless, he will be quite content with the results of his work.

Appraisal for Results

Counseling ideally occurs each time a manager communicates in whatever context, even during day-to-day operations. In any event it is highly desirable to review the total results that have been achieved—a process commonly referred to as performance appraisal.

The performance appraisal interview should not be a catch-all for sins of omission in the past. Psychologists indicate that the time to correct a child is just after he makes a mistake, not a week or two later, and the same thing is true of adults. Appraisal should highlight successes and needs without dredging up the past in minute detail. If a machine is not functioning properly, the supervisor doesn't wait till the next major overhaul; he takes corrective action immediately. If an employee has a problem that is disrupting his unit's performance, the time to take action is when the problem is first recognized. Similarly, when an employee has made a significant contribution, it should be recognized immediately through positive action. Provided this rule is diligently adhered to, the periodic developmental counseling session can be anticipated without misgivings by both manager and employee. It can focus on praising, not appraising, in the knowledge that praise without performance may be futile but that performance without praise is worse.

Thousands of hours and millions of dollars have been spent by staff departments in devising intricate systems for helping line managers develop their people's full potential by appraising—generally —their strengths and weaknesses. These systems provide guides on how to conduct the appraisal sessions, special forms for appraising each employee, and controls to assure that the appraisals are duly carried out. Often the information is coded and fed into a computer for future reference in considering candidates for promotion. Yet all such systems fall short of meeting the basic needs of the line manager, the individual employee, or the company, simply because the manager is asked to discuss both strengths and weaknesses.

Because the employee knows he will be appraised on both, no amount of praise will overshadow the so-called constructive criticism. He knows that "no man is perfect" and his manager is bound to make suggestions for improvement. By past experience the employee is pretuned to criticism and, however adroitly it is phrased, will tend to overlook whatever praise is given.

For his part, the manager often spends the bulk of his preparation time wondering how he can communicate weaknesses without unduly disturbing an employee who is otherwise making a satisfactory contribution to the unit's results. He tends to dread the coming session, and to build up emotionally for it, just as much as the employee. He may even rebel against conducting appraisal interviews at all.

So let's put some common sense into performance appraisal, make it desirable from both the manager's and the employee's standpoint, and get some tangible benefits from it. Essentially, the objectives of employee, manager, and company are identical here—to convert the individual employee's latent potential more fully into productive, results-oriented activity. This will help both him and the organization meet their basic goals. All that is needed is a few guides with a minimum of special forms and controls.

Praise the Man for His Strengths

Many people who work together for years never get around to telling each other how they enjoy it and praising each other for their separate contributions. There seems to be a feeling that to tell another person you appreciate him as a human being is a sign of weakness. Sadder yet, an all too common reaction on the part of the person being praised is to ask himself, "What does that so-and-so want of me?" instead of accepting the compliment at face value.

And this isn't true just in business. How long has it been since you told your wife you love her? From the columns of newspaper and magazine space devoted currently to marital relations, it would

DEVELOPING A TOUGH-MINDED CLIMATE

appear that many wives would like to know they are appreciated. You may retort, "If I did tell her, she would immediately think I'd been up to something." True, she might, if it had been a long time since you last reaffirmed your love, but even this initial reaction need not rule out candid discussion and broadened personal communication. And so it is in the business situation.

But how do you praise a man for his strengths? By way of preparation you simply take a blank sheet of paper and write down his good points. For example:

- What do you consider is the man's value to the company?
- What has been his contribution to company results?
- What traits does he have that you personally value?
- What are his strengths as a man?
- Why do others in your organization value the man?
- What have been his specific achievements not connected directly with the results expected from his position?

In other words, develop an exhaustive list of pluses, remembering that no matter how bleak the record may appear, all men have some strengths.

The first part of the appraisal session should focus on these strengths and contributions; it should not refer to weaknesses at all. This may take real persistence and courage on your part, but will build your personal image as a real leader—a man for whom the person being appraised will move mountains.

This image will become even more vivid when you ask your man to help you help him by pinpointing ways in which you or other members of management can help him to realize his personal objectives more completely through his work. You will speak frankly, seeking constructive ideas and hoping that he will take advantage of the climate you have established and ask you to reciprocate by giving him your ideas on how he can be more effective.

If he doesn't, don't be disturbed. Perhaps it will happen the next time. Meanwhile, he will concentrate on using his strengths, and the weaknesses will in all likelihood tend to fade into the background— or the new climate with its ease of communication will stimulate him to improve himself without criticism from you. If he does ask for help, you should use extreme restraint, again assuming the role of a

COUNSEL, DON'T ADVISE

manager who is helping a man to help himself. Don't stress his weaknesses. If you do, you will find the familiar barriers being erected. Instead, ask him to elaborate on where he feels the need for strengthening—and, ordinarily, he will be quite accurate in pinpointing his weak spots. You will then be in a position to help him do something about them.

What About the Problem Employee?

The great majority of employees, as we have said over and over, want to know what is expected of them, want to work, and want to know their work is appreciated. These are the ones who have unlimited potential and in whom you, as a manager, should invest the majority of your time.

However, you will always have other employees with problems that must be corrected. A tough-minded, hard-hitting approach is the only way to attack these problems. The manager who has praised his staff, when such praise is due, will have no qualms about pointing up the difficulties that arise. He will know that his own performance standards require him to take decisive action and that this will increase the respect his subordinates have for him. In his session with the problem employee, he will

1. State the problem and its symptoms concisely from his viewpoint and make it clear that the sole purpose of the meeting is to answer the question: "What can we do about this situation?"
2. Discuss the problem with the employee until agreement is reached on its nature and the reasons for its existence. The employee should have ample time to ask questions.
3. Help the employee to work out a solution that builds on his strengths and indicates clearly just what specific results will be expected, when they must be accomplished, and what failure to meet the agreed-upon commitments will mean. *Accountability must be fact, not fiction.*

Simplification of employee appraisal by, first, praising when praise is deserved and, second, hitting problems head-on as soon as they arise will open new vistas of human relationships for you and allow you and your staff to work in harmony, helping each other to achieve tangible satisfactions from the job. However, this is no more a one-shot cure for the troubles of an organization than any other management tool or technique. Continuous reinforcement is required as new strengths emerge and new problems come to light.

SUMMARY AND ACTION STEPS

The manager who provides counsel instead of advice has an intangible plus. Not only has he developed the necessary confidence in himself, but he has the satisfaction of being able to entrust his staff with complex tasks in the certainty that they will perform effectively. In fact, he can be sure that even when he has not perceived a need, his practice of counseling the whole man and instilling sound principles in his staff will result in men who will sense the need and act without specific orders. This in itself is proof of the fact that you can never give more than you will receive in return. The manager gives through his counsel and receives not only results but the opportunity to expand his horizons still further through his work, his community, and his home.

The basic differences between the manager who counsels others and the manager who provides advice only can be summarized as follows:

COUNSELOR	ADVISER
Helps the other person recognize the need. Encourages him to ask for help.	Provides advice whether asked for or not.
Obtains all pertinent facts.	Provides advice with only selected facts.
Obtains feedback on receptivity to counsel during the entire process.	Obtains compliance or encounters opposition.
Helps the other person understand the *why* of an action he takes.	Explains what is expected, but is sketchy about why.
Is truly interested in the results achieved.	Takes pride in the answer he develops and "sells" to the extent that a better answer which could be arrived at by both may be overlooked.
Knows the counsel will be acted upon if properly given.	Finds that advice is sometimes rejected.

Builds people; is motivated to help others help themselves.	Is often motivated by self-interest.
Is sure that the person to whom he has provided counsel has learned and is capable of solving future problems.	Will often find repeated requests for basically the same solutions.

How do you become an effective counselor? Here is what you do:

1. Know yourself.
    a. Think about yourself.
    - What do you believe in?
    - In your estimation, what are your potentials?
    - What are your objectives? What do you want to achieve during the next 5, 10, 15 years? During your lifetime?
    - How long do you plan on living?
    - Why do you want to achieve anything?
    - Are you afraid to fail?
    - Are you afraid to succeed?
    - Are you truly happy?
    - Have you developed a basic philosophy and understanding of the meaning of life?
    - Are you giving yourself the best chance to use your physical and mental strengths?
    - What limits have you placed on achieving your full potential?
    - What particular habits and traits are most characteristic of you?

    b. Objectively measure your strengths and beliefs.
    (1) Consider the feasibility of consulting with a professional counselor and taking a battery of psychological tests and interest and skill inventories.
    (2) Audit your physical condition by having a complete physical examination.

    c. Obtain feedback on yourself from your associates.
    (1) Ask them to tell you about yourself candidly.
    (2) Discuss your answers to the questions under "*a*" to get their opinion of them.
    (3) Think back to any advice they may have tried to communicate to you previously.

    d. Put in writing the picture you have gained of yourself through self-appraisal. This will be helpful for comparison purposes in the future.

DEVELOPING A TOUGH-MINDED CLIMATE

2. Improve your knowledge of people.
   a. Review your conversations with associates in relation to Step 1c of your self-analysis and determine what their answers to the questions you asked yourself would be.
   b. Ask a close associate to write an independent appraisal of a man you both know well and whom you too have appraised. Compare the appraisals and discuss their similarities and differences.
   c. Ask people that you come in contact with plenty of questions to determine why they do what they do and say what they say.
   d. Pick up a simple, practical book on human motivation, read it, and discuss its contents with acquaintances. Try out its ideas in practical business situations.

3. Broaden your knowledge through reading.
   a. Set aside a few minutes each day to read. At this point it isn't important what you read; the object is to get into the *habit* of reading.
   b. After each session, think about what you have read.
   c. Discuss what you have read with others to achieve a better understanding of it.
   d. Obtain three books you have been meaning to read, but haven't found time for—or a book you wouldn't ordinarily be attracted to. Read them one at a time. Think about them and discuss them with others.
   e. Gradually broaden your reading to include books that stretch your thinking, especially on topics with which you are not especially familiar or comfortable.

4. Develop yourself as a listener.
   a. In daily conversation, purposely concentrate on what the other person has to say, not on what you plan to say in return. If what you have to say is worthwhile, you will remember it and it will fit in naturally when the time comes for you to speak.
   b. Ask plenty of questions beginning with *who, what, why, when, where,* and *how.* Don't be afraid of silence. Let the other person express himself fully before you comment.
   c. Practice the habit of thinking comfortably during lags in conversation. It will most likely improve the quality of what you ultimately say. In other words, think before you speak.

5. Practice developing an emotional context in your contacts with people.
   a. Ask questions (and make statements) and observe the reactions to them.

b. Practice phrasing your questions and statements carefully so as to arouse emotions progressively on the part of those with whom you talk.
   c. Take an unpopular position and advance its merits in conversation.
   d. Develop a keen awareness of the visible signs of emotional involvement in people. Do they appear fidgety or nervous? Do they look away?
   e. Whenever you have participated in or have observed a situation in which emotions have risen to the surface, think back and try to identify the physical reactions that preceded your actual recognition that a person had become emotionally involved.

From this point on what you need is practice. To judge from attitude surveys in hundreds of companies, employees badly want to know what is expected of them and how well they are doing. This is fertile ground for practice even if you have just completed your periodic appraisal sessions.

Does this outline sound too juvenile? Then read it again. Remember that topnotch men in every type of endeavor find it necessary to revitalize themselves from time to time by going back to the basics of their professions. Review the principles of counseling and appraisal when you encounter problems and keep in mind that truly big men learn from their mistakes.

CHAPTER XVII

The Uncommon Man

THE TOUGH-MINDED MANAGER IS DEDICATED TO DEVELOPING ORDINARY men into extraordinary men—an opportunity for service which is one of life's most exhilarating and most challenging experiences. And, since development is really *self*-development, the tough-minded manager must motivate others by creating the sort of stimulating work environment that will make them strive for individual, measurable growth. To this task he directs his total drive and strengths.

The purpose of an organization is to cause common men to do uncommon things. Management leadership can change common men into uncommon men.

Values and Voltage

Leadership, when supplied to a man in business by a manager of business, can cause a man to grow beyond himself; to reach for and move toward goals which previously were only distant visions; to improve his performance beyond all expectations; to develop an interest in, even a glowing enthusiasm for, work and life far in excess of any previously imposed limitations.

The leader who can give of himself sufficiently to be an inspirer, a developer, of uncommon men must first *be* an uncommon man. This he is able to do because he has become thoroughly acquainted with himself and, as a result of this intimate acquaintance, has established some deeply felt personal values. It is not his design to take from others; rather, he is constantly seeking ways to give of his talents and abilities so that others may grow and prosper.

The uncommon man is a whole man who is receiving great satisfaction from all facets of life. He is stimulated by his work and proud of his accomplishments. He is self-critical only when he has not given his best. He is growing continuously and is using his physical resilience and well-being and his alert mental capacities to nurture the development of his subordinates and associates productively. He knows this is good business because, for example,

- Suggestions for improvements received from subordinates have, when installed, resulted in substantial monetary savings.
- When a key man was injured and away from the job over an extended period, his assistant was able to step in and maintain a high productivity level.
- Reports come back from about town indicating strongly the enthusiasm each employee has for his job and the company.

The uncommon man has developed a level of self-discipline which allows him and encourages others to work wholeheartedly and without compromise toward predetermined objectives. He has set personal and organizational goals which, not readily attainable but always in sight, call for that extra ounce of effort. He is the uncommon man not only in business but in his community, in his church, in his political activities, and most of all in the family. He "devotes his life to the interests and welfare of others so that they will respond in a way that will assure attainment of the goals of his leadership."*

The "Square" Executive

Everyone who has been in the business world for any length of time has worked with or for a few people who, through their actions, have succeeded in obtaining top-drawer effectiveness from those about them and, at the same time, commanded a respect bordering on reverence. What distinguishes these outstanding executives from others who do not inspire the same performance, the same taut ship?

There is no mystical power that a tough-minded manager possesses. He does embody many physical, mental, and personal assets which can be identified as risers on the ladder of achievement: integrity, candor, stamina, courage, ambition, vitality, empathy, ability, knowledge, and so on *ad infinitum*. However, two attributes which stand out above the others are *wisdom* and *honesty*. Webster defines wisdom as "ability to judge soundly and deal sagaciously with facts,

---

* Lawrence A. Appley, *Management in Action*, American Management Association, Inc., New York, 1956.

especially as they relate to life and conduct." The "square" executive—the balanced manager—has this wisdom gained from experience, from indoctrination under fire, and strengthened by undeviating honesty. He deals with problems honestly; he represents himself and his beliefs honestly and with candor; his word is truly his bond. In short, he is a square shooter who can be depended upon.

The man who can stand foursquare may be in the minority today. In days past he was the rule, not the exception. Handshakes between men of integrity bound business deals which nowadays would require a battery of lawyers and reams of paper. There are partnerships, still existing today, that came into being when two men said simply, "Let's do it!" Surely there can be no better time than now for each of us to consider the present trend of public and personal integrity, to reappraise the place honesty occupies in his life and the importance he personally attaches to wisdom. Dedicated men can reverse a trend and change an environment substantially by permeating it with personal values.

This is true, of course, not only of the manager in a responsible position but of the rank-and-file worker in plant or office. For example, a machine operator didn't appear to be himself physically. He was getting his share of the work out, but he wasn't his usual ebullient self—he seemed to be forcing himself to produce. His foreman, asking whether he were feeling all right, discovered that he had been sick during the night and still wasn't quite well. Why hadn't he stayed home and used his sick leave? The man's reply went something like this: "We have the finest sick leave plan I've ever seen, but it's for people who are *really* sick. I wouldn't want to abuse it because that wouldn't be honest."

And then there's the worker who frequently stayed at his bench five to ten minutes after the quitting bell. It was simply his way of making sure that he put in all the time he was being paid for.

The beatnik, the hipster, will never be any competition or threat to the "square."

Basic Equipment

There are proven tools available to the manager just as there are for the craftsman: marketing research, performance appraisal, budgeting, value engineering, employee selection techniques, and many more. These tools must be kept sharp; they must be modified and improved as necessary; they must be kept in their proper perspective, and new ones must constantly be acquired. However, the acquisition and even the proficient use of these basic tools may bring laudable returns, but they cannot guarantee total, contained success. For a sound foundation upon which growth can proceed in the tough-minded environment, the manager must obtain additional tools and employ them effectively.

What are these additional tools? Empathy, reliability, vision, creativity, guts, and of course honesty—though not necessarily in that order. The whole man could not omit even one of them.

Let's apply these tools to the operation of a personnel department. The manager of a profit center, let us say, is not getting cooperation from his subordinates in meeting commitments. Production schedules are lagging; rejects are running higher than usual. A good personnel manager will attack the problem analytically. He will most certainly consult with the manager and his people, remembering to listen rather than talk but moving in forcefully to locate strengths and recommend necessary changes with candor, honesty, and consideration for the individuals involved.

Since management, as defined by Lawrence A. Appley, is "the development of people and not the direction of things," the real equipment needed consists of those qualities of leadership which will make an associate stretch. They are, it will be noted, personal characteristics and not acquired management skills; in fact, they are the automatic recall attitudes which make possible the effective use of the acquired skills. The basic tool could be likened to a hammer, the acquired skill to a nail. The nail cannot perform its function until it is driven into place by the hammer. The acquired management skill produces results when hammered home by strong use of the manager's personal equipment.

A commanding officer during World War II was a man with well-honed leadership tools. Very early in life he had developed a high level of self-discipline which allowed him to separate facts and acts from personality and person. Grasping the error or the omission quickly, he would bring a person to task—but always candidly and constructively. More often than not, a few hours later, he would drop by the tent with a first-name greeting and a boisterous "Hurry up! Let's take in a movie!" He was and is a respected friend because he gave a part of himself so that others might grow. He had both the basic equipment and the courage to use it effectively.

Standards Which Pull and Stretch

Unless performance standards, ethical standards, and, in fact, all the goals of life are set out of immediate reach, no one will grow and everyone will be reduced to mediocrity.

There seem to be daily complaints that the quality and quantity of instruction in American schools today are geared to the average of the class. If this is true—and one suspects it is—many students are not being challenged by their teachers. It is also possible that they are being mentally and emotionally injured by being held back, while the average students are merely riding along with little excitement or enthusiasm and certainly no measurable growth. The below-average students are being stretched, but they may not be receiving the help they need to absorb the learning experience and are therefore even more frustrated than their classmates.

We have all heard the statement, "It's not so much whether you win or lose, it's how you play the game." But isn't it sad to think that people may actually be encouraged to lose rather than to expend the additional effort which would enable them to win? Win, that is, with dignity and compassion. Only the hard man glories in the defeats of others.

It is time for business executives, at least, to be forceful in establishing performance standards for themselves and their associates which are geared to improvement. There must be no joy in losing when winning is a possibility. The free enterprise system demands the best from all of us at all times. The future is for those who can compete and win.

The tough-minded environment can provide the stretchers if the tough-minded manager will supply the proper spirit and leadership —with distinct emphasis on high levels of conduct and justice and established standards which stress building on strengths rather than weaknesses. For the productivity climate has its real foundation in people who are effectively and enthusiastically applying themselves to meet performance standards which pull and stretch and to achieve the desired results. Too often the few companies that have conscientiously attacked the organization of functions by defining and describing jobs have created *activity* standards and rewards rather than results standards and rewards. Position descriptions can increase individual effectiveness only when they are accompanied by performance standards based on the results expected. Traditionally, a job description tells *what* is to be done, while a management performance standard tells *how well* the job is to be done. The tough-minded manager blends these two tools into a dynamic force.

Only by establishing goals, ideals, and standards which require real growth and challenge can the manager himself grow as an individual. But, when he grows, he creates a dynamic atmosphere which will be an inspiration to everyone associated with him.

Positive Attitudes

A person who concentrates his whole being on strengths has no time or inclination to clutter his mind up with weak, negative attitudes. A manager who looks at himself confidently in the mirror each morning, who anticipates the day's challenges eagerly, will react with zest to its problems. He will make excuses neither for himself nor for his subordinates. He starts from the premise that the job can be done, the problem solved, the obstacles overcome. This is the basis for positive leadership.

Ben Hogan, at the peak of his success in golf competition, was severely injured in an automobile accident. He was never expected to play golf again, but within a couple of years he returned to the tournament trail and again won major tournaments. Today Ben is a successful businessman and is still playing sub-par golf. He attacked his return to productive life with determination and zest.

The bald fact is that there are far more big jobs than there are big men. And if big men are in such demand, what is there that differentiates the big ones from the rest? A big man thinks positively. He has determined his purpose in life; he has high standards of personal conduct which will guide him toward the attainment of that purpose, he possesses the required knowledge and skills; and he gets tremendous satisfaction out of his job.

The successful manager is made up of many parts. These parts, like those of a jigsaw puzzle, are different in size and shape, but each is needed to complete the picture. It is impossible to conclude that any one part is more important than any other. Perhaps, however, moral responsibility and vision—more than any other two qualities—define the big man, the tough-minded man. He can give others vision and a sense of responsibility. He has the positive approach to life which rules out dwelling on weaknesses. He has the time—and takes the time—to counsel subordinates, associates, friends, and acquaintances on their problems, ideas, and interests.

A man may be outwardly gruff, cold, and stern. He may talk as though he had little or no concern for others. Very few of his associates will be aware of the tremendous heart behind this superficially cold exterior—the heart that may now and then prompt him, for example, to find a youngster on the street who looks hungry and whose clothes are shabby, take him to lunch, buy him some clothes and a toy, and send him on his way. Such a man may be a big man, living a big life. But a warm interior surrounded by a warm exterior would make him a bigger man.

The Abundant Life

A productive life, a meaningful life, must include a strong, worthwhile relationship to one's work. A person who is activity-oriented, who merely occupies a spot on an organizational chart, putting in the minimum time required, is wasting not only his time and talents but others'. The man who does not stretch, who does not develop himself, is as surely withering away as an unused muscle.

A purposeful life for the executive who aspires to be a whole man involves a balance of activities and interests all hinged upon his business responsibilities. Certainly he should have a fine relationship with his family which will occupy much of his time and thought. He should also assume his share of responsibility for his church, his community, and his nation, and he must have time for relaxation and recreation—time for refueling the tank of energy which supplies the enthusiastic drive.

We are told that doctors and ministers outlive business executives. Is this because of their dedication to work: work that means giving

> ## MY CREED
>
> I do not choose to be a common man. It is my right to be uncommon—if I can. I seek opportunity—not security. I do not wish to be a kept citizen, humbled and dulled by having the state look after me. I want to take the calculated risk; to dream and to build, to fail and to succeed. I refuse to barter incentive for a dole. I prefer the challenges of life to the guaranteed existence; the thrill of fulfillment to the stale calm of utopia. *I will not trade freedom for beneficence nor my dignity for a handout.* I will never cower before any master nor bend to any threat. It is my heritage to stand erect, proud and unafraid; to think and act for myself; to enjoy the benefit of my creations and to face the world boldly and say, this I have done. All this is what it means to be an American.
>
> —DEAN ALFANGE, *This Week Magazine,* December 30, 1951

of their talents—indeed, their very lives? Possibly. Such dedication could well be a major contributor to longevity in their case, but we might further conclude that men of these disciplines are equally dedicated to other phases of life, and that it is this which makes their careers particularly full and meaningful. They must, above all, have clearly understood and thought-out *values.*

Herbert Hoover, who lived to be 90 years old, kept his mind and body completely active and productive in his work as an engineer, as a businessman, as a welfare administrator, as the President of the United States, and at the last as a tremendously respected and regarded elder statesman—an adviser to others. He is proof that dedication to useful work, plus a balanced diet of other activities and interests, makes for an abundant life.

A person who exists below his optimum level of productivity, who does not use his talents and his intelligence to the utmost, is a cheat. He is cheating his family by denying them a fuller life. He is cheating his associates because they are unable to profit from his gifts. He is cheating himself because he is not the whole man he was intended to be. His life lacks zest and verve.

The Fresh Wind of Individualism

During the past years it has become increasingly difficult to recognize anyone as an individual. So many efforts have been made to blur him into a group, a mass, or a collection. So many changes have taken place in schools, in government, and in unions to glorify the many and the average and to minimize the individual. Togetherness, committee-itis, and group decision making in business and in the family have reduced a person's chances of growing as an individual. The danger is that he may not long have the courage or stamina to fight back.

It appears that all too many of us have lost sight of this basic need of a man for recognition as a single human being, not to mention the tremendous possibilities inherent in utilizing the strengths of individuals and molding their efforts together to accomplish common goals.

When we speak of an individual, we do not, of course, mean the rebel who knows what he is *against* but doesn't know what he is *for*. He is the man who tears things down by emotional negativism. The real individual works diligently to build solid accomplishments on a basis of positive values. He has set realistic goals for himself toward which he is striving. He is a whole man with the courage and self-discipline to be an individual.

Certain encouraging signs on the horizon suggest that not all of us are allowing ourselves to be lost in the group or to go along with the crowd without first knowing the reason why. There are businessmen who are no longer accepting the traditional when the new can be proved superior. There are tough-minded businessmen who want the productivity climate in which individual performance is measured quantitatively and qualitatively in terms of individual contribution to profits. And it appears that there are school administrators and teachers who are throwing off the shackles of educational obsolescence and trying hard to provide stretch for all, not just the average, students.

We in our country must establish an overall climate in which all our citizens can develop positively as individuals. The problem is to insure that these same individuals function effectively as a team

DEVELOPING A TOUGH-MINDED CLIMATE

which will demand for each member the best of the strengths he possesses.

SUMMARY AND ACTION STEPS

How can a common man become an uncommon man? How can he change a routine, drab life to a dedicated, abundant one? How do real values, backed up by energetic application, produce a big man?

A serious attempt has been made here to identify the positive characteristics and actions which distinguish the uncommon man who produces uncommon results. By identifying these attitudes and attributes we have made the first step toward answering our questions. We can now develop further steps.

There can be no start toward improvement in any area without an uncompromising analysis of self in depth. A person must look at the life he has led and is leading. He must question his goals, if he has any, as they affect each facet of his existence. He must evaluate his actions and thoughts in relation to these goals and this life, and the conclusions which he reaches at the end of this process will be his guide to future action.

He must above all ask himself unequivocably whether he is satisfied with what his analysis uncovers. Are the methods he has been using to achieve his goals wholly ethical and beyond reproach? Are the values and standards which have characterized his past life the right ones? If the past is not to be a model for the future, and if the individual is convinced of the need for a change, then he is ready for the next step.

At this point he should draw up a blueprint, not just in the mind but on paper, as a constant reminder and record. This blueprint will be a word picture of the desired results—a picture of the uncommon man. If he will look objectively at his strengths and weaknesses, he can produce a plan which will be the right route to follow, establishing the appropriate changes, the actions to be taken, the values needed to reach the objectives. To be most effective, this plan must be spelled out in detail with a realistic timetable. Part of it could look like this:

1. I will read a worthwhile book each week.
2. I will take a course in better report writing and complete it within three months.
3. I will volunteer to teach a Sunday School class. (I have been offered the chance many times.)
4. Jean and I will discuss finances and establish a workable, mutually agreeable family budget by January 1.
5. I will analyze my job in detail to determine how I can be more productive. I will have this analysis finished two weeks from today.

Obviously, any objective that is established must have a stretching effect, as must each step of the plan, so that change and growth are accomplished. And, for this systematic approach to tough-mindedness to be workable, there can be no compromising of principles or lessening of values. Nor can any barrier or obstacle in the way be considered a deterrent to personal progress that cannot be surmounted. Courage and self-discipline, in large proportions, are what is needed to carry out the well-laid plan step by step.

Beyond this, it should hardly be necessary to add that

1. Goals must be the result of vision and reflect complete integrity and honor.
2. The means of achieving both ultimate and intermediate goals must be honest and reflect true consideration of others.

In this plan the individual will clearly be establishing a way of life which will include business, social, political, civic, and immediate family relationships and activities. It must be dynamic; its goals, results-oriented, must be moved further out as intermediate objectives are attained. There is, he will find, no end to real growth.

CHAPTER XVIII

Management Horizons

THERE IS ONLY ONE WAY TO VIEW THE HORIZON. THAT IS TO LIFT your eyes and your head and look far beyond what's immediately in front of you. There is only one way to pursue that horizon, and that is to move forward, looking to see where you're going, not where you've been.

These statements may seem trite and obvious. It's doubtful that any of us would dispute them; however, many of us constantly violate them in our pursuit of far horizons. This is especially true in business organizations. For example, company management will often use historic figures to forecast future performance. When actual performance closely approximates the forecast, management is pleased, feeling that the effectiveness of its planning has been demonstrated. Seldom does such a situation cause concern, even though it may be repeated year after year. Only occasionally does a thoughtful executive reflect over the possibility—indeed, the probability—that performance bears out a forecast because we make it do so. Not by exploiting breakthroughs or wringing out the most from our opportunities, because breakthroughs and opportunities are difficult to predict, but by doing tomorrow what we did yesterday.

The only time when historic data can effectively predict future performance is when the same old methods are used within the same climate in the same way that generated the historic data. When this is the case, growth is limited and often accidental.

The primary job of top management is not to administer the annual plan or to promulgate the current organization, policies, and procedures. Its primary job is to visualize conditions as they will exist in the relatively distant future; determine the changes in organization methods, products, and people that will be necessary; and skillfully time the changes in phase with the changing environment. Since few of us are clairvoyant, our vision of the future will always be vague and cloudy. However, to the perceptive individual certain signs and general trends will usually be discernible.

DEVELOPING A TOUGH-MINDED CLIMATE

The Coming Burden on Management

It is quite clear that the future of the free enterprise system in this country, as in the world, rests squarely on the shoulders of its representatives, the chief executives of the companies that make up that system.

It is equally clear that the free enterprise system with all it implies is to be tested in the coming decades as it has never been tested before. The world is becoming less and less the property and captive market of a few dominant and industrially mature countries. It is becoming more and more a splintered, fragmented complex of nations: some young, awkward, adolescent, seeking to struggle up out of poverty and oppressive colonialism; some aging, living in the past, and pretending that nothing has changed; and some—like our own country—bursting with strength, vigor, and enthusiasm and boldly seeking new frontiers.

There is no doubt that free enterprise can withstand future tests, as it has those of the past, and grow stronger as a result. But, if it is to do so, we must develop a degree of creativity and innovation far greater than any we have ever known before. No longer are we servicing only markets in which people necessarily think the way we do, act the way we do, and need what we need. We are servicing many markets where people, though they may want what we have, are not in a position to use, buy, or pay for it. These markets are of many varied types, and our products must be designed to accommodate all the variations. Our pricing structures, our cost factors, our channels of distribution, even our basic methods of management must be re-evaluated in terms of these world markets, not only as they are today, but as they will be tomorrow and many years into the future.

Then there is the factor of change. We must recognize that the world is experiencing an increasingly dynamic process of change and predicate the development of our organizations upon change, not upon obsolete concepts designed to maintain the *status quo*. The whole notion of fixed organizational lines of authority and precise functional assignments is an attempt to achieve a static condition and cannot possibly measure up to the challenges of a dynamic, changing business environment. Organization in the future will more and more have to assume an identity of its own; a structure which, like the human body, constantly builds new cells, develops new muscles, changes its internal chemistry, and learns new patterns of behavior. The challenge of the future is to design this organism in such a way that change is self-perpetuating and predicated on the realities of the environment.

In many cases today, companies are in a constant state of change, but the change often stems from superficial understanding of management concepts or personal politics. Quite frequently an organization—which may be among the greatest and best known in the world—will establish a rigid structure and pattern of business practice—and stick with it until it becomes so dislocated from its contact with the realities of the market that a major shake-up is required. New managers are brought in, new distribution channels are established, whole divisions are added or eliminated, and new products replace old ones. A chaotic, painful period ensues until all these elements are again molded into another orderly pattern of rigid organization and stereotyped performance which is suited to current needs. Yet, in a few more years, this organization too will become disoriented and another shake-up will take place.

Consider the concept of centralization and decentralization. Many companies have gone through the process of centralizing their organization structure, then decentralizing it, and finally recentralizing it in complete disillusionment. This doesn't work. A fixed organization structure is like a photograph, portraying a momentary state of being which is already past and will never exist again.

Enjoyment, Not Just Results

So the real challenge facing us as managers today is to determine how we can go about building the organization of the future that will be conditioned to change and thrive on it; the organization that will change routinely and continuously as the demands of its environment and its people change. This will require enriching our current concepts of management by objectives, which are just beginning to be effectively applied, with management by *process*, where the accomplishment of tasks and objectives is secondary—a natural by-product of the company climate and the way its employees pool their strengths for maximum productivity. We have to develop in people the desire and capability to not only accept a climate of change but enjoy it; to gain real satisfaction from working with others, not only for the attainment of objectives, but for the sheer enjoyment of doing the work necessary to meet goal after goal.

Much dissatisfaction has been expressed by those in top management positions who say: "We try for a profit margin of 10 per cent and then, when we hit that, for 12 per cent—and even 15 per cent. Where will it all end? We never seem to be content—the minute we achieve one goal, we set another, still higher one." True, the setting and achieving of goals is not enough in itself to give individuals a full measure of personal fulfillment. This can only be gained through enjoying the process of getting results as well as the results themselves.

There is a certain danger in evaluating a man only in terms of specific results, however often this book may have stressed the importance of objectives and results requirements. Why? Because it may lead a man to judge himself solely by the same criteria, and because it can and often does make him simply endure or tolerate his work, gaining satisfaction only when the work is done or the task completed. It may, for some of us, require a great change in our way of thinking to achieve a climate in which we derive real joy from the process of getting things done as well as the things themselves.

Motivation, Tired but Still Untapped

If we are to expand our thinking from management by objectives in the direction of an increasingly meaningful management process, we have to look carefully at what it is that makes people want to do things and what it is that gives them enjoyment and satisfaction as against what tends to detract from this sense of enjoyment and satisfaction. We must look into the basic principles of human motivation as they apply not only to the job situation but to life itself.

It is important to ask ourselves this question: Would we work if we didn't have to? Think of the people who have become independently wealthy at a relatively young age. Do they sit back and quit working? Do they golf, swim, eat, and indulge themselves generally to the exclusion of all productive activity? By no means.

Either these people find ways of making some worthwhile contribution to the world, or they wither and decay. They found charitable organizations, they go into politics, they take the lead in civic causes, they become prominent in clubs and religious organizations. They evidently find that material or economic security is not enough; they are motivated by something else.

Yes, we would work even if we didn't have to. Why is this so? Why must people be productive? There are two basic reasons: the need for human companionship and the need to be an important part of something greater than ourselves. There are surely few people who are satisfied, let alone happy, to be always by themselves. It is a fundamental drive to want to share one's feelings, thoughts, and ideas with others; to want to share both successes and failures; to want to contribute to others' success and happiness; to have a reason for existing. In fact, it is apparent that this need and desire to work with others toward the attainment of common goals, or to indulge in common activities, is of much greater motivational value than money. This being the case, it is obvious that, for all our talk about motivation in recent years, we have not even begun to tap our human resources.

Most of our compensation plans are based solely on money. We grade jobs in terms of their value to the organization in dollars. We reward people for the objectives they have attained, the results and contributions they have made, primarily in terms of dollars. Once in a while we give them a pat on the back, a new office, a company automobile, an expense account; but all these again are weighed in terms of dollars or other tangible value. How often, in how many places, do we see any appreciation of the greater motivational advantage of providing a climate where people can satisfy their basic need for human companionship? How often do we offer individuals the opportunity to feel they are an important part of a smooth-running, powerful, highly productive group whose impact is far greater than the sum of the individual's own effort? To inspire personal excellence and obtain consistently exceptional performance, these two motives must be recognized and satisfied.

Occasionally, by coincidence or intuition, the right ingredients are thrown together and the results are spectacular. The right size of group, the right mix of personalities, the right type of work, and perhaps other elements which have yet to be identified are combined, and some form of human chemistry produces a superlative living machine. The basketball team, together virtually unbeatable, no one of the five a star. The pennant-winning baseball team without a man on the All-Stars. The night crew on the freight dock that always seems to have the trucks ready to roll by morning regardless of volume. The manufacturing division management that always beats production schedules despite breakdowns or last-minute snags. The sales team that's always first in the market with the most.

These cases are rarer than they need be. When they do occur, the group's phenomenal success is usually attributed to the competitive spirit, exploited but not analyzed. Seldom do we study successful performance to see why it is successful; we only study failure to punish the guilty and eliminate the cause. Yet what has been interpreted as the fruits of the competitive spirit is not that at all. It is a group of people who have accidentally found a supremely compatible environment; a combination in which the strengths of one man completely balance the weaknesses of another, so that working together gives each individual a feeling that what he is doing is natural to him. The competitive spirit may well be the catalyst that welds the group together and initially spurs its members to a high level of performance; but, if it is not replaced by a sense of joy and fulfillment derived from the process of achieving excellence as a team, the exceptional performance cannot be sustained.

Search your organization, search your own relationships within it. Are you finding joy and fulfillment in the pursuit of excellence as a member of a smooth-working team? Are you actually going to work with a keen anticipation of the companionship you will have that day, that week, that month? Will you go home at night feeling that you have been a part of something greater than yourself? That you've blended your efforts with those of others while still retaining your inherent integrity and individuality? If you have found this harmonious and purposeful existence, guard it jealously. Few men are as fortunate.

Self-Confidence and the Team

It is possible, within a company, to develop a climate which recognizes these motivational factors, which stresses a system of values and working methods that help to satisfy people's needs for human companionship and purposeful existence. The size of the group, the meshing and balancing of strengths and weaknesses, the merging of personal and organizational objectives—all are important. But there is at least one other absolutely essential ingredient which, when coupled with the rest, can enable an organization to transform itself from a rigid, static entity, comfortable only in the *status quo*, to a vital dynamic organism, continuously achieving higher levels of excellence and productivity. This critical ingredient is deep and pervasive self-confidence—individual self-confidence and *team* self-confidence. It is the feeling that *I* and *we* can meet and master each challenge, exploit each opportunity, solve each problem. It is the recognition that, although *I* and *we* shall occasionally fail, our total efforts will result in both psychological and material success.

The concept of team self-confidence is not new, but it has yet to be applied effectively in industry. In the world of athletics it is a phenomenon which often upsets the odds makers. Even here, however, it is elusive. A team may have it one week and lose it the next. Most startling upsets, we can be sure, result from its development to a high degree. What we in business and industry must do is to find ways of developing the same sort of individual and team self-confidence and apply it on a sustained basis.

Self-confidence is the one ingredient that is most lacking in the world today. Its absence is what most inhibits and restricts our ability to make full use of our basic talents and prevents us from grasping more than a fraction of the opportunities available to us. It is keeping us managers from making the most of our greatest resource—human beings. How do we develop deep and pervasive self-confidence? How do we erase the fears that bar people from trying things which they are more than likely to succeed in doing? Unless we can find the secret to this dilemma, we will never gain the full measure of our own talents, nor will we realize the unlimited productivity that comes from joint human effort.

Self-confidence. Now we have it; now we don't. In certain situations we are confident; in others we are not. Why is it so difficult to seize this essential ingredient and hold on to it? What causes it to keep slipping away from us as individuals, as managers, and as people? What does it take to build a sustained and sustaining self-confidence? It takes, above all, an unshakable faith grounded in a set of values and beliefs tempered into a state of invulnerability to external pressures. Before any man can have any measure of self-confidence, he must know very firmly what he believes in. He cannot be plagued by self-doubts. This sort of unshakable faith cannot be developed, moreover, without exposing oneself to a wide range of experiences. A man must experiment, must try principles in a number of situations, discarding those which do not hold up and clinging to those that meet the test of varying conditions.

Self-confidence, in other words, begins with the development of values and beliefs, but it matures through applying them constantly on the job, at home, and in all aspects of life—and through finding that they really do bring success, satisfaction, and happiness.

Gearing for the Space Age

As the world and the universe expand about us, we must also expand or we will quickly find ourselves shut off from the mainstream of life. Today we're not talking about the problems of transportation across oceans; we're no longer concerned with the distance from here to California, or from here to Paris. Today we are concerned about the distance to other planets, and tomorrow it will be other planetary systems. We may, in the future, even leave our galaxy and seek new ones. We may be faced with new and different forms of life, different metals and minerals, different concepts—perhaps some that we cannot comprehend because they are entirely foreign to our way of thinking. We will be meeting situations and conditions that do not follow the laws and principles of our current science, either human or physical.

We are now building spacecraft designed to land on the Moon, on Mars. We are producing equipment with such fine tolerances as to virtually preclude any acceptance of error. Such minute objects as a discarded cigarette butt, a lock of hair, or a burr on a metal valve may completely destroy a multimillion-dollar spaceship and cut short the lives of its occupants. And all this makes external, procedural quality control almost impossible. More and more the importance of the simple statement that "quality is built in, not inspected in" becomes apparent. Never before have we been able to recognize so clearly the fact that each individual must set his own standards of excellence and maintain them. We cannot force people to be accurate, to be careful; accuracy and care can come only from internal motives: the desire to excel, the willingness to recognize and assume the consequences of one's laxity and errors.

Never before, in short, have we been so vividly aware of the need for each of our employees to have his full measure of self-confidence and so be willing and able to do his job fully and completely. All the more important, then, that we focus even more closely on the need for developing people to their greatest potential and for quickly recognizing when our demands exceed that potential. We are approaching the time when the enforcement of accountability will be more than a desirable concept; when it will, in fact, be an absolute prerequisite to effective management. Thus the degree of our success as we enter the Space Age will rest solely and directly upon our ability to build the faith of the individual in himself, to help him arrive at solid beliefs, to release his capacity for self-directed excellence, and to match his abilities carefully with requirements.

Our nation, which has so long stressed the value and the rights of the individual over those of the state or the organization, will dominate the Space Age. We will lead the way because we are seeking and will make breakthroughs in human understanding and motivation—breakthroughs which will enable us to realize the creative and productive potential of our people—as long as we never lose faith in ourselves and our ability to innovate.

Management and the Millennium

The management leader in generations to come will not be the man who has mastered a discipline, the man who has achieved a graduate degree or two. He will not be the financier, supersalesman, or expert at analysis. He will be the man who is able to inspire others, who can weld together many individuals of wide and diverse experiences and abilities into a tight, cohesive group with singleness of purpose and unity of direction.

With this man as leader, people will know they can find no greater satisfaction than that which comes from belonging to a group, from judging themselves constantly by the excellence of their day-to-day work as part of that group and the richness of their day-to-day relationships. The climate in which they function will recognize the difference between conformity in behavior and unanimity in concepts. It will encourage them to innovate, to try new ways of applying fundamental principles; it will tolerate occasional failure within the total context of excellence in the belief that only a fallible human leader can inspire other fallible human beings.

Finally, leadership in the world of tomorrow will fall to those who are able to identify individuals with the basic stuff of wisdom, warmth, and tough-mindedness; who can put five such people together and get out of them more than five times the productivity of any one of them alone; who can exploit opportunities; who can erase the line between superior and subordinate and never miss it, rising above management by authority. These future executives must be able to identify and communicate the purpose of the organization, the goals to be accomplished, and the philosophic guidelines within which people will operate. Above all, they must inspire in their employees a vision of personal excellence, stimulate each individual to seek the satisfaction of being a member of a highly productive team, and provide the climate that will enable him to realize personal fulfillment in the process of achieving job goals.

All organizations, if they survive long enough, pass through three progressively higher levels of maturity. On the first or lowest level the entire organization is dominated by a single personality who directs all the major functions and makes all the major decisions. The second or next higher level is characterized by diffused management receiving direction through a sophisticated system of objectives, policies, procedures, and controls. On the third or highest level of maturity we find a diminution of functional organization, rigid policies, and controls—along with self-motivation, self-direction, self-confidence, and self-control *in each and every employee.*

Today, some companies are still in the first stage of maturity, but they must soon move to the second stage or they will cease to exist. When the head is gone, the body will die. The majority of successful companies are currently in the second stage of maturity; they have yet to attain the third and highest level. It is still in the distance—visible but only vaguely on the approaching management horizon. Managers must choose their course: Is it to be yesterday's, today's, or tomorrow's?

CHAPTER XIX

A Reaffirmation of Faith

I think it is safe to say that the human raw material available to this country, expressed in terms of mental capacity, is not substantially different from the equivalent in any other nation. What we have done is to increase the fruitfulness of our spiritual soil by providing the fertilizer of incentive to each of our citizens.

—CRAWFORD H. GREENEWALT
The Uncommon Man
McGraw Hill Book Co., Inc., New York, 1959

SINCE MAN'S EARLIEST BEGINNINGS HE HAS DEPENDED ON TOOLS TO carry out his ideas. The painful progress—slow but accelerating enormously of late—from stone hammers and spears to computers, jet aircraft, and nuclear fission has been an infinitely varied history of inspiration, experimentation, innovation, development. However, the basic factor in the creation of stone, metal, plastic, and other physical tools has always been the human mind.

We have seen, moreover, that the tools of the tough-minded manager are the personal attributes that make him a whole man and, to a lesser extent, his acquired skill in the recognized techniques of management: planning, organization, coordination, execution, and control. And, in the same sense, the real tools of men in general are the applied principles and laws of human behavior. Nothing is of such pressing and overriding importance in this century as the understanding and use of these tools.

The Tools of Enterprise

The real tools of enterprise in our country will be only adequate without a deeper understanding of the free enterprise system and its foundations by a vastly greater number of businessmen.

DEVELOPING A TOUGH-MINDED CLIMATE

In one recent management clinic a visitor to the United States, the executive vice president of a European company, pointed out with considerable asperity, "You don't have free enterprise here—you have equal parts of socialism and capitalism. You have about the most security-conscious people in the world." One after another, the American executives who were present attempted to answer the visitor—only to be cut to pieces by his quick, practiced arguments. It was all too clear that most of these Americans understood the meaning of the U.S. Constitution only vaguely, and in a grade school way. Few of them could recite even a few words from this most vital of all American documents, yet it was and is the very keel, superstructure, and stuff of our free enterprise system.

What was wrong? For one thing, our Constitution is currently and widely interpreted to mean freedom of economic enterprise only, whereas, in precise reality, it provides for economic, social, political, and spiritual freedom as a unified, dynamic whole. For another, there is prevalent today a narrow emphasis on materialism—an uncertain, compulsive, and fearful preoccupation with purely material trappings of success—coupled with a failure to recognize that fear and insecurity will be our constant companions as long as we focus only on material success as their antidote. And such a sterile concept of free enterprise completely ignores the requirements of the whole man who wants from his business or his job the full thrill of creating, building, giving, and living in daily, constructive interaction with other people.

Is this a situation with which we can temporize? Absolutely not! What do we do, then? Here are some results-getting steps to unleash the tools of enterprise:

1. Structure internal communications media so as to include a steady and stimulating series of helpful discussions, illustrations, and anecdotes. Of course these must be introduced appropriately if management is not to be accused of invading its employees' privacy and demanding conformity with its particular political views.
2. Scrupulously avoid such meaningless and nonsensical terms as "Leftist" and "Rightist." Focus only on how to be an increasingly effective *Enterpriser!*

A REAFFIRMATION OF FAITH

3. Make sure that all the company's employees know and understand the basic beliefs and principles of the top executive. More importantly, if you are that top executive, make sure that those basic beliefs and principles are stimulated, clarified, and enlarged by a deep understanding of the great manifestoes of Americanism. You don't want to force everyone to believe as you do, but you hope the example you set will bear out the validity of your beliefs.
4. Structure all external media to reflect, and even to promote, the idea that yours is a company or a division that expects and rewards *enterprise* in every job right down to the bottom of the organization. The newest and perhaps most poorly educated employee needs to be enterprising, and unless he can express this need within a climate of productivity, you will never obtain his full effort and enthusiasm.

We cannot achieve the "great society" through government dole and legislation. We can achieve it only through enlightened individuals who understand the tools of enterprise and how to use them. The tough-minded approach therefore calls for

1. Understanding the "free" nature of "enterprise" (the very word implies readiness, courage and energy, venturousness, boldness in starting projects), including its political, social, and spiritual aspects.
2. Understanding the "every day" meaning of "enterprise" as it applies to business operations.
3. Establishing a results-oriented climate to encourage and stretch people and require the daily use of enterprise.
4. Very important—refusing to provide raises and recognition for subordinates who have long relied simply on seniority, diplomas, color, creed, and general "nice-guyism."

The tough-minded manager knows that people who are fully motivated and challenged to exercise economic, political, social, and spiritual enterprise, to direct their initiative freely toward demanding business goals, are by far the most valuable and happy employees. He knows that economic or financial profit usually is greatly increased by a workforce that is gaining a full measure of social, political, and spiritual profit. In short, he regards an expenditure of time and effort on the fundamental tools of enterprise as a sound investment. It takes ingenuity and it takes guts, but the rewards can be astonishing.

The head of a large food-processing company protested: "Look—all I want is more profit. Show me how to increase sales, cut costs, and keep the blasted union out of my hair. Let's talk later about building a climate."

This man was a conscientious, hard-working executive. He had insisted on quality products, good equipment, sound cost accounting, budgets, marketing research, modern plant layout, and just about all the techniques of modern management. In addition, he had sent numerous key executives to outside seminars and had inaugurated an in-company program of management development. But the company did not operate harmoniously or in phase; real pride, enthusiasm, and *esprit de corps* were noticeably absent; the atmosphere was pallid and sterile. A job was just a job. It took the development of the productivity climate in an orderly way, with emphasis on carefully thought through and clearly communicated values and expectations, to make the profit picture crackle and glow. Only then did executives who had felt conflicting or negating emotions about their jobs, who had seen no soul-stirring reason to commit themselves totally to company success and profit, snap into gear.

Throughout the length and breadth of our country, thousands upon thousands of people are going home each night with their energies almost completely unexpended. Often they feel it imperative that they engage in "good works" outside the job to satisfy their hunger and thirst for a feeling of purpose, contribution, and dignity. Yet every alert and courageous top executive—with the tools of free enterprise—can harness this unexpended drive in the achievement of company goals.

We must not forget that our country, which is still so young in comparison with the Old World, is above all a nation of *total* free enterprise. Only when this total concept is systematically built into every segment of business can we begin to assume with real assurance that we are worthy and capable of retaining our privileges as a nation of free and honorable men.

All the more regrettable, then, that it has become "square" to teach young people a better understanding of free enterprise, of integrity and hard sweaty work—in short, of the individuality and other values that are basically American. Once it was a good and pleasant thing to say of a man, "He's a square shooter." "He stands four-square." "He puts in a square day's work." These values must be brought back into focus, made popular in both business and other circles. Young men—and some not so young—must be taught that our free enterprise system does not need to be defended with elaborate public relations devices. It needs only to be understood and *practiced.*

When executives realize that our whole way of doing business, with emphasis on the necessity of profit, is based entirely on positive and basically American values and that failure to define and practice these values can have a distinct impact on their pocketbooks, balance statements, and security, they will come alive with a snap. For these values are *the basic architecture of our whole business.* Many of our successful entrepreneurs would fail completely in a smothering collectivist society. We must be individuals, true, but let's remember that the climate established by the Constitution makes it all possible.

If a company president should want deliberately to devitalize his business, he could do this readily by stressing profit only, without stating *why* it is essential and *why* it is American. True productivity is never achieved by teaching only the procedural techniques of management and scrupulously rejecting any discussion or understanding of the values underlying the enterprise. Free enterprise relies essentially for success on a system of morality, and a whole set of beliefs and principles is necessary to provide the fabric of truly tough-minded management. And only tough-minded people can meet the requirements of tomorrow.

The Tools of Faith

Managers, from first-line supervisors up to top executives, are full of questions these days. And, invariably, their questions narrow down to the individual's own concept of success. With startling regularity, statements like these are made:

- "I've got plenty of money now for my own personal security—two cars, a fat bank balance, a nice home, kids graduating

- from good colleges—but something is missing. I feel kind of restless and futile."
- "The only way I can get rid of my inhibitions and relax is with a couple of double martinis. Something is wrong—I know this isn't the way to live. All it's going to accomplish is cirrhosis of the liver. What can I do about it?"
- "My business is successful, but I'm not. I'd like somehow to feel a little more significant."
- "I don't drink and I don't smoke, and my people think I'm a glacially efficient decision maker. But I'm not—I'm so tense sometimes I could yell. I think this job may be too big for me, but I'm trapped."
- "How on earth can I set the style and tone of my company when I don't even know, in reality, why I'm in business? Sure I know that profit is the 'name of the game'; but, honest to goodness, I can't imagine what I'm going to do with more money."

These comments and hundreds like them add up very plainly to the stark realization that something is badly out of kilter in our business community. As the executive vice president of one of the nation's largest companies says:

> I've waited for years to see evidence that some of my smart young comers want something other than to claw their way past their peers and push for increasingly big offices, big salaries, and exclusive club memberships. I've got to select a successor soon, and it won't be any of these eager and self-centered hustlers. I've got to find a man who has depth, wisdom, energy, and some kind of an internal gyroscope that gives him the ability to reason coolly and objectively and yet stay completely dissatisfied with the *status quo*. Darn it, I guess I want a man who's tough-minded.

Clearly a flexible, pliant, durable—in short, tough—quality of mind is something to be eagerly and assiduously sought. Without tough-mindedness, a man is doomed to mediocrity. With it no obstacle can be too big. But how is it achieved?

At the very core of the tough-minded man is faith. Time after time, in the business maelstrom, tired, dispirited, jaded executives

A REAFFIRMATION OF FAITH

have reviewed their accomplishments only to recognize that, while the sum total of their work has yielded material rewards in abundance, it has failed to provide bone-deep satisfaction. And what is the missing ingredient? Most often it is the sort of abiding faith that supports a man in every facet of his life—a belief in God that transcends day-to-day material considerations.

Is this theory? Is it pious posturing? Emphatically no! To lead others effectively, a man must first know himself. And, to know himself, he must have faith; he must know how to lose his self-preoccupation in a deep personal commitment to eternal truths and values—to his God. Here are some attributes of two types of executives:

Possesses a living, breathing faith:	*Lacks a real and meaningful faith:*
Mental health.	"Gray sickness."
Vigor.	Self-doubt.
Optimism.	Cynicism.
Personal power.	Sarcasm.
Confidence	Self-concern.
Vitality and endurance.	Low energy level.
Convictions.	Apologistic attitudes and manner.
Drive.	Poor motivation; tendency to want something for nothing.
Integrity.	Little sense of values; reputation for politicking.
Candor.	Evasiveness.
Continuous renewal.	Progressive physical and mental weakness.
Inspiration for others.	Little leadership ability; knack for making the simple seem complex.
Concentration on the strengths of others.	Concentration on the weaknesses of others.
Positive attitude.	Negative attitude.

The tough-minded manager must continuously communicate—by both word and example—that profit is essential, that it is honorable, and that it is impossible to generate too much of it as long as the full requirements of management by integrity are met. But—even more challenging—*he must blast the fallacy that you must compromise integrity to run a truly profitable business.* The converse is true in spades! Companies will almost always make more money when they employ the full arsenal of the tools of enterprise with strongest emphasis on dynamic personal faith.

The president of a vegetable-processing company lamented:

> Both our unions have gotten out of hand. We have featherbedding, grievances by the dozen, high turnover, supervisors with paralyzed initiative. You name it—we've got it. And the whole problem is people. Our facilities and equipment are above average. Our reputation for quality is based on years of satisfaction. There doesn't seem to be any real hostility or open distrust—just a messy and cloudy atmosphere which has smothered the enthusiasm of my executives. Two have had heart attacks, one has had a nervous breakdown, and the others have become defensive and indecisive. What's wrong?

The question wasn't really what was *wrong* but, rather, what should be *better*. The president had to carry out systematically the steps necessary to build a climate of enthusiasm based on challenging goals, results measurements, hard-hitting candor, emphasis on individual strengths, an understanding in depth of what free enterprise really is, and, finally, *faith*.

At this point the cynical manager will demand, "How on earth can I mix 'religion' with my business?" He can't and he shouldn't. The tough-minded manager in no way tries to introduce his church into his business. But he nonetheless proceeds on the following facts:

1. The privileges of entrepreneurship and capitalistic endeavor have been made possible by our Constitution with its Bill of Rights.
2. Our founding fathers fashioned the Constitution to provide, through government, a way of life based squarely on the Ten Commandments.
3. The Ten Commandments are the foundation of all law and, therefore, provide a universal basis for management by integrity.
4. These two manifestoes provide a framework for profit. There is no dichotomy between the two; they are indivisible.

Certainly it takes vision, skill, and hard work to build this kind of "electric" climate, but it can be infinitely satisfying, infinitely rewarding, and it can help insure that the American businessman will become a true force for both world peace and total human enterprise in an age that cries out desperately for strong sure leadership.

The Tools of Humanity

As the destructive capacity of nuclear fission grows, we stand literally on the brink of oblivion. The boiling ferment of ill-fed and ill-understood millions has created worldwide tides of hate and fear that cannot be met simply with newer and better electronic devices. Indeed, the continued existence of a livable world virtually depends on whether we continue to concentrate on improvement of the sophisticated electronic mechanisms which can send missiles hurtling throughout the world or whether we apply ourselves with terrible urgency to the clarification of the values which control the hand on the button.

Our nation has led the world in material abundance. Our plants, machine tools, chemical processes, and assembly-line methods have been far in the vanguard of the world's efforts. But, although we have learned to circle the world in minutes, we find it inconvenient to visit a sick employee in the hospital across town. We have moved from engine lathes and blacksmith's techniques to automated factories, yet we have devoted precious little time to determining what truly motivates the people involved. We have developed vastly improved printing processes only to fill airport terminals with a collection of paperbacks which appall visitors from other countries. We have spawned an increasing conglomerate of labor relations legislation, and yet we know very little about why many workers join unions (some with dubious reputations) rather than insist on their own individuality. We have continued to build increasingly imposing churches and cathedrals, and at the same time many of the people who have contributed the most money to them have done so to keep from taking a penetrating and uncompromising look at their own mixed-up and ill-defined values.

From all parts of the continent intelligent, experienced executives are asking what they can do to make sure their time on this planet is really well spent. What they can do boils down roughly to this:

DEVELOPING A TOUGH-MINDED CLIMATE

1. Know what you stand for—and why. Whether you are chairman of the board or a shipping clerk, you owe this to your country, your enterprise, and yourself.
2. Learn much more about our country. The late Harry Bullis stated in *Manifesto for Americans:*° "To defeat organized tyranny in the world we must continue to achieve a more highly educated society and preserve its freedom of inquiry and expression.... Democracy is enormously more than a form of government. An expression of the human spirit at its best, some of democracy can be written into law, but its essence is in such attitudes as tolerance and fraternity and such processes as discussion and cooperation. The method of democracy is to rely on the collective judgment of a well-informed citizenry."
3. Settle for nothing less than management by integrity in your own business and job. There is no better way to launch worthwhile state and nationwide projects than to operate from a base of strength—a tough-minded, profitable business that truly illustrates free enterprise in action.

Armed with a positive *philosophy*, girded with *principles*, guided by *practice*, and sustained by *faith*, resolve to live life to its fullest. Walk tall—with the sure knowledge that the world needs and is hungry for the big, tough-minded individual.

° Harry A. Bullis, *Manifesto for Americans*, McGraw Hill Book Company, Inc., New York, 1961.

GLOSSARY OF TOUGH-MINDED TERMS

As Used in a Productivity Climate

accountability—the extent to which one is answerable to one's superior for the results requirements of his position. A statement of accountability in the productivity climate includes the stipulation of penalties for failure to perform.

activity—action, motion, force which proceeds in a nondirective manner; movement carried on for the sake of movement rather than for achievement or result.

calculated schizophrenia—a studied and reasoned ability to view one's own motives and actions with a high measure of detachment and objectivity.

candor—an impartial use of the truth; communication used to build up rather than tear down; a constructive focusing on the positive rather than the negative aspects of a situation. Communication which usually includes the **why**.

communicate—to transmit views or facts to another person so that he will know and understand them. Real communication takes place only when the recipient wants to do something about the information.

communication—the process of transmitting views or facts to another person; the result of such communication; a message. **Batten's Law of Communication:** "When the communicatee does not understand exactly what the communicator intended, the responsibility remains that of the communicator."

consistency—harmony and uniformity of action to achieve clearly understood results requirements or objectives.

control—to measure and evaluate the use (or performance) of men, money, materials, time, and space in achieving predetermined objectives; the process of such measurement or evaluation. The prime purpose of control is to determine not where we have been but where we are going. The best possible control is achieved through enlightened people who know the **what, where, when, who, how,** and **why** of their jobs and want to get the desired results.

counsel—to provide information and suggest a course of action to another person in a manner which makes him want to do something about it. Includes **why** and sometimes **how**, whereas advice often deals only with **what**.

dignity—excellence of character; an awareness of intrinsic worth.

discipline—training which corrects, molds, strengthens, or perfects. In the tough-minded climate, discipline focuses on what can be done rather than on what can't be done. It ranks the "punishment" aspects of discipline second to the development aspects.

emotional context—a blend of various emotions such as fear, anger, disgust, grief, joy, and surprise to achieve learning or modification of behavior. A blank relationship between two people in a business environment seldom results in much real learning.

empathy—the imaginative projection of one's own consciousness into another being for purposes of positive accomplishment.

free enterprise—freedom of individual action to chart and accomplish a full measure of individual achievement—economically, politically, socially, and spiritually; freedom to develop the whole man and apply his full talents to stretching work assignments.

go-giver—a positive term replacing the cliché "go-getter" to mean a type of tough-minded person who knows he can achieve much more as an efficient "whole man" when he directs his major energies toward giving encouragement, knowledge, inspiration, and understanding to others rather than seeking self-aggrandizement only.

grace—a special warmth felt and expressed toward all other human beings; an absence of pettiness and self-concern. A living manifestation of the belief that man should devote his major energies to doing something for others and not to others.

hard—firm, rigid, solid, contracting and rigidifying with pressure, breaking under great pressure. The hard personality often becomes increasingly defensive and negative.

individual—in the truest sense, a person who knows and is primarily motivated by what he is for, not what he is against.

individuality—the quality of knowing what one is for, rather than against, and being guided accordingly.

integrity—that quality of a man or woman which requires that the only real purpose of any thought, word, or deed be to build persons or things in order to achieve positive and ethical results.

loyalty—allegiance and obedience that must be earned. Tough-minded people do not and cannot require—or expect to receive—loyalty in excess of the loyalty they themselves demonstrate.

management process—the applied belief that all five elements of management (planning, organizing, coordinating, executing, and controlling) exist for just one purpose: positive accomplishment.

motivate—to act so as to achieve motive. A person must motivate himself; the superior can only provide the type of climate which stimulates him to make wise and maximum use of his energy to achieve his motive. Motivation requires a tough-minded blend of pull (goals) and push (accountability).

GLOSSARY OF TOUGH-MINDED TERMS

negative—retreating from the challenge and discipline required to achieve positive results.

nice guy—one who is affected, self-deprecating, insincere, overly subtle; hence, evasive and untrustworthy. Used in this context to mean a person who chooses the easier alternative and rationalizes this action with "nice" clichés. One who retreats from the requirements of demanding self-discipline.

organize—to arrange the resources of a business in the manner best suited to achieve its objectives.

performance—the achievement of results required to meet established objectives; level of excellence expressed in positive accomplishment.

phony—a person who purports to be something he or she isn't.

plan—to schedule accomplishments for the purpose of producing a total result greater than the sum of its parts; a schedule so established.

positive—directed toward the accomplishment of goals (specifically, the objectives of the company). Used to describe thought and energy.

presence—a total appearance or impression created or projected by an individual which emanates confidence and effectiveness and inspires the confidence of others.

productivity climate—an operational blending of philosophy, principles, and practices which produces a high measure of results; a talented and pervasive use of resources to accomplish and exceed the objectives of the enterprise.

profit planning—the process of determining the required amount of profit from each principal unit of the business.

rebel—a person who knows, and is primarily motivated by, what he is against as opposed to the one who knows what he is for; to know what one is against and be motivated accordingly. See also **individual; individuality**.

results—an end consequence which is a product of planned, directed, and controlled action; achievement of targets, goals, or objectives.

self-confidence—the scarcest ingredient in business today; a belief in one's abilities to meet and surmount the problems and challenges of life. **Team self-confidence:** a cohesive union of individual talents and beliefs in the accomplishment of positive results, reflected by such slogans as: "The difficult we do today; the impossible takes a little longer." "When the going gets tough, the tough get going."

self-discipline—self-training which stresses the expansion and growth of all resources to achieve positive goals. It is based on the premise that confidence and competence increase much more rapidly when the individual continuously welcomes formidable challenges.

social gestalt—a dynamic interweaving of individual behavior patterns which produces group accomplishment greater than the sum of its parts.

sophisticated—artificial, highly complicated, refined; maintaining a façade which obscures the basic truths of the situation.

square—a person who conditions and guides all his actions in conformance with fundamental truths, as distinguished from the beatnik or hipster who consistently adapts to expediency and cynicism.

system of values—a complete and functionally compatible combination of essential truths. Values are the subjective interpretation of the immutable laws of the universe which shape and guide human reactions. The orderly expression and transfer of tough-minded values into practices is the essential process involved in building a climate of productivity.

taut ship—a company, division, or department which has installed and is effectively carrying out all the requirements of the productivity climate.

team—a group of people who share a common toughness of mind directed toward the accomplishment of individual purpose through the attainment of skillfully developed goals.

theory of crutches—the premise that serious weaknesses and problems within all organizations are not and cannot be identified or corrected because expedient and compensatory measures are informally effected to minimize the consequences of the weaknesses without eliminating the weaknesses themselves.

tool—here, an instrument for achieving qualitative results: philosophy, values, concepts, principles, laws, etc.

tough—flexible, pliant, lasting, durable, high-quality, difficult to break; expanding, strengthening with experience. The tough personality has an infinite capacity for growth and change.

vital—bursting with life and positively directed energy.

warmth—overt evidence of a desire to build and give to another, as reflected in tone of voice, facial expression, and the free expression of positive emotion.

"we" feeling—the feeling that one is part of a hard-hitting team that gets results. This is possible only when most or all of the people feel like individuals—with individual purposes, values, and dignity fused and focused on a common goal in which they believe.

wisdom—a knowledge of fundamental truths and the ability to use them in a meaningful, developmental, and positive way, producing a course of action which achieves desired results.

www.ingramcontent.com/pod-product-compliance
Lightning Source LLC
Chambersburg PA
CBHW050351230426
43663CB00010B/2070